FAILED STATES AND THE ORIGINS OF VIOLENCE

To my mother

Failed States and the Origins of Violence

A Comparative Analysis of State Failure as a Root Cause of Terrorism and Political Violence

TIFFIANY HOWARD
University of Nevada, Las Vegas, USA

Routledge
Taylor & Francis Group
LONDON AND NEW YORK

First published 2014 by Ashgate Publishing

Published 2016 by Routledge
2 Park Square, Milton Park, Abingdon, Oxon OX14 4RN
711 Third Avenue, New York, NY 10017, USA

Routledge is an imprint of the Taylor & Francis Group, an informa business

British Library Cataloguing in Publication Data
A catalogue record for this book is available from the British Library.

The Library of Congress has cataloged the printed edition as follows:
Howard, Tiffian .
Failed states and the origins of violence : a comparative analysis of state failure as a root cause of terrorism and political violence / by Tiffiany Howard
pages cm.
includes bibliographical references and index.
ISBN 978-1-4724-1780-0 (hardback) – ISBN 978-1-4724-1781-7 (ebook) – ISBN 978-1-4724-1782-4 (epub) 1. Failed states–Case studies. 2. Political violence–Case studies. 3. Terrorism–Case studies. I. Title.
JC328.7.H679 2014
363.32–dc23

2013032359

ISBN 13: 978-1-4724-1780-0 (hbk)

FSC www.fsc.org MIX Paper from responsible sources FSC® C013985

Printed in the United Kingdom
by Henry Ling Limited

Contents

List of Figures

List of Tables

Appendices

Acknowledgments

The journey from a tiny idea to a completed manuscript is one with many winding roads, twists and turns. In my case there are a number of people who have traveled this arduous path with me who deserve my wholehearted gratitude. Therefore, I would like to begin with my colleagues and friends, Michelle Kuenzi, David Damore, Ken Fernandez, John Tuman, Ted Jelen, Dennis Pirages, Jonathan Strand, Liam Frink, Ann Cammett, Marcia Gallo, Todd Robinson, Kevin Dawson, and Mark Padoongpatt who listened to my ideas (or more generally listened to me complain about my inertia in completing my manuscript) and read various drafts at various stages. Your constructive input and advice were invaluable to me over the past several months as I worked to complete and submit my manuscript. I would also like to thank Ted Gurr and Barbara Harff, who graciously allowed me to visit their graduate course at UNLV to run some of these ideas by them and our graduate students. I would like to thank Brendan Morris, Nerses Kopalyan, Jason Mitchell, David Snyder, Eugene O'Neal, Jonathan Doc Bradley, Doug Abbott, Kate Eugenis, Autoosa Kojoori-Saatchi, and Kenny Retzl, with whom I engaged in some spirited debates regarding the arguments contained within this work. Finally, a special thanks goes to Susie LaFrentz and Melissa Rodriguez who have the unenviable task of trying to keep me organized, which is no small feat!

Beyond my UNLV family, I have been blessed with friends and family who have provided unwavering love and support throughout my career in general. That is why words cannot even begin to express how grateful I am for April, Margean and Nagoster Franks, Bina Pittman, Roxanne and Rosita Galloway, Melynda and Melanye Price, Menna Demessie, Lisa Aubrey, Caressa Peterson, Errol Henderson, Mark Sawyer, Sheletha Drew, Gwen Tucker, Joan Maldonado, Tosin, Alao, Ingrid Porciuncula, Lynn Stewart, Jennifer Brinton, Alonda Thomas, Kia Oparah, Tavona Boggs, and Silvia Stepp. Many of whom are scholars themselves, at various stages you provided feedback on my work, but in general you provided what I needed the most, which was your love and friendship during very challenging moments over the past few years.

For those who know me, they know I strive for a well rounded balance within my life. Consequently, my physical resilience has undoubtedly strengthened my resilience in all other aspects of my life. It is for that reason, I would like to thank my Crossfit Las Vegas, Team Bombshell, Fit Fizeeks and CAC families for keeping me grounded, balanced and enriching my personal life. However, a special thanks goes to Tamra O'Halloran, Wendy Butler, Manish Saija, Courtney Cox (yes, that's her real name), Jon Afalla, Shamaine Commins,

Cory Bence, Sonia Lucas, Neil Ryan Guieb, Villi Uyema, Marc and Michael Ty, Jose Berumen, Michelle Saberton, Michele Gano, Michael BenShimon, Aaron and Shanon Pahk, Dylan Turalva, Danielle Sigman, Leslie Hernandez, Karrina Francis, Tarah Mitchell, Yen Nguyen, Heather Sumpter, Tiffany Gaston, Alissa Parker, Lisa Maloy, Tiffany Wilkerson, Bridget Row, Lisa Marie, Krystal Bladecki, Erin Frame, Jea Jung, Arlin Rodriguez Mossholder, Jan Kae, Hank Vose, Kristin and Eddy Gifford, Amy and Grayson Gearin.

Last but not least, I would like to thank freelance editor, Jami Carpenter who has worked with me on this and other projects to fine tune my work, my editor at Ashgate, Rob Sorsby for investing in this project and keeping me on deadline, and the anonymous reviewers who provided feedback that ultimately led to a stronger, more concise and much more refined and polished final manuscript.

Chapter 1
Breeding Grounds: Failed States and the Origins of Terrorism and Political Violence

Introduction

What are the factors that give rise to a terrorist? From what conditions is a violent extremist born? Is an individual inherently predisposed to be attracted to political violence, given a combination of specific genetic traits, or does an individual's exposure to a certain environment, generally one containing traumatic experiences of violence, desensitize that person in such a way that political violence, and specifically terrorism, represents a viable mode for addressing political grievances? From historians to psychologists, socio-biologists and political scientists, nearly every social science discipline has grappled with the dilemma of understanding how a seemingly rational individual makes the decision to support and engage in political violence and terrorism.

In 1968, Gurr set forth a proposition in his now classic work, *Why Men Rebel*, that individuals resort to political violence because of perceptions of relative deprivation. In essence, Gurr argues that an individual's frustration regarding perceived deprivation (hence it being relative) fosters aggression within that person which can then manifest itself in the form of acts of political violence, such as rebellions, riots, revolutions, and terrorism. Since the publication of Gurr's work, many have challenged this argument and have postulated other approaches to understanding the factors that compel an individual to terrorist action. Some scholars have asserted that political violence, but specifically terrorism, is rooted in basic human physiology and in many ways see terrorism as an extension of aggressive behavior that is learned in the same manner as all other behaviors (Hubbard, 1983; Oots and Wiegele, 1985). A counter to the physiological position is one rooted in a more environmental approach, which suggests the actions of individuals are based upon their subjective interpretation of their environment (Morgan, 2001; Crenshaw, 1981; Johnson, 1978; Jenkins 1979). Thus, environments conducive to terrorism will naturally give rise to terrorists.

Many scholars have approached the root causes of terrorism from a diverse set of lens; however, what all these works have in common is that there is no consensus among them regarding how a terrorist originates. At best, there remain two divergent paths: nature vs. nurture. Terrorists are either born and there is nothing one can do about their physiological mapping or they are shaped by their environments. Most political scientists would argue it is the latter; the only problem with that position is that little empirical work has been done to test this assertion and ultimately fully understand what types of environments give birth to terrorists.

A proponent of the environmental trajectory, Jenkins (1979) cites certain conflicts as the environmental preconditions for terrorism. He notes the failure of rural guerrilla movements in Latin America forced rebels into metropolitan areas, which led to the emergence of urban violence. He also cites the defeat of Arab nations in the 1967 Six-Day War, which forced the Palestinians to resort to terrorism after having witnessed the failure of conventional warfare (Jenkins, 1979; Hudson, 1999; Morgan, 2001). While Jenkins is one of the few to identify specific environmental factors, the main problem with his argument is that he does not explain how the socio-political landscape of a country can change, while similar patterns of terrorism remain. Case in point: if rural guerilla movements have failed, then what explanation is there for the continued existence of The Revolutionary Armed Forces of Colombia (FARC),and that instead of fading away, they have reorganized, expanded, and remain a thriving enterprise in the rural areas of South America?

Continuing along this vein of thought—that environmental conditions are salient to the makings of a terrorist—Johnson (1978) and Crenshaw (1981, 1995, 2007, 2011) identify permissive causes of terrorism that have their origins in the environment. These factors include urbanization, the transportation system, communications, media, weapons availability, and the absence of security measures. The first problem with their position is that because these are technology-based conditions, they will evolve over time and terrorists with them. The emergence of narco-terrorism and cyber-terrorism are illustrative of this evolution of modality. Twenty years ago, these modes of terrorism were virtually non-existent, but are becoming increasingly more prevalent today. Cyber-terrorism, especially, has garnered a great deal of interest and attention with the growing importance of computers, the internet, and social networking. To focus specifically on situational conditions that will change in time is limiting, and at no point gives us insight into the societal factors that give rise to terrorists, which is the second problem with the position taken by Johnson and Crenshaw. The factors identified by Johnson and Crenshaw, such as media and transportation systems, are essentially correlate factors. Simply put, the evolution of modern transportation does not explain to us why a person decides to engage in terrorism.

At the same time, and despite my critique, I do acknowledge the influence of the media and that exposure to radical views through social networking and the internet are relevant considerations that have largely given birth to homegrown terrorist threats in Western society (Bjelopera and Randol, 2010; Beutel, 2007; Johnson, 2010). Further, I do not dismiss the importance of the media and the internet and its impact on influencing extremist thought and action. At the same time I argue there are specific situational factors unique to each scenario of homegrown terrorism that cannot be captured by a unified analysis, such as this one. In other words, why are some people in Western society susceptible to extremist messages originating from the media and internet, while others who consume the same information are not? While it is a compelling question and undoubtedly related to this work in that it posits why stable states also give rise to terrorist threats—to address the origins of homegrown terrorists in Western society would move us beyond the scope of this work.

Setting situational conditions aside, one of the most salient environmental propositions is poverty. Even Gurr (1968) and his proponents (Davies, 1973; Margolin, 1977; Lichbach, 1990) take the position that poverty, and other similarly related factors such as inequality and lack of education are at the root of terrorism. A number of recent works have discounted education, inequality, and poverty as sufficient preconditions for terrorism (Sandler and Enders, 2001; Taylor and Horgan, 2000; Krueger and Maleckova, 2002; Kendall, 2005; Walker and Smith, 2001; Silber and Verme, 2010, 2012; Hopkins, 2008; Kuegler, 2009) pointing to terrorists from educated, middle to upper class socio-economic backgrounds; yet at no point do the authors provide sufficient alternative theories to the dilemma and that is—if not poverty, then what are the socio-political and economic factors that give rise to terrorism?

As of yet, this question remains largely unanswered. There is a general consensus among the terrorism and political violence literature that individuals who are exposed to a particular environment exhibit a greater likelihood of engaging in political violence and terrorism, but there is no unified understanding, or even agreement regarding the features of this environment. Yes, we would expect terrorists and violent extremists to be born out of experiences of political instability and violence, but neither psychologists nor political scientists have worked to establish any empirical norms to establish this assertion. One of the greatest weaknesses of the field of terrorism and political violence is the lack of empirical research in general (Hudson et al., 1999; Silke, 2004; Borum, 2004). At the risk of being mired down by large N datasets and statistical analyses, there is a dearth of quantitatively oriented research regarding the origins of strategic political violence and terrorism that provides an explanation as to why there is a lack of consensus among scholars, if only because it is difficult to establish generalizations from specific case studies and phenomenological historical accounts.

Failed States and the Origins of Violence

The lack of quantitative research on terrorism, and the absence of a consensus regarding the environmental conditions that foster terrorism and political violence, was what originally gave rise to this work. To answer the query posed at the onset of this chapter—the conditions under which a terrorist emerges—I first identify the climate of state fragility as the ideal environment to give rise to political violence, and in certain cases, it specifically leads to terrorism. And from that position, I argue that the living conditions within weak and failed states are so psychologically damaging and physically threatening that such an unstable climate ultimately drives one to obtain tangible political and economic resources through the use of violence[1]. Thus, the crux of this work is that state failure represents the impetus for political violence, in that it makes weak and failing states the volatile breeding grounds for terrorists and violent extremists. Moreover, I contend that this dynamic is so problematic because the majority of states where this phenomenon is present are situated in the developing world.

As research has shown, 'bad neighbors often make for bad neighborhoods' in that fragile states in fragile regions are a recipe for disaster (Zartman, 1995; Weiner, 1996; Howard, 2010b; Rotberg, 2003, 2004; Miliken, 2003; Chestermen et al., 2005; Debiel and Klein, 2002). One failed state can collapse an entire region, as has been the case in the Horn of Africa, and along the Western coastline of sub-Saharan Africa with the failure of Sierra Leone, Liberia, Guinea, and Côte d'Ivoire. Additionally, there is the widely accepted belief that terrorism flourishes in failed states (Howard, 2010, 2011; Freedman, 2002; Linden, 2002; Rabasa et al., 2007).

For the purposes of this work, the assertion that failed states are attractive to terrorists is one to address, because the connection between the two is a logical one. Given the absence of a governmental and military presence, such a climate of disorder naturally would allow entities that existed beyond the scope of governance to establish a quasi set of norms and rule of law in pockets of territory (Howard, 2010a). I do not argue that point. However, I challenge the simplicity of such an argument.

While such an assertion may explain the *movement* patterns of transnational terrorists, it does not offer any reasoning for the emergence of domestic terrorist threats from failed states. I would go so far as to argue the proponents of the former position conflate these two very distinct groups, which could explain why many scholars are so convinced that failed states are attractive to terrorists, when really they have missed a critical component of this relationship.

I do not argue that failed states are attractive to transnational terrorist groups, because they are, but the relationship between terrorism and state failure is more nuanced than existing studies have demonstrated. This work focuses specifically on *why* is it that failed states have given rise to such deadly terrorists groups. I assert that earlier studies of the relationship between state failure and terrorism overlook the probability that existing terrorists groups find failed states so attractive, not only because of the absence of a functioning government and security forces, but also because of the recruitment potential. This argument will be fleshed out in the following chapters. The important point is that previous studies have examined

1 At several points throughout this work, I refer to obtaining tangible economic and political goods as the primary motivation of individuals to engage in acts of political violence. However, there is no measure for this intervening variable of wanting to obtain political and economic resources as an individual's motivation for political violence. This is merely a hypothesis (of which several could be made regarding this relationship), and it is one which is not tested in the study, which is noted here.

the movement patterns of terrorist groups into failed states, but they have missed the micro-level dynamic of the impact fragile states have on the psyche of an individual living in such a devastated state. The sexual violence in the Democratic Republic of the Congo (DRC) represents a tragic example of this phenomenon. After decades of state failure, subsequent conflict, and mass forced migration, the DRC has given rise to some of the most brutal acts of internal violence the world has witnessed since Rwanda.

In Chapter 2, I delve deeper into the violent conditions observed in the DRC, which are deeply rooted in its legacy of state failure. Beyond the DRC, I evaluate the region of sub-Saharan Africa as a whole. This text begins with sub-Saharan Africa for one main reason: that it is a region of chronically failed states. If ever a region should give rise to terrorists, and it has, it is sub-Saharan Africa. At the same time, however, I discuss why the political violence in sub-Saharan Africa, which is generally not transnational, oftentimes is not classified as terrorism, the reasoning behind this politically motivated decision, and the implications this has for the region. In this chapter, I build the argument that grounds the subsequent chapters: that failing and failed states breed terrorists and violent extremists. Utilizing Afrobarometer data, I evaluate respondent support for the use of political violence and draw inferences from these findings. Several points one should take away from this chapter is that despite widely held beliefs, there are terrorists and there is terrorism in sub-Saharan Africa, this terrorism is rooted in a long legacy of state fragility, and most importantly, in recent years these groups have been exposed to extremely deadly internationally sponsored terrorists, which have made domestic terrorists in the region more extreme in their violence. I conclude this chapter with the warning that given the complexities of state decay in the region, if more attention is not given to the increasing political violence in sub-Saharan Africa, terrorism in this part of the world could evolve into an uncontrollable phenomenon, the magnitude and severity of which the global community has yet to witness.

Within Chapter 2, I test the hypothesis that failing and failed states breed terrorism and political violence by evaluating a region of chronically failed states, whereas, in Chapter 3 I observe this phenomenon, utilizing terrorism as my critical variable of interest. The Middle East and North Africa (MENA) region has given birth to some of the most violent terrorist organizations in the form of Hamas and Hezbollah. Moreover, this part of the world has also born witness to bloody insurgent and rebel movements against repressive regimes, most notably, in Iran, Algeria, and Syria. Beyond the political violence against brutal dictators and imperial forces, the Middle East and North Africa remain the site of some of the most protracted conflicts in the world, and host two of the most tragically failed states—Iraq and Syria. Given the prevalence of political violence, the protracted nature of this violence, and its intensity, the MENA region represents an ideal region of observation for this analysis. The question I pose in this chapter is similar to the one posed in the preceding chapter, but diverges somewhat. Instead of trying to understand what type of violence emerges *from* a region rife with failed states, in the case of Chapter 3, I am most interested in what are the most salient features of the states in a region that has produced the deadliest forms of terrorism the modern world has ever seen.

Chapter 4 follows the concept set forth in Chapters 2 and 3. Yet, what is unique about Southeast and South Asia is that it does not exist at any extreme. In other words, it is neither the region of the most or worst failed states, as is the case in sub-Saharan Africa, nor is it the region with the most or the worst terrorism. Instead, Southeast and South Asia hover in between these two regions in that they are comprised of chronically weak states that have consistently suffered from acts of political violence.

What is probably most interesting about South Asia and Southeast Asia is the stark dichotomies that exist between states in this region. For example, South Asia can produce a violent ethno-separatist terrorist organization in the form of the LTTE or Tamil Tigers, or give rise to an Afghanistan—inarguably a failed state, one that has been in a state of failure for many decades—yet still coexist in the same region as India, a state with the fifth largest economy in the world that is continuing to grow and thrive. If state failure is contagious, and bad neighbors make for bad neighborhoods, then why has India not suffered from the continued failure and ongoing violence of its not-so-distant neighbors? This is a question I address in Chapter 4.

South Asia aside, Southeast Asia presents a similar conundrum, probably one that is even more perplexing, because of all the regions I evaluate in this work, Southeast Asia is undoubtedly the most resilient with regards to socio-economic indicators, though the incidents and threat of terrorism in Indonesia remain a genuine security concern, as well as the growing dissent in Malaysia and Thailand. Despite the problems facing the region, Singapore remains a shining example of prosperity and stability in a region that, while it is not the worst of the bunch when it comes to either terrorism or state failure, it consistently hovers in unstable space. Thus, the obvious question would be why incorporate Southeast and South Asia in the analysis?

The main argument that grounds this entire study is obviously evident in both regions, although South Asia is a stronger case in that the failed states of Sri Lanka, Afghanistan, and Pakistan have been more fertile breeding grounds for terrorists than perhaps Southeast Asia; and there is undoubtedly much to learn from the states that produced the Tamil Tigers and al-Qaeda. A part of this study is also predictive in that I speculate on which regions will give rise to the next generation of internationally sponsored terrorists. The analysis I present in Chapter 2 touches upon these speculative suppositions, but in Chapter 4 is where I really build my case regarding my predictions concerning the future breeding grounds for terrorism—and Southeast Asia, especially, is central to these assertions.[2]

2 To date, the Asian Barometer, and despite claims on their site, has yet to release any data on South Asia. Upon investigation of their actual datasets, it remains the case that their data are primarily limited to East Asia and SE Asia (http://www.asianbarometer.org/newenglish/surveys/DataRelease.htm). I acknowledge this in my chapter on S/SE Asia

In comparison to the other regions, where we clearly can observe a relationship between state failure and terrorism, Latin America presents the most challenging case of them all. That is because within Latin America there is a confluence of a number of factors that complicates the linear relationship between the two variables of interest. Since the 1950s, Latin America has had to contend with the festering dissent of the indigenous population. This group has historically occupied the lowest rung of the ethnic caste system and has traditionally been relegated to rural areas, where inequities in wealth distribution and property ownership have marginalized them, and locked them into the agrarian sector of the economy, where there is very little opportunity for upward mobility. As a consequence, the indigenous population has effectively been consigned to poverty, generation after generation.

This climate of ethnic and economic inequality was the ideal catalyst for the Marxist revolutionaries that mobilized the indigenous and rural masses during the sixties. The Cuban Revolution and the rise of Fidel Castro sparked others, like Che Guevara, to initiate their own movements, with the rural poor as their main base. The National Liberation Army (ELN) and FARC in Colombia emerged within this context, but with the fall of the Soviet Union and the essential death of Marxist ideologies, the ELN and the FARC had seemingly two choices: fade away into obscurity or become a legitimate political party in the new government based upon semi-democratic principles. The choices made by the FARC and ELN diverged sharply from its contemporaries and does much to explain why these two groups still exist today, while other leftist revolutionary organizations in Latin America have all but disappeared.

In Chapter 5, I discuss the decision of the FARC to transform itself from a revolutionary group in protest of the treatment of the rural poor into a narco-terrorist organization, a decision that has kept Colombia embroiled in violence for decades now. Consequently, it is this dynamic of competition over the drug trade that has made analyzing the relationship between state failure and political violence in Latin America so complex.

In the preceding chapters, I examine the political violence that is perpetrated against the state in response to the failure of that state to provide a basic standard of living for its citizens. However, in Chapter 5, owing to the absence of a perfect linear relationship between state failure and political violence, I must take into account the presence of non-state actors involved in the drug trade, and the influence these groups have on the state with regards to the violence created by this mitigating factor, and its impact on the decision-making process of an ordinary citizen. Further, while several states have made concerted efforts to combat the

---

and in my concluding chapter. Therefore, upon arriving at the chapter on this region, background accounts of India and Sri Lanka are presented in order to give readers a sense of the South Asia region and highlight the features of state failure which are present given my inability to observe the relationship of interest using statistical analysis. I will further elaborate upon this in Chapter 4.

presence of these groups involved in drug trafficking, the question for this analysis is do the citizens of Latin American states that are specifically impacted by the drug trade recognize and appreciate the efforts of the state authorities, or do they blame the state for allowing the drug trade to gain such a strong foothold in their state? That is a question I pose in Chapter 5, the answer to which is central to our understanding of how Latin America functions as a breeding ground for political violence and terrorism.

Failed States and a Typology of Terror

In the following section I discuss in greater detail the definitions of terrorism that are relevant to this analysis—of which there are hundreds. The only universal definition of terrorism upon which scholars can agree is that *one doesn't exist.* Nonetheless, for the purpose of this work, I establish that terrorism is politically motivated strategic violence against the state for the purpose of forcing tangible economic and political concessions, including state autonomy, but not limited to absolute authority over the state (i.e. the entire displacement of the regime in power). This definition will be fleshed out in greater detail in the subsequent section, but for now, it is important that I point out that while this definition establishes the working parameters of my analysis, and is thus intentionally broad, there are important limitations to this definition as well.

The main limitation is that not all forms of terrorism originate in the breeding grounds of failed states. There are notable exceptions in the right-wing terrorism that is epitomized by white supremacists and anti-government rhetoric found in the United States and the majority of western democracies.[3] Additionally, the ethnic-nationalist/separatist violence exemplified by the IRA[4] also does not fit 'neatly' within the framework of this model, and certainly not state-sponsored violence that is characterized by genocide and politicide. Instead, the type of terrorism that one finds in the breeding grounds of fragile states is overwhelmingly political violence indicative of what David Rapoport identifies as the fourth wave

3 While not all right wing white supremacist terrorism is rooted in radical Christianity, a number of groups, especially in the United States (i.e., the KKK, the Christian Identity, and the Aryan Nations) often cite Christian religious doctrine as justification for their terrorism, which according to Rapoport's definition, would be considered a fourth wave or form of terrorism. I only mention right wing groups in the context of this analysis to illustrate that despite that this type of terrorism would be considered religious terrorism, I argue that a certain type of religious terrorism originates in fragile and failing states, of which right wing religious terrorism is excluded.

4 Although a peace agreement was forged between Sinn Fein and the British Unionists/Loyalists in 2005, I mention the IRA because this form of terrorism did not originate in a failed state. However, it is often characterized as religious violence, which according to Rapoport's definition would be considered a fourth wave/form of terrorism, despite its emergence as a terrorist organization in the early 1900s.

of terrorism (Rapoport, 2004). This type of violence is characterized by religious zeal, of which Islam is at the center (Rapoport, 2004). According to Rapoport, even if a group is not explicitly motivated by religion, many secular groups still manage to emerge in response to "excessive religious zeal" (Rapoport, 2004; Horgan and Braddock, 2012, p. 51). Even the right wing and ethno-separatist terrorist movements mentioned earlier can trace their origins to religion and religious tensions.

Yet, despite the saliency of religion to these very diverse terrorist movements, it is important to make these necessary distinctions, because there will be those who challenge this work for its grand sweeping assertion that all failed states give rise to all types of terrorism, when that is not true. The fundamental argument I make is that fragile states function as breeding grounds for radical religious terrorism typically grounded in Islam, which has been responsible for the "most significant, deadly and profoundly international attacks" (Horgan and Braddock, 2012, p 51; Rapoport, 2004).

There are exceptions within this analysis, most notably that of Latin America and sub-Saharan Africa where there remain remnants of both the second and third waves of terrorism, which are characterized by either anti-colonial revolts (second wave) or grounded in leftist ideology (third wave). At this point my argument diverges from that of Rapoport for I do not believe either the second or third waves have come to an abrupt or screeching end as he does, and this is evident by the examples of political violence and terrorism currently observed in sub-Saharan Africa and Latin America. Instead, I contend that while it has declined sharply, these two regions provide evidence that the violence from anti-colonial revolutionary movements has simply transformed into terrorism against impotent post-colonial regimes, but at the root of the violence is frustration and resentment over the damage done by the process of colonization. In states such as Rwanda and Sudan where there is a protracted legacy of the colonial powers manipulating the political power structure—even after their departure from these states—we have seen ethnic-class struggles that have been especially brutal given the deeply rooted divisions and bitterness between the warring factions—divisions that were artificially created by their colonizers.

Similarly, in Latin America, the third wave leftist Marxist revolutionaries, who gave birth to the FARC and Sendero Luminoso (Shining Path), have simply shed their ideological rhetoric in favor of the more practical ideal of tangible financial gain. The Shining Path, thus far, has been subdued, but has not disappeared and many speculate there could be a resurgence in their influence under the right circumstances. Moreover, the FARC has not been subdued at all. Instead it has adapted to the evolving socio-political landscape of the region given its current involvement in narco-terrorism.

The second and third waves of terrorism may have ended according to Rapoport's assessment, but I argue that neither the organizations that were born during these waves have died, nor have the seeds of dissent. These groups and their grievances have simply evolved, like the FARC, which has been reinforced by the failing Colombian state, along with the numerous rebel groups across Africa that once fought colonial powers but now engage in brutal acts of terror to undermine the weak regimes of their fragile states.

Defining An Act of Terror-Establishing the Working Parameters of Terrorism and Political Violence

As previously discussed, there exist strong divisions within the literature regarding the definition of terrorism. This is mainly because of regional and cultural differences that manifest themselves within the research and literature. What one scholar defines as terrorism, the other considers a resistance movement. This polarization within the literature can be attributed to the notion that the word 'terrorism' in itself is fraught with a myriad of racial and religious complexities. It is that duality of perception that makes the process of arriving at a unified definition extremely challenging.

The usage of the term terrorism can be traced back to the French Revolution, and the contemporary Oxford English Dictionary illustrates this within the definition of terrorism as it references the French Revolution as an example:

> Terrorism: A system of terror. 1. Government by intimidation as directed and carried out by the party in power in France during the revolution of 1789–1794 (Hoffman, 2006, p. 2).

At the time of the French Revolution, terrorism was viewed as a positive action to demonstrate dissatisfaction with the government. The widespread view was that the resistance of the people against the government was legitimate in light of the atrocities the government committed against the people. The same ideals were adopted during the American Revolution, which the French went on to borrow. However, because of the violence that took place during the French Revolution, the French concept of terrorism has come to represent the basic tenant of terrorism—violence against the government.

Yet, violence against a regime in and of itself does not represent terrorism. That is a contemporary concept, which considers any act against a government as terrorism. This perception of terrorism represents how politicized the term has become, while the early notions of terrorism considered violence against a corrupt and oppressive government as perfectly acceptable. The tension that exists regarding what should be defined as terrorism and what should be considered a legitimate resistance movement or revolution has plagued scholars for many years, and there still remain sharp divisions within the literature (Chomsky, 1988; Craig, 1988; Long, 1990; Rapoport, 1999; Zanini, 1999; Cooley, 2000; Wilkinson, 2000; Cillufo et al., 2001; Addison, 2002; Franks, 2004; Hoffman, 2006).

While much of the literature on political violence has focused on terrorism, it is important to point out that there are two strategic types of terror: the singular difference is the ideology of the acting group. Insurgent groups[5] often organize within ungoverned territory, just as terrorist groups; however, the goals of insurgents are vastly different from the goals of terrorists, despite the conflation of these two groups.

Insurgency is defined as "an organized movement aimed at the overthrow of a constitutional government through the use of subversion and armed conflict" (Rabasa et al., 2007, p. 3). Although insurgents rely upon terror as a coercive tool, their overall goal is to conduct military operations through the use of guerilla tactics, or some other strategy, for the sole purpose of seizing and acquiring territory where they can create a 'liberated zone' or 'counter-state' (Rabasa, 2007). Insurgents also tend to rely upon the aid and support of the mass population, from which they recruit members, enjoy popular support, and provide material resources as compensation. Ideal examples of this dynamic can be found in Lebanon and the Occupied Territories of Palestine, where Hezbelloh and Hamas, respectively, enjoy considerable popular support and legitimacy.

However, in contrast to insurgents, terrorists are often isolated, and they operate in small, clandestine networks. Although their aims may benefit the populace, they do not tend to insert themselves within the mass population as insurgents do. A classic example of this dynamic was the isolated and remote presence of al-Qaeda operating in Afghanistan and Pakistan.

Further, terrorists are often characterized by their attacks, which are generally targeted at non-combatants, hence the widespread outrage and reaction to large-scale terrorist attacks. Finally, the aims of terrorists are sometimes viewed as "millenarian, unachievable," and idealistic (Rabasa, 2007, p. 3).

However, while terrorists and insurgents are organized around different agendas and maintain varied objectives, their actions and use of terror as a strategy are nearly identical. Consequently, I acknowledge the ideological and fundamental differences between insurgents and terrorists, but at the same time, I do not distinguish between the two groups in this analysis, nor do I distinguish between other variant forms of political violence.

Therefore, adopting the definition set forth by Hoffman in *Inside Terrorism* (2006), I define acts of terror as "[an] abhorrent act of violence perceived as directed against society …" (2006, p. 1). Whether or not these groups are classified as insurgents, rebel groups, drug cartels, paramilitary organizations, revolutionary movements, or ultimately as terrorists, for the purposes of this analysis I consider any strategic activity with the intent of inducing fear, based upon coercion, and for the purpose of threatening harm with the goal of forcing political or economic concessions, to be an act of terror and a form of political violence.

As I acknowledge in the previous section, this working definition is intentionally broad, and some may challenge the conflation of these distinct types of political

5 Resistance movements are considered non-violent and represent those groups that engage in civil disobedience. When they begin to use violence, they transform into rebel or insurgent groups.

violence. That is a legitimate critique of this work, yet I argue for such a broad definition because the impact of all acts of terror and political violence on a society are identical. In the wake of the devastation created by a violent attack, the greater populace does not distinguish between rebel groups, narco-terrorists and violent radical Islamists, nor do they genuinely care about the grievances of these groups—these delineations are reserved for academics. Additionally, to make the distinction between the variant forms of political violence would move me into a discussion of the strategic motivations that compel these groups to organize and act. This type of discussion would take this work down a very different path from that of its original intent; and that is to determine the role state fragility and failure play in the emergence of deadly political violence, and in specific cases, terrorism.

Finally, and most importantly this work is specifically focused on domestic political violence and terrorism. The main assertion of this analysis is that state failure fosters support for political violence against the state—in which an individual lives. At the same time this work has larger implications regarding transnational terrorism which I discuss at various points throughout this work, particularly in Chapters 2 and 4. I also expand upon the centrality of this work to the discussion of transnational terrorism in the concluding chapter. Yet, beyond this discussion, it is important to firmly assert, while this work touches upon the relationship between transnational terrorism and state failure, it does not empirically test this relationship. Instead, this research advances our understanding of state fragility and failure as a root cause of domestic political violence and terrorism through the process of theory building and statistical modeling.

Understanding the Concept of State Capacity and State Failure

Studies dedicated to understanding state building and state capacity are prevalent throughout the political science literature. Scholars Charles Tilly and Mancur Olson have devoted a great deal of their research to understanding how a nation develops and how and why empires fail (Olson, 1982, 2000; Tilly, 1992). In *Coercion, Capital and European States*, Tilly examines how capital-intensive and coercion-intensive paths of state formation over time produced radically different types of states in Europe (1992). He also argues the state system fashioned in Europe has not always existed, and that it will not endure forever (1992). Like Tilly, Olson also seeks to understand the development of nations and the factors that contribute to their decline (1982). There are two distinctions between the work of these scholars and the goals of this study: 1) Tilly is more interested in the development of the state in general, therefore he focuses exclusively on European states, where the Westphalian state model originated, although state failure is less a problem in Europe than it is in the developing world; and 2) Olson's work primarily focuses on the political organization of the state, therefore his unit of analysis is the regime or empire, as opposed to the actual nation-state and its economic, cultural and political institutions.

Tangential to the study of states is the study of the efficiency and efficacy of political institutions. A classic study of the development of political institutions, the foundation for state formation, is Robert Putnam's analysis of the development of political institutions in Northern and Southern Italy (1993). The basic premise of Putnam's argument is that social capital and a highly developed civil community affects institutional performance and promotes democratic institutions, ultimately determining whether a democracy will succeed or fail. Putnam's analysis provides insight into how a state can succeed and how a state can fail. While there is a vast difference between a failing institution and a failing state, both are related, and Putnam demonstrates that a strong state has effective and efficient institutions. Like Putnam, Easterly also arrives at similar conclusions regarding the quality of institutions and the role they play in the capacity of the state (2000). According to Easterly, high quality institutions, such as rule of law, bureaucratic quality, freedom from government expropriation, and freedom from government repudiation of contracts, mitigate the adverse economic consequences of ethnic fractionalization. In countries with sufficient institutions, ethnic diversity does not lower growth or worsen economic policies. High quality institutions also reduce war casualties on national territory and lessen the probability of genocide, given the presence of ethnic fractionalization (Easterly, 2000).

As previously stated, institutional quality affects the capacity of the state, but weak and ineffective institutions are not solely responsible for the failure of a state. Among the state failure research available, there is body of literature that attempts to explain this phenomenon utilizing forecasting models of social conditions. Utilizing data from 1955 to 1999, the State Failure Task Force (currently the Political Instability Task Force) estimates a global forecasting model of state failure that, based upon data two years in advance of the event, distinguishes between states likely to fail or experience failure, and states likely to remain stable or in their present state (State Failure Task Force Report, 1995, 1998, 2000). According to the State Failure Task Force a state failure event consists of: 1) revolutionary wars, 2) ethnic wars, 3) adverse or disruptive regime transitions, and 4) genocides and/or politicides. Given the State Failure Task Force's definition, 136 state failures occurred between 1955 and 1999. Out of more than 75 statistically relevant explanatory variables, the State Failure Task Force develops a global forecasting model as their best model that includes three variables: the level of democracy, the degree of trade openness, and levels of infant mortality. The Task Force concludes that this model specification correctly identifies about two-thirds of state failures.

Based on the results of their model, the State Failure Task Force arrives at the following conclusions: 1) that while high infant mortality consistently appears to be linked to state failure, there is no direct causal relation. Infant mortality serves primarily as an indicator of the overall quality of material life;[6] 2) the effect of trade openness on increasing the likelihood of state failure is greater in

6 As an indicator of overall quality of life, low infant mortality rates would be linked to state success just as high rates have been linked to state failure.

less democratic nations; 3) levels of trade openness and infant mortality show no statistical relationship; and 4) partial democracies are at a greater risk of failure than either full democracies or full autocracies (State Failure Task Force Report, 1995, 1998, 2000).

The State Failure Task Force's first phase of results in 1995 sparked the emergence of two major complementary works: *State Failure and State Weakness in a Time of Terror* (Rotberg, 2003) and *When States Fail: Causes and Consequences* (Rotberg, 2004). Edited by Robert L. Rotberg, both volumes function as a complement to the findings of the Task Force. Instead of statistical modeling, the authors utilize case study analyses to identify mitigating factors that further explain the breakdown of the state. Rotberg et al. (2003, 2004) further develops and expands upon the indicators of state failure described in the Task Force Report (1995, 1998, 2000).

This competing body of literature asserts that the State Failure Task Force's definition of state failure is narrow because it is limited to solely conflicts, and ignores more tangible human security concerns. In contrast, this collection of studies relies upon a broader definition of state failure (Rotberg et al., 2003, 2004). This body of work defines state capacity by a nation's ability to provide the public good of security, which allows for the emergence of other essential public goods and institutions such as a healthcare system, a transportation system, facilities for commerce, an educational system, and an open (or relatively open) political system. Thus, according to Rotberg and others (2003, 2004), the failure to provide the public good of security represents the failure of the state.

Defining State Failure—Failing and Failed States[7]

From the existing state formation and state failure literature, we develop a sense of the important roles of the state—the main one being to provide security to its citizens. However, while scholars differ on how security is defined and measured, they all seem to agree that at the root of state failure is an overall lack of security. Without security, states are unable to complete other basic tasks, such as, maintaining its physical infrastructure in the form of roads, schools, and the delivery of fundamental public goods. Thus, the state's primary goal and duty to its citizens is to provide the public good of security. A strong state ensures that its borders are secure and that its citizens are not engaged in internal conflict. The delivery of a host of other public goods can only be achieved when a reasonable measure of security has been sustained within a state's borders. In addition to

7 In this analysis I use several descriptive terms of state failure interchangeably. Failing states are sometimes referred to as weak or fragile states, whereas failed states are sometimes referred to as collapsed states. See Howard 2008 and 2010b for further discussion regarding the arbitrary distinctions between terms given the observation of states in decline in the global system.

security, another essential public good is access to government with citizens having the ability to fully participate in politics and the political process. Strong states allow for a political system that has regular and open elections, a functional court system, and a method to address the protection of fundamental human and civil rights.

In contrast to strong states, failing states include a broad continuum of states that are inherently weak due to geographical, political, or economic constraints; where they may be temporarily or situationally weak due to internal conflict, management weakness, corruption, despotism, or external threats (Rotberg, 2003, 2004). Failing states typically exhibit ethnic, religious, linguistic or some other type of intercommunal tension that has yet to erupt into uncontrollable violence. Urban crime rates tend to be high or on the rise, physical infrastructure networks, such as roads or the mail delivery system, have deteriorated, schools and hospitals show signs of neglect, and per capita GDP and other indicators of economic prosperity have all declined, typically at a very dramatic rate. Furthermore, greed and corruption are rampant, especially among government officials.

While the failing state is in a precarious position of deteriorating circumstances, the failed state lacks all signs of security and order. Failed states exhibit characteristics similar to failing states, the only exception is that the conditions are significantly worse, to the point where a failed state is indistinguishable from a state plunged into anarchy. The majority of "failed states are tense, deeply conflicted, dangerous, and contested bitterly by warring factions" (Rotberg, 2003, p. 5). Essentially, failed nation-states are unable to control their borders, their economy has deteriorated, they are involved in bitter violent struggles, there is no evidence of a functioning physical infrastructure, and their political institutions lack any form of legitimacy. In most cases, the government of a failed state experiences multiple rebellions and civil unrest, communal conflict, and a host of discontent directed towards it (Rotberg, 2003). In other words, a failed state represents a polity that lacks the ability to perform the fundamental tasks of a nation-state in the modern world.

Operationalizing the Definition of State Failure

According to the Rotberg et al. studies, state failure occurs in stages and can be classified as: 1) weak, 2) failing, 3) failed, and 4) collapsed (2003, 2004). While this classification is applicable to the Rotberg et al. studies, it diverges sharply from the classification of states employed by the State Failure Task Force (1995, 1998, 2000). The scholars that comprise the State Failure Task Force simply distinguish between a failed state and a non-failed state. They employ this distinction because it allows them to include more cases in the dataset. Another important distinction between the Rotberg et al. studies (2003, 2004) and the State Failure Task Force is that Rotberg and his contributors classify a state as failed according to its ability to provide essential public goods whereas the State Failure Task Force denotes a state as failed if it experiences a revolutionary war, an ethnic war, an adverse or disruptive regime transition, or genocide(s) and/or politicide(s) in a given year (1995, 1998, 2000).

While I consider the findings of both studies compelling, I believe it is important to arrive at a comprehensive definition of state failure, which I argue neither study does adequately. Providing the public good of security does not exclude a nation-state from failure, as Rotberg et al. suggest (2003, 2004), whereas the presence of conflict does not always put a nation-state at risk of failure, which is what the State Failure Task Force would have you believe. For example, Rotberg and associates classify Sudan as a failing state because it provides public goods in the northern region only, whereas the State Failure Task Force classifies Sudan as a failed state because it has been embroiled in a civil and ethnic conflict for more than 20 years.[8] Similarly, Colombia, which boasts a high crime rate, would be classified as failing state by Rotberg and associates given that it provides the public good of security in its urban areas, but the State Failure Task Force classifies Colombia as a state not at risk for failure because it does not exhibit the presence of the conflicts identified as failure. Also, while Rotberg and associates classify Haiti as a weak state because it provides public goods to certain groups in urban areas, the State Failure Task Force identifies Haiti as a state at risk for failure because of the presence of revolutionary war and abrupt regime transitions. The discrepancies between the two studies are driven by the fact that they define state failure very differently, and yet I argue neither definition is sufficient in its characterization of state failure.

This work takes a position between these two overarching bodies of literature and echoes a similar position advanced by another vein of literature which focuses on states that lack either effectiveness or legitimacy (Chandler, 2006; Chesterman, Ignatieff, and Thakur, 2005; Debiel and Klein, 2002; Goldstone, 2008; Goldstone et al., 1998, 1999; Howard, 2008, 2010b; Miliken et al., 2003; Zartman, 1995). Consequently, states relying upon legitimacy can fail when they "reveal themselves to be corrupt, incompetent, too dependent on foreign powers, or become perceived as unjust through their policies or actions" (Goldstone, 2008, p. 286). Similarly, states which rely upon effectiveness can fail when they are no longer able to provide security, along with "the economic benefits or coercive strength that sustains them" (Goldstone, 2008, p. 286). This vein of literature focuses on a state's ability to achieve *both* effectiveness and legitimacy. Therefore, the absence of one or both of these factors reflects a state that is failing or has failed, respectively.

Yet, how does one operationalize effectiveness and legitimacy? In this work I contend that the absence of the public good of security, the absence of state governance as evidenced by ungoverned territory, a weak or illegitimate state authority, and a basic failure to provide for comprehensive public goods represent the components of state failure (Howard, 2008, 2010b).

8 This was prior to creation of the independent state of South Sudan in July 2011.

Thus, failed states are characterized by this analysis as those states that are performing poorly across all, or the majority of these indicators, an illustrative example being that of Somalia. Whereas, failing states report weak (but not poor) performances across several of the indicators, but not all of them. The aforementioned Colombia once again provides an ideal example of a failing state as it struggles with ungoverned territory, a weak central state authority, and in the provision of public security, yet it manages to provide public goods to a substantial majority of its populace.

In subsequent chapters I further flesh out these definitional measures of state failure that are employed in this work given my earlier research on this phenomenon (Howard 2008, 2010b). Nonetheless, these indicators of state failure function as explanatory variables for the dependent condition of individual support for political violence. Consequently, the basic tenet of this work, which I test statistically, is that failing and failed states have an impact on fostering support for political violence.

The Larger Implications

Using survey data from the Global Barometer project, I argue that there is an insidious pattern of deprivation within failing and failed states that drives ordinary citizens to support the use ofpolitical violence, and in several specific cases, terrorism against the state. Up until now research has focused on the macro-level, seeking to understand how to address insurgencies and terrorist activity and broader transnational threats. I argue that this approach is flawed. It ignores the most basic and fundamental component of human psychology—the desire to survive. Failed states threaten individuals' survival, which ultimately drives them to obtain tangible political and economic resources through the use of violence.

Beyond the obvious implications of this work, and that is pinpointing those factors that influence an individual's decision to support the use of political violence and terrorism, this researchalso brings together the rich data amassed by the Global Barometer projects. Thus, this work is unique in that it examines the micro-underpinnings of individual support for political violence, and it utilizes the entire Global Barometer project to do this. This is an exploratory work, searching for the role that state failure plays in generating specific security threats, rooted in political violence and terrorism. Therefore, at the end of this study, what we have is an examination of four diverse regions that have been plagued by a combination of failing and failed states, and political violence, and we draw parallels between these regions whereby we arrive at a single conclusion—failing and failed states are breeding grounds for political violence, violent extremists and terrorists. Consequently, while counter-terrorism measures have their merits and should certainly never be abandoned, through the process of this text, I contend that attention shouldalso be given to pursuing serious state-building efforts.

Chapter 2
And They All Fall Down: The Pandemic of Political Violence and State Failure in sub-Saharan Africa

Introduction

With the global war on terrorism, Africa has been dragged into the middle of the contentious discussion, despite that the majority of conflicts and terrorist activity in the region are not connected to internationally sponsored terrorism or a comprehensive agenda against a specific target in the West. The Lords Resistance Army in Uganda, the insurgents in the Niger Delta, the extremists in Kenya and Nigeria, the militias in the Democratic Republic of the Congo, and a collection of rebel groups and insurgent movements throughout the region are the principal security threats to the citizens of Africa—not al-Qaeda, Hamas, or any other internationally recognized terrorist organization on the U.S. State Department's list. Yet, Africa has become a target in the global war on terror, but Africa's greatest offense has been that its network of failed and weak states are simply unable to sufficiently monitor its borders or govern its territory, thus opening the door for internationally sponsored terrorist networks to take up residence within the region, where they have gone on to plan attacks against American, European, and Israeli targets, built local cells with the capacity to attack in Africa or recruit for operations elsewhere, and found sympathetic agents within the population to provide safe haven and financial support for terrorists and their operations (Harbeson and Rothchild, 2008).

Africa is undoubtedly plagued by systematic state failure in that the region lacks strong governance, comprehensive economic development, and fails to provide security to its citizens, and order in its territories. As a result, Africa's failed states have helped facilitate internationally sponsored terrorist networks and operations. However, until recently, this type of activity was primarily relegated to North Africa and the Horn, because that region of Africa is mostly comprised of states collectively known as the Maghreb, which share historical, cultural, and religious ties with the Middle East. Thus, North Africa and the Horn are far more integrated into the network of international extremist Islamic terrorist activity than sub-Saharan Africa. For example, Algerians and Moroccans have consistently been involved in many attacks in Europe, and comprise the majority of Africans who have reportedly traveled to join the *jihadist* movement in Iraq. Further, the development of the radical Islamic Courts Movement in Somalia has reinforced the economic, political, religious, and ethnic linkages between the Horn of Africa and the Middle East, as people, arms, money, and materials move from the Arabian Peninsula, across the Red Sea, through Somalia[1] and Sudan into the heart of Africa.

What was once a seemingly 'benign' terrorist presence in sub-Saharan Africa is starting to transform into a movement, with states such as Nigeria, Sierra Leone, Liberia, and the DRC now lending arms, financial support, and radical militants to the extremist *jihadist* movement of internationally sponsored terrorist organizations such as al-Qaeda. Furthermore, with the recent bombings in Kenya and Somalia, and the failed bombing attempt on a U.S. airliner by a Nigerian national, it is becoming increasingly evident that internationally sponsored terrorist networks have found a permanent home in sub-Saharan Africa and within the hearts and minds of its people, which pose significant challenges for the international community, given the region's patchwork of failed states, where terrorists can easily hide and thrive.

Thus, while internationally sponsored terrorist organizations have been present in sub-Saharan Africa for the past 40 years, the region has seemingly been immune to terrorist attacks, but that is changing. With successful independence movements, and the emergence of democratic states, the people of sub-Saharan Africa were hopeful for the region's future, but with constant civil wars, brutal dictatorships, and violent struggles for power, sub-Saharan Africa has degenerated into a region of failed states. As a consequence of sustained failure in the region, the people of sub-Saharan Africa have become disillusioned with its leadership and political institutions, making them more susceptible to the radical ideologies of internationally sponsored terrorist groups which promise economic prosperity and political power; and it is this phenomenon which represents the crux of this analysis.

In this chapter, I discuss how the conditions of state failure have fostered support for political violence in sub-Saharan Africa. Terrorist groups are now actively recruiting more militants from within the region, and support for extremist acts is on the rise in sub-Saharan Africa. Thus, I argue sub-Saharan Africa could soon play host to the next generation of terrorists and usher in the next wave of lethal terrorist activity.

Main Argument

Unlike other regions, such as the Middle East and South Asia, where extensive research has been conducted on the conditions that foster popular support for political violence and terrorism, there is a glaring absence of research on this phenomenon and its presence in sub-Saharan Africa. This is largely because acts

1 Due to Somalia's geographical and cultural ties to the Maghreb, I acknowledge it could be included in the following chapter that examines North Africa, but my designation of states to specific regions is driven by the United Nation's classification.

of terrorism are not as prevalent in this region as they are in the rest of the world, but in recent years that has begun to change with major incidents in Mombasa, Kenya, Mogadishu, Somalia, and Mali.[2,3,4]

In this chapter, I evaluate the relationship between state failure in sub-Saharan Africa and the growing presence of terrorist and insurgent groups in these states, along with growing support for the use of political violence, in an effort to illustrate the very real likelihood that Africa's failed states will soon become the breeding ground for extremist ideologies and a new generation of terrorists.

While it is tempting to reduce the argument to the simple explanation that weak and failed states would naturally be attractive to terrorist groups and insurgents, given the absence of a functioning security force, I assert the relationship is more nuanced than this. There is certainly the element of a pull factor present—in that actors engaging in political violence are better able to carry out operations in failed states, and up until now, the majority of studies have remained solely focused on this element—the attractiveness of failed states to terrorists and insurgents (Newman, 2007; Freedman, 2002; Linden, 2002; Menkhaus, 2002). However, another argument in this dynamic is the possibility that citizens of failed states are attracted to political violence because of the deteriorating conditions within this type of state. A critical element that has remained absent from this discussion is the decision-making process of ordinary citizens to support terrorist and insurgent activity because the state can no longer fulfill its responsibilities to its citizens. I argue that individuals living in failed states are attracted to political violence because the system is broken—the state has failed in its duty.

Rather than evaluate the patterns of political violence in relation to Africa's failed states using event data, my goal is to examine individual support for the use of violence as a political tool when the state has failed. Using barometer survey data, I find there is an insidious pattern of deprivation within failed states that drives ordinary citizens to support the use of political violence. This study helps further scholarly discourse by suggesting an alternative root cause of this type of violence that has been overlooked by global indicator models of terrorism, because up until now they have ignored individual level data, and have also ignored the basic tenets of human psychology and what drives seemingly rational human beings to commit irrational acts of violence.

---

2 Mohammed, Ibrahim. (2009). "Somali Police Warn of More Suicide Bombings." *Reuters*. Dec. 7. http://www.reuters.com/article/idUSTRE5B63DV20091207. Accessed, December 10, 2009.

3 Snowdon, Ben and David Johnson. (2007). "Primer on the Embassy Bombings and the U.S. Strikes on Sudan and Afghanistan." http://www.infoplease.com/spot/newsfacts-sudanstrikes.html. Accessed, December 10, 2009.

4 Similar to Somalia, due to Mali's (as well as Chad, Niger and Mauritania) geographical and cultural ties to the Maghreb, I acknowledge it could be included in the following chapter that examines North Africa, but my designation of states to specific regions is driven by the United Nation's classification.

Failed states threaten individuals' survival, which ultimately compels them to obtain tangible political and economic resources through other means, including the use of political violence. Further, the major implications for the international community are that this pattern of deprivation leaves individuals in these states more susceptible to the influence of internationally sponsored terrorist groups. As a consequence, failed states function as breeding grounds for terrorists, who then export their radical ideologies to other parts of the world to create terrorist threats across the globe. Thus, I argue the global war on terrorism will remain a futile endeavor if the international community ignores the importance of comprehensive state building that incorporates the sustained development of strong political and economic institutions within developing societies (Howard, 2008, 2010b).

Now the importance of this research is twofold. First, this work joins the existing body of research on weak states, fragile states, and failed states (Rotberg, 2003, 2004; Esty, 1995; Goldstone et al., 1998, 1999; Miliken et al., 2003; Howard, 2008, 2010b; Debiel and Klein, 2002; Chesterman, Ignatieff, and Thakur, 2005; Chandler, 2006; Zartman, 1995) in that it outlines a discrete set of indicators of state decline. However, it goes beyond these works by evaluating how these factors work together to weaken a state and create chaos and anarchy within a nation where terrorism and violence then become legitimate avenues to obtain political and economic resources.

Beyond establishing a typology of state failure, this study is also particularly timely and unique from other works on terrorism in its approach to understanding alternative root causes of this type of violence beyond the typical factors given, such as economic decline, religious radicalism, and levels of frustration (Martin, 1987; Huntington, 1991; Sorli, Gleditsch, and Strand, 2005; Piazza, 2006, 2007; Newman, 2007; Tikusis, 2009). I argue that unlike previous works, which focus on macro-level terrorist incidents and specific country cases that paint a broad picture of how weak states contribute to political violence, this study probes deeper and seeks to understand what is it about the features of state failure that influence an individual's decision to support and commit an act of political violence.

Africa's Failed States

This chapter restricts its unit of analysis to sub-Saharan Africa, because the region represents a unique case when it comes to the discussion of state failure and political violence. State failure is an apparent pandemic in the region of sub-Saharan Africa. With the exception of Western Sahara and Swaziland, 52 of Africa's 54 countries are on the 2011 Failed State Index as states at the critical levels of warning or alert. It is believed that state failure remains such a problem in Africa because the region was never organized along the contemporary state model that we recognize today. As a result, Africa must now struggle to build political and economic institutions capable of sustaining a functioning state.

Research dedicated to understanding post-colonial African states acknowledge that many political scientists try to impose a concept of statehood based upon the models of Weber that are not appropriate given the context of ethnic and tribal identities unique to post-colonial African nations (Jackson and Rosberg, 1982; Bates, 1981; Widner, 1995; Herbst 1996). Africa was never comprised of classically defined Westphalian sovereign states that maintained a monopoly over the territory within its boundaries. Furthermore, many colonial powers that established a presence in Africa made no effort to extend the administrative authority of the government beyond the capital city. "In most cases, the colonial governments were little more than elementary bureaucracies, with limited personnel and finances, and were more comparable to rural country fiefdoms in Europe than modern independent states" (Jackson, 1993). After achieving independence, several African nations continued this trend and did little to extend the administrative authority of the government beyond the urban centers.

Consequently, considering Africa's historical background, Herbst argues that the failure to resuscitate failed states or prevent weak states from failing in Africa is the result of the international system's legitimization and recognition of several African nations that were really never states to begin with (1996). The vast majority of reports and analytic studies that examine the state continue to use existing nation-states as their unit of analysis. Yet, borders manufactured by colonial powers make the concept of statehood in Africa very difficult to achieve. Given that post-colonial Africa lacks a history of state development, it is very difficult for these contemporary states to create strong states. Many post-colonial African nations are experiencing episodes of state failure because they simply lack a blueprint. It is a challenge for states that lack a history of prior state development to establish strong and effective states today because the political and economic institutions necessary to promote state building were never cultivated in the past (Howard, 2010b).

Terrorism, Insurgency, and Political Violence in Africa

Political violence in Africa is more widespread and commonplace than many may realize. Africa's most tragic failed states, the DRC, Sierra Leone, and Somalia are all well-known sponsors of terrorism, and at various time periods in their histories have all provided safe haven for dangerous terrorist networks, such as al-Qaeda.

As if managing terrorism in sub-Saharan Africa is not difficult enough, this region must also contend with insurgent activity. Insurgent movements in sub-Saharan Africa have waged a campaign of terror against citizens within their own countries, which could rival the attacks of any international terrorist operation. For example, while some would classify Sierra Leone's Revolutionary United Front (RUF) as primarily an opposition movement, the U.S. State Department has named the RUF as a terrorist group, pointing to the violence that characterized their campaign of terror against the weak government during the nineties.

Yet regardless of one's position on the appropriate classification of the RUF, the RUF's relationship with al-Qaeda through their diamond smuggling operation, and its harboring of members of this terrorist organization within Sierra Leone is well known.

Given the presence of political violence in Africa, this analysis is focused specifically on determining the impact the economic and political climate in the region has on individuals' acceptance of political violence as a legitimate political tool. The Afrobarometer survey allows me to do this in that it relies upon a measure of political violence, whereby it asks respondents to indicate whether or not they sometimes consider it necessary to use violence in support of a just cause. The only limitation of the survey on this issue is that no distinction is made between the variant types of political violence that typically come in the form of rebel or insurgent activity, and terrorism. The conflation of all types of political violence into a single measure raises the issue of whether or not individuals actually make the distinction between the variant types of violence. I argue that while there are unique motivators for each type of violent act, insurgent activity and terrorist attacks are often times indistinguishable. Therefore, while insurgent activity and terrorist activity are discrete types of political violence, I contend that these are simply labels and that individuals affected by political violence often do not make a distinction between the variant forms.

Hypotheses

The main hypothesis that guides this entire analysis is that failing and failed states foster political violence. This is because of the weak rule of law in these fragile states and the complete absence of a security infrastructure capable of monitoring territorial borders.

State Failure

As discussed at the opening of this work, strong states provide one basic, fundamental public good that fragile states lack: the public good of security. Without security, it is difficult for states to provide other basic goods that indicate a state is stable. Therefore, I set forth five hypotheses that capture the dimensions of state weakness.

The Public Good of Security

H1: Individuals who feel that the state does not provide adequate personal security are likely to support the use of political violence

This hypothesis is grounded in the assertion that individuals who have been victims of a violent act will turn to political violence as a means to achieve some measure of security. This is because the state has failed to provide security. Consequently, these individuals are more likely to support groups that may commit violent acts, but at the same time provide ad hoc security. This particular phenomenon is based upon what some sociologists have identified as the key factor that contributes to gang membership. Studies have found that adolescent males who have witnessed violence or have been a victim of violence no longer believe the state and its security personnel are capable of protecting them (Adamson, 1998; Akers, 1998; Akers and Gang, 1999; Elliot and Menard, 1996; Flannery and Huff, 1999; Klein and Maxson, 2006; Seifert, 2006). As a consequence, they seek protection from alternative groups, such as a gang, to provide this protection, even as the gang goes on to commit violent acts. Seifert applies this particular cognitive behavior not only to the recruitment of members into gangs, but into cults and terrorist organizations as well (2006). She argues that adolescent exposure to war and genocide leads to an increased likelihood that these individuals will grow up to become violent and participate in social violence, such as terrorist organizations (2006). Thus, personal insecurity has the potential to lead to support for the use of political violence.

The Presence of the State

H2: The greater the presence of the state, the less likely an individual will support the use of political violence

In every known case of state failure, the absence of the state's influence is captured by the existence of ungoverned territory. Ungoverned territories are characterized by large stretches of land within a state that are without rule of law exercised by the central government. These spaces are typically located in rural areas, beyond the influence of the central government, or in mountainous locations where there is rough terrain (Rabasa et al., 2007; Howard 2008, 2010a). The existence of ungoverned territory within a weak state is particularly problematic. Without the presence of the government and security forces, non-state actors such as rebel groups, terrorist cells, paramilitary units, and insurgents can organize themselves in these spaces and engage in illegal activities without having to contend with the presence of the central government.

Given what we know about ungoverned territory, I hypothesize that the greater the presence of the government throughout the state, the willingness of an individual to support the use of political violence is less likely.

State Authority

H3: The greater the authority and legitimacy of the state, the less likely an individual will support the use of political violence

The logic behind this hypothesis is that the leadership of a state sets the tone for the state. If the state authority is perceived as corrupt, or as having seized power through illegitimate means, it becomes difficult for the state to convince citizens to adhere to basic laws and institutional rules (Levi, 1988). The only exception is when state leaders use violence and coercion to maintain authority and legitimacy in lieu of functioning institutions. In those cases, states only maintain power and authority through oppression and the use of repressive tactics. In the end, however, state repression can only subdue the populace for so long in the face of deteriorating conditions because of state failure. Political violence becomes the only alternative for repressed citizens of a failed state, and a perfect example of this phenomenon is provided in William Reno's study of Sierra Leone (Rotberg, 2003).

Reno illustrates that because of the corrupt actions of her leaders, widespread conflict was inevitable in Sierra Leone, and yet the emergence of internal conflict did not immediately threaten the power of those whose actions generated the violence (2003). Instead, the political authorities used their own brand of violence and insecurity, in lieu of political institutions, to control their citizens for several years. "These techniques included manipulating access to remaining economic opportunities, instigating local tensions and factional divisions, and using disorder as a political instrument to divide potential challenges to their authority" (Rotberg et al., 2003, p. 71).

In the absence of bureaucratic institutions, political authority in Sierra Leone was based upon controlling markets and manipulating access to economic opportunities. The state authority's capacity to privatize state assets played a key role in its ability to exercise authority and legitimacy. Yet, eventually the state authority could only maintain a minuscule degree of strength in the presence of bureaucratic weakness, corruption, and economic scarcity. When the façade faded, the government's strategy to hang on to its position of power was based upon its ability to undermine the security of its citizens. Given the state's interest in creating a security dilemma, conflict became inevitable. With the ineffective leadership of Stevens and the APC (All Peoples Congress), Sierra Leone was dragged from failure into complete collapse once the RUF seized control of the government through the use of terror and political violence.

The Provision of Public Goods

H4: When citizens are provided with tangible public goods, they are less likely to support the use of political violence

Beyond the provision of the public good of security, the provision of other tangible goods such as an education system, health care, transportation systems, mail delivery, and basic services, are essential responsibilities of the state (Debeil and Klein, 2002; Kreijen, 2004; Rotberg et al., 2003, 2004; Zartman, 1995). When states fail to provide these fundamental services, individuals must seek alternative ways in which to access these public goods (Azam, 2001). This may be in the form of resorting to political violence themselves as a way in which to obtain these goods, or throwing their support behind terrorist organizations and insurgent groups because they believe these groups will succeed where the state has failed.

The Protection of Private Property

H5: When citizens are provided with adequate protection of their private property, they are less likely to support the use of political violence

According to Boone (2007), tensions born out of territorial disputes and environmental stresses are more likely to result in conflict. Bates makes a similar argument. He finds that violent consequences of state decline become evident when private property becomes insecure (2007). This hypothesis is twofold. First, in states where the state authority engages in rent seeking and predatory behavior, citizens are less likely to feel their property is protected. They may rely upon violent organizations to provide this protection, or they may engage in violent activities in order to protest the state authority's corrupt behavior concerning private property. At the same time, when individuals feel another group or individual is threatening their property, they may turn to organizations that engage in terror and violence to remove this threat, which is often at the root of ethnic and genocidal conflicts.

Data and Methodology

Data

The data for this analysis come from the Afrobarometer survey that collects data from several sub-Saharan African countries, with approximately 1,200 respondents of voting age from each state. The survey was conducted in three rounds and gathered using face-to-face interviews based upon a random representative national sample. For the purpose of this study, I use the third round (2005–2006), which consists of a total of 18 cases (N~1200 for each case): South Africa, Namibia, Botswana, Lesotho, Ghana, Zimbabwe, Nigeria, Zambia, Tanzania, Uganda, Malawi, Mali, Cape Verde, Kenya, Mozambique, Senegal, Benin and Madagascar.[5]

As discussed at the opening of this chapter, the overwhelming majority of Africa's nations are considered failed states. An examination of the 2008 Index of State Weakness reveals that with the exception of Cape Verde, South Africa, and Botswana, the remaining 15 cases in the sample rank in the bottom three quintiles[6] (Figure 2.1). The 2011 Failed State Index reports similar findings, except that it ranks all 18 of the cases from the Afrobarometer's survey as either a state in the phases of warning or alert[7] (Figure 2.2). The indexes illustrate that as a unit of

5 It is important to note that the Afrobarometer survey data are intentionally biased toward liberalizing regimes; therefore, authoritarian regimes and countries embroiled in conflict are underrepresented.

6 This analysis classifies states as failing or failed that are ranked in the bottom three quintiles on the Index of State Weakness (See Howard and Morris, 2013).

7 This analysis classifies states as failing or failed that are ranked at "warning" or "alert" respectively, on the Failed State Index (See Howard and Morris, 2013).

analysis, Africa presents a unique opportunity to observe the impact state failure has on the support for political violence. Furthermore, the sample is representative of this particular phenomenon in the region, which is why all 18 cases are included in the analysis.

Table 2.1 The 2008 Index of State Weakness rankings for the country cases in round three of the Afrobaromoter survey

Country	Index of State Weakness Ranking	Quintile
Zimbabwe	8	Bottom Quintile
Uganda	27	Bottom Quintile
Nigeria	28	Bottom Quintile
Zambia	32	2nd Quintile
Mozambique	39	2nd Quintile
Malawi	46	2nd Quintile
Madagascar	49	2nd Quintile
Kenya	50	2nd Quintile
Mali	52	2nd Quintile
Lesotho	53	2nd Quintile
Tanzania	55	2nd Quintile
Senegal	68	3rd Quintile
Benin	71	3rd Quintile
Namibia	82	3rd Quintile
Ghana	84	3rd Quintile
Botswana	102	4th Quintile
South Africa	110	4th Quintile
Cape Verde	123	5th Quintile (The Highest)

Note: Rankings based upon a total of 141 countries.

Table 2.2 The 2011 Failed State Index rankings for the country cases in round three of the Afrobaromoter survey

Country	Failed State Index Ranking	Quintile
Zimbabwe	2	Alert
Kenya	14	Alert
Nigeria	15	Alert
Uganda	21	Alert
Malawi	28	Alert

Table 2.2 *Concluded*

Country	Failed State Index Ranking	Quintile
Zambia	60	Warning
Lesotho	67	Warning
Madagascar	68	Warning
Tanzania	70	Warning
Mozambique	72	Warning
Mali	83	Warning
Cape Verde	84	Warning
Namibia	96	Warning
Benin	97	Warning
Senegal	102	Warning
Botswana	116	Warning
South Africa	122	Warning
Ghana	124	Warning

Note: Rankings based upon a total of 177 countries.

Description of the Variables

Dependent Variable—Political Violence

The dependent variable is a measure of political violence. It captures individuals' attitudes regarding the use of political violence as a legitimate tool to secure tangible goods or concessions from the state. The measure for political violence is based upon the following question in the Afrobarometer survey:

> Question (Variable=Violence): Which of the following statements is closest to your view? Choose Statement A or Statement B.
>
> A: The use of violence is never justified in [respondent's country] politics.
>
> B: In this country, it is sometimes necessary to use violence in support of a just cause.
>
> Value Labels: 1=Agree Very Strongly with A, 2=Agree with A, 3=Agree with B, 4=Agree Very Strongly with B, 5=Agree with Neither, 9=Don't Know, 98=Refused to Answer, -1=Missing Data.[8]

8 All missing data, including the value label "-1=Missing Data" are removed from the analysis.

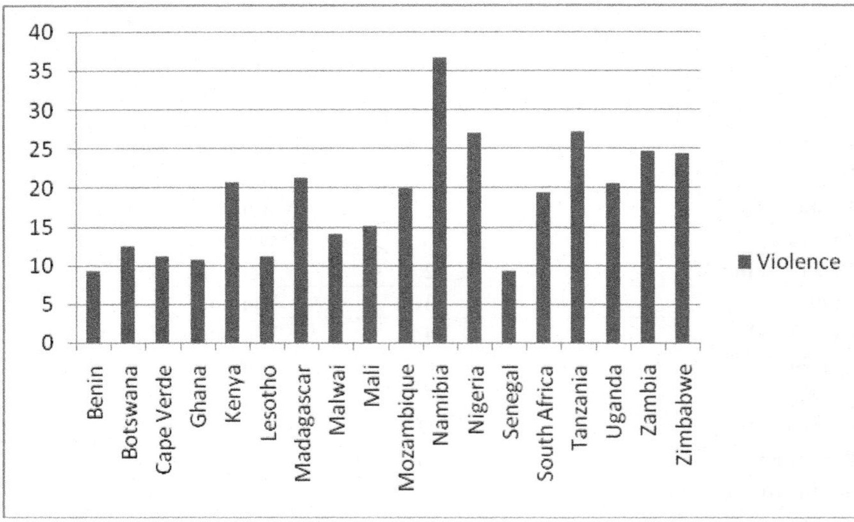

Figure 2.1 Percentage of respondents who support the use of political violence (2006)

In order to estimate the model, I set the values "1" and "2" to zero, values "3" and "4" to one, and code the remaining values as Missing Data. This leaves me with 23,993 observations out of an original 25,397 observations. My reasoning for coding the variable in this manner is because I am only interested in those respondents who favor the use of violence in relation to those who do not. I do not know the motivations of respondents who do not have an answer, or agree with neither statement, so this information is not useful to me. In the end, the transformation of the variable allows me to determine which dimensions of state failure increase the likelihood that individuals will support the use of political violence. Therefore, the value "1" indicates the respondent agrees with Statement B and supports the use of political violence, whereas the value "0" indicates the respondent agrees with Statement A and does not support the use of political violence.

Explanatory Variables

The public good of security

The first explanatory variable I will discuss is based upon two measures of the public good of security. Together, these measures capture individuals' opinions regarding how secure they feel. The belief is that if individuals' feelings of personal insecurity are great, the more willing they are to turn to political violence against the state which has failed to protect them. They are also more willing to support groups that engage in political violence because they believe these groups will provide protection for them. For example, in a survey taken in July 2006 the Beirut Center for Research and Information found that approximately 87 percent of the Lebanese citizens polled supported Hezbollah, a known terrorist organization, and their actions against Israel.[9] The same was true regarding Palestinian support for Hamas and Hezbollah. Following the capture of an Israeli soldier in 2006, a July 24 survey conducted by An-Najah University in the West Bank town of Nablus found that 91 percent of Palestinians supported the militants' demands that the soldier only be released in exchange for prisoners held by Israel.[10] It is widely believed that Hezbollah and Hamas[11,12] enjoy the support of the Lebanese and Palestinians largely because these terrorist organizations are perceived as "protectors from Israeli aggression."[13,14,15] Therefore, the greater the feeling of insecurity, the more likely individuals are to support the use of political violence.

The measures for the public good of security are based upon the following questions in the Afrobarometer survey:

> Question 1 (Variable=Security1): Over the past year, how often (if ever) have you or anyone in your family feared crime in your own home?
>
> Value Labels: 0=Never, 1=Just once or twice, 2=Several times, 3=Many times, 4=Always, 9=Don't Know, 998=Refused to Answer, -1=Missing Data.
>
> Question 2 (Variable=Security2): Over the past year, how often (if ever) have you or anyone in your family been physically attacked?
>
> Value Labels: 0=Never, 1=Just once or twice, 2=Several times, 3=Many times, 4=Always, 9=Don't Know, 998=Refused to Answer, -1=Missing Data.

In order to estimate the model, I code the values of "9" and "998" as Missing Data for both variables. By removing these values, I am left with a scale that

---

9 —— (2006). "Poll Finds Overwhelming Majorities in Lebanon Support Hezbollah, Distrust U.S." *World Public Opinion: Global Public Opinion on International Affairs*. August 2. http://www.worldpublicopinion.org

10 Ibid.

11 Wilson, Scott. (2006). "Hamas Sweeps Palestinian Elections, Complicating Peace Efforts in Mideast." *The Washington Post Foreign Service*. January 27.

12 —— (2009). "Palestinian Support for Hamas has not Declined. *The Jewish Institute for National Security Affairs Report, No. 850*. January 27.

13 Aslan, Reza. (2006). "Hezbollah is Nobody's Puppet." *Los Angeles Times*. July 25.

14 Jamail, Dahr. (2006). "Hezbollah Could be Gaining Strength." *Inter Press News Service*. July 26.

15 The role Hamas and Hezbollah play in providing security and material goods to the Lebanese and Palestinians, while important, it should not overshadow that Hezbollah and Hamas also enjoy popular support because of the deeply felt resentment and hostility the Lebanese and Palestinians feel toward Israel.

indicates an increase in perceived insecurity. Given the measurement of this explanatory variable, a positive coefficient indicates that a higher level of perceived insecurity increases the likelihood that a respondent will support the use of political violence.

The presence of the state

The second explanatory variable, the presence of the state, is based upon three measures of this dimension. Together, these measures capture individuals' opinions regarding the frequency and duration of contact with their elected officials. The belief is that the more visible the government, the more likely the state is present, especially in the case where the survey asks respondents to indicate how often they have contacted their local and national government in the past year to solve a problem. Individuals are less likely to contact their government officials to solve a problem if they perceive the government's presence in their daily lives to be negligible. This situation would support our hypothesis regarding the presence of the state and ungoverned territory. A state where the elected officials are perceived as present, active, and visible, the less likely the region these officials are governing would be considered ungoverned territory. The measures for the presence of the state are based upon the following questions in the Afrobarometer survey:

> Question 1 (Variable=Presence1): During the past year, how often have you contacted any of the following persons for help to solve a problem or to give them your views: a local government councillor?
>
> Value Labels: 0=Never, 1=Only once, 2=A few times, 3=Often, 9=Don't Know, 98=Refused to Answer, -1=Missing Data
>
> Question 2 (Variable=Presence2): During the past year, how often have you contacted any of the following persons for help to solve a problem or to give them your views: a member of Parliament/National Assembly representative?
>
> Value Labels: 0=Never, 1=Only once, 2=A few times, 3=Often, 9=Don't Know, 98=Refused to Answer, -1=Missing Data
>
> Question 3 (Variable=Presence3): How much time does your member of Parliament/National Assembly representative spend in this constituency?
>
> Value Labels: 0=Never, 1=At Least Once a Year, 2=At Least Once A Month, 3=At Least Weekly, 4=Here Almost All of the Time, 9=Don't Know, 98=Refused to Answer, -1=Missing Data

In order to estimate the model, I code the values of "9" and "98" as Missing Data for the three variables. By removing these values, I am left with a scale that indicates an increase in the perceived presence of the state for all measures. Given the measurement of these independent variables and my hypothesis, a negative coefficient indicates that the perceived *absence* of the state increases the likelihood that a respondent will support political violence.

The state authority

The third explanatory variable, state authority, is based upon seven measures of this dimension. Together, these measures capture individuals' opinions regarding the legitimacy of the government and its elected officials. The belief is that if the state authority is perceived as corrupt, or as having seized power through illegal or unconstitutional means, it is difficult for the state to convince citizens to adhere to basic laws and institutional rules. In support of our hypothesis, a corrupt or illegitimate state authority encourages citizens to engage in political violence against the state. The measures for the dimensions of state authority that capture government corruption are based upon the following questions in the Afrobarometer survey:

> Question 1 (Variable=Corrupt1): How many of the following people do you think are involved in corruption, or haven't you heard enough to say: the President/Prime Minister and officials in his office?
>
> Value Labels: 0=None, 1=Some of them, 2=Most of them, 3=All of them, 9=Don't Know, 98=Refused to Answer, -1=Missing Data.
>
> Question 2 (Variable=Corrupt2): How many of the following people do you think are involved in corruption, or haven't you heard enough to say: members of Parliament/National Assembly representatives?
>
> Value Labels: 0=None, 1=Some of them, 2=Most of them, 3=All of them, 9=Don't Know, 98=Refused to Answer, -1=Missing Data.
>
> Question 3 (Variable=Corrupt3): How many of the following people do you think are involved in corruption, or haven't you heard enough to say: local government councillors?
>
> Value Labels: 0=None, 1=Some of them, 2=Most of them, 3=All of them, 9=Don't Know, 98=Refused to Answer, -1=Missing Data.
>
> Question 4 (Variable=Corrupt4): How many of the following people do you think are involved in corruption, or haven't you heard enough to say: national government officials?
>
> Value Labels: 0=None, 1=Some of them, 2=Most of them, 3=All of them, 9=Don't Know, 98=Refused to Answer, -1=Missing Data.

Question 5 (Variable=Corrupt5): How many of the following people do you think are involved in corruption, or haven't you heard enough to say: local government officials?

Value Labels: 0=None, 1=Some of them, 2=Most of them, 3=All of them, 9=Don't Know, 98=Refused to Answer, -1=Missing Data.

In order to estimate the model, I code the values of "9" and "98" as Missing Data for both variables. By removing these values, I am left with a scale that indicates an increase in the perceived presence of corruption among elected officials for all measures. Given the measurement of these independent variables and my hypothesis, a positive coefficient indicates that the perceived presence of government corruption increases the likelihood that a respondent will support political violence.

Turning now to the other dimensions of state authority, I employ a set of measures that also capture the legitimacy of the state authority by measuring the process by which officials are elected to office, and if this is a fair and equitable process. The measures for the legitimacy of the state authority are based upon the following questions in the Afrobarometer survey:

Question 1 (Variable=Legitimate1): Think about how elections work in this country. How well do elections ensure that the members of Parliament/National Assembly representatives reflect the views of the voters?

Value Labels: 0=Not at all well, 1=Not very well, 2=Well, 3=Very Well, 9=Don't Know, 98=Refused to Answer, -1=Missing Data.

Question 2 (Variable=Legitimate2): Think about how elections work in this country. How well do elections enable voters to remove from office leaders who do not do what the people want?

Value Labels: 0=Not at all well, 1=Not very well, 2=Well, 3=Very Well, 9=Don't Know, 98=Refused to Answer, -1=Missing Data.

In order to estimate the model, I code the values of "9" and "98" as Missing Data for both variables. By removing these values, I am left with a scale that indicates an increase in the perceived legitimacy of the state. Given the measurement of these independent variables and my hypothesis, a negative coefficient indicates that the perceived *absence* of government legitimacy increases the likelihood that a respondent will support the use of political violence.

The provision of public goods

The fourth explanatory variable, the provision of public goods, is based upon three measures of this dimension. Together, these measures capture individuals' opinions regarding the state's ability to provide citizens with essential public goods. The belief is that if the state cannot provide essential public goods, individuals begin to perceive that state as weak or impotent, and turn to other means of obtaining these essential goods. Resorting to crime, corruption, and the black market economy are just a few ways in which individuals gain access to these goods; political violence represents another such avenue. In support of my hypothesis, a state that does not provide essential public goods to its constituency encourages citizens to engage in or support political violence as a means of gaining access to these necessary goods. The measures for the provision of public goods are based upon the following questions in the Afrobarometer survey:

> Question 1 (Variable=Goods1): Over the past year, how often, if ever, have you or anyone in your family gone without: enough clean water for home use?
>
> Value Labels: 0=Never, 1=Just once or twice, 2=Several times, 3=Many times, 4=Always, 9=Don't Know, 998=Refused to Answer, -1=Missing Data
>
> Question 2 (Variable=Goods2): Based on your experience, how easy or difficult is it to obtain the following services? Or do you never try to get these services from the government: a place in primary school for a child?
>
> Value Labels: 1=Very difficult, 2=Difficult, 3=Easy, 4=Very easy, 7=Never try, 9=Don't Know, 98=Refused to Answer, -1=Missing Data
>
> Question 3 (Variable=Goods3): Based on your experience, how easy or difficult is it to obtain the following services? Or do you never try to get these services from the government: medical treatment at a nearby clinic?
>
> Value Labels: 1=Very difficult, 2=Difficult, 3=Easy, 4=Very easy, 7=Never try, 9=Don't Know, 98=Refused to Answer, -1=Missing Data

For the variable *Goods1*, I code the values of "9" and "998" as Missing Data. By removing these values, I am left with a scale that indicates the increasing ability of the government to provide the public good of clean water. Given the measurement of this variable and my hypothesis, a negative coefficient indicates that the perceived inability of the government to provide the public good of clean water increases the likelihood that a respondent will support the use of political violence.

For the variables *Goods2* and *Goods3*, I code the values of "9" and "98" as Missing Data. And instead of dropping value 7, which indicates citizens do not try to obtain certain basic services from the government, I recode it as "0." I do this because I do not know the motivations behind an individual's reasons for not attempting to obtain these particular services from the government.

In some cases, wealthy individuals do not need to obtain certain basic services, such as education and health care from the government. The government may provide the service, they simply don't use it, whereas individuals living in poverty may need these services, but are apathetic toward the government and its ability to provide them with these services. Since I do not have any insight regarding why these respondents never seek to obtain these services from the government, I cannot drop this value. I would lose important information if I did this, which is why I code the response as zero. After recoding this variable, I am left with a scale that indicates the increasing ability of the government to provide the public goods of education and health care. Given the measurement of this variable and my hypothesis, a negative coefficient indicates that the perceived inability of the government to provide thepublic goods of health care and education increases the likelihood that a respondent will support political violence.

The protection of private property

The fifth explanatory variable is based upon a single measure of the protection of private property. This measure captures individuals' opinions regarding the security of their private property. The belief is that if individuals' feelings of property insecurity are great, the more willing they are to turn to political violence against the state which has either taken their property through illegal means or allowed their property to be illegally seized by others. Similar to the actions of individuals who lack personal security and their support for groups who engage in political violence; individuals are also more willing to support these violent groups because they believe these organizations will provide property protection for them or help them regain access to their property (Bates, 2007). The measure for the protection of private property is based upon the following question in the Afrobarometer survey:

> Question 1 (Variable=Property): What if anything, would you do to try and resolve each of the following situations: someone wrongly seized your family's land?
>
> Value Labels: 1=Don't worry, things will be resolved given enough time, 2=Lodge a complaint through proper channels or procedures, 3=Use connections with influential people, 4=Offer tip or bribe, 5=Join in public protest, 6=Other, 7=Nothing, because nothing can be done, 9=Don't Know, 998=Refused to Answer, -1=Missing Data

In order to estimate the model, I code the values of "9" and "98" as Missing Data for both variables. I also drop the value "6" and recode value "7" as zero.[16] In the case of value "6," which represents "Other," I remove this because it offers no substantive information for this analysis. In the case of value "7," which represents "Nothing, because nothing can be done," I choose to set this value to

16 By dropping a value, I code it as Missing Data.

zero, because as far as tangible meanings regarding the scale, it is similar to value "1" which represents "Don't worry, things will be resolved given enough time." Both options indicate that nothing is done; the only difference is the motivation behind why the respondent chooses not to act. By setting value "7" to zero, I am left with a scale that moves along the continuum from doing nothing out of apathy to actively protesting. The transformation of this variable indicates an increase in the support for more radical actions, given the loss of private property. Given the measurement of this variable and my hypothesis, a positive coefficient indicates that the more radical the action a respondent is willing to take if his or her private property has been seized increases the likelihood that a respondent will support political violence.

Table 2.3 List of variable names and description of the concepts measured

Variable Name	Indicator Concept
Violence	Measures Political Violence
Security1	Fear of Crime
Security2	Personally Attacked
Presence1	Contacts local government to solve problems
Presence2	Contacts national government to solve problems
Presence3	Time the national government leaders spends with the constituency
Corrupt1	The President/Prime Minister is corrupt
Corrupt2	The National Assembly/Members of the Parliament are corrupt
Corrupt3	The Local Councillor is corrupt
Corrupt4	National government officials are corrupt
Corrupt5	Local government officials are corrupt
Legitimate1	Members of the national government govern according to the mandate of the people
Legitimate2	The ease with which citizens can remove ineffective leaders from office
Goods1	Gone without clean water
Goods2	Government provides education
Goods3	Government provides medical treatment
Property	Illegal seizure of private property
Education	Respondent's highest level of education
Gender	Gender
PersEcon	Respondent's current economic level
Ethnic	The respondent' ethnic group and their current level of economic status in relation to other ethnic groups
Urban	Respondent is from an urban or rural area

Controls

I operationalize a series of control variables that capture the socioeconomic conditions of the respondents. I argue that one of the most salient differences between the respondents in this study is socioeconomic level. Otherwise stated, I believe that support for political violence is more likely among the "have nots" and the marginalized populations of society. Therefore, I include the variables, level of education, personal economic situation, ethnic groups' economic situation, gender, and whether the respondent lives in an urban or rural area. I argue these control variables serve as ideal indicators of an individual's socioeconomic position within that state. See Appendix C for a description of the control variables and their measurement.

Model

I conduct cross-sectional analysis using logistical regression in order to determine which dimensions of state failure increase the probability that an individual will support and/or engage in political violence in the selected country cases. In order to test my assumptions, I estimate a logit model that captures respondents' support for the use of political violence.

Logit Model

$$Model1 = h\left(\frac{p_i(violence)}{1 - p_i(violence)}\right) = \beta_0 + \beta_1 Security + \beta_2 StatePresence + \beta_3 StateAuthority + \beta_4 StateLegitimacy +$$
$$\beta_5 SPublic\ Goods + \beta_6 Property + \beta_7 Education + \beta_8 Gender + \beta_9 PersEcon + \beta_{10} Ethnic + \beta_{11} Urban + e$$

Figure 2.2 State failure model of support for political violence

Findings

Descriptive Statistics

In Figure 2.3, I report the trend of terrorist activity in sub-Saharan Africa for a 30-year time period between 1977 and 2007. Figure 2.3 reveals that in the seventies and early eighties, incidents of terrorism in the region were relatively low, with attacks averaging around 50 per year. However, as we moved toward the end of the eighties and into the nineties, there was a sharp increase in terrorism. I argue that this was because of the failure of the post-independence governments to promote stability, comprehensive democracy, and economic development.

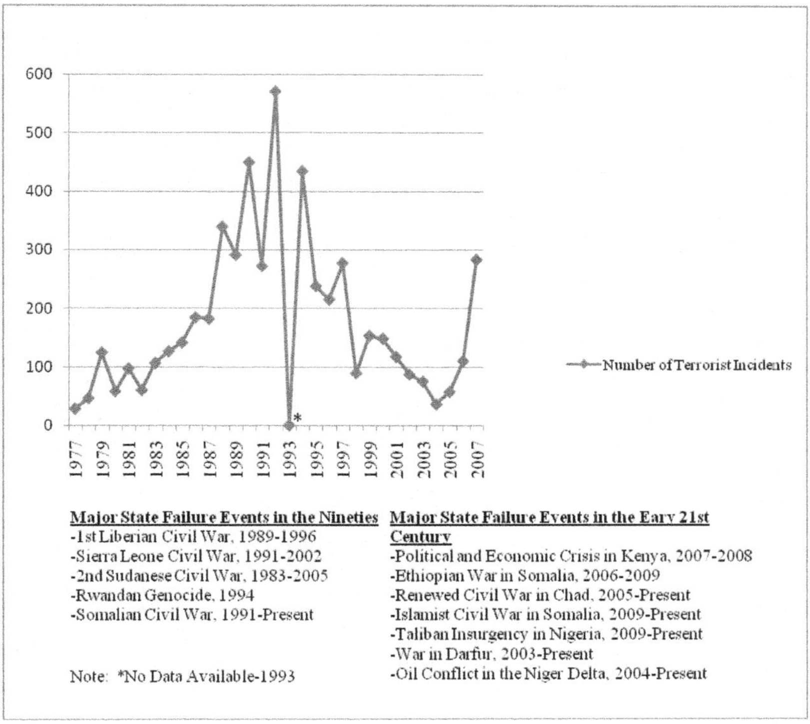

Figure 2.3 Number of reported terrorist incidents in sub-Saharan Africa, 1977–2007

With the majority of African independence movements taking place in the sixties and seventies (Figure 2.4), there was about a 15-year period in the region where leaders struggled to implement democracy and promote stability. However, when these attempts failed, rebel groups emerged and civil war erupted, plunging many of sub-Saharan Africa's states into failure. As a consequence, political violence erupted during these periods of failure, one of which occurred during the tumultuous period of the nineties. Another era where we can observe a spike in political violence has begun in the early part of the twenty-first century. This is largely the result of the failure of post-civil war peace agreements. Again, the people of Africa have been disappointed by the corruption and polarizing factions of the political leadership, thus opening the door for terrorist groups to offer an alternative strategy for obtaining political and economic goods that the state has failed to provide. The major problem with the current surge in political violence and the growing presence of terrorist organizations in the region is that unlike the period before in the nineties, radical Islamic ideologies have found a home in sub-Saharan Africa and have begun to take root, making the presence of these groups, coupled with the failure of African states, a very deadly combination that the international community must now contend with.

Figure 2.4 Map of African independence

Statistical Results

Table 2.4 Binary logit estimates of support for political violence

Variable	Restricted Model	Full Model
Security1	-.004 (.021)	-.0045 (.022)
Security2	.171*** (.035)	.175*** (.036)
Presence1	-.004 (.027)	-.008 (.028)

Table 2.4 ***Concluded***

Variable	Restricted Model	Full Model
Presence2	.029 (.041)	.035 (.041)
Presence3	.114*** (.021)	.093*** (.022)
Corrupt1	.165*** (.038)	.185*** (.040)
Corrupt2	-.028 (.045)	-.040 (.046)
Corrupt3	-.005 (.041)	-.029 (.042)
Corrupt4	-.072 (.046)	-.060 (.047)
Corrupt5	.060 (.043)	.056 (.044)
Legitimate1	-.030 (.032)	-.040 (.033)
Legitimate2	-.072** (.029)	-.064** (.030)
Goods1	.009 (.018)	.024 (.019)
Goods2	-.049** (.022)	-.049** (.023)
Goods3	-.033 (.026)	-.054** (.027)
Property	.132*** (.031)	.129*** (.032)
Gender	—	.040 (.049)
PersEcon	—	.056** (.021)
Education	—	.048*** (.013)
Ethnic	—	-.07** (.025)
Urban	—	.057 (.053)
Constant	-1.61*** (.120)	-1.67*** (.173)
Observations	11380	10789
Pseudo R^2	.0139	.0178
LR χ^2	159.37	194.08
Prob> χ^2	.000	.000

Note: ***p < .01 for two-tailed test; ** p < .05 for two-tailed test; *p <0.1 for two-tailed test; standard errors in parentheses.

Turning now to the statistical results, the findings echo the trends observed in Figure 2.3. The conditions of state failure foster individual support for the use of political violence. In Table 2.4, I report the binary logit estimates for the model, which indicates the probability that a respondent will support the use of political violence.[17]

Findings that are Statistically Significant and Support the Hypotheses

Regarding the statistical findings, the first set of variables I discuss are those that are both statistically significant and provide support for the stated hypotheses. The first of such variables is *Security2.* This variable indicates whether the respondent, or someone in the respondent's family, has been personally attacked in the past year. The findings suggest that a higher level of perceived physical insecurity increases the probability that a person will support the use of political violence.

In terms of the concept of state authority, the variable *Corrupt1* indicates whether the respondent perceives the national government as being corrupt. The findings suggest that a higher level of perceived corruption within the national government increases the probability that a person will support the use of political violence.

The second measure of state authority is legitimacy, and the findings suggest that the more difficult it is for voters to remove an ineffective leader from office, the more supportive they are of using political violence as an option.

Turning now to the provision of public goods, the findings suggest that the more difficult it is for respondents to receive the public goods of education and health care from the government, the more supportive they are of using political violence as an option.

As far as the protection of public property is concerned, the more radical the action respondents are willing to take if their private property has been seized increases the likelihood that respondents will support political violence.

With regards to the control variable, *Education*, it can be interpreted either way. The prevailing belief is that low levels of education are associated with poor living and economic conditions (Smith, 2005; Sen, 1982; Brady, 2003; Danziger and Weinberg, 1994; Berliner, 2005; Becker and Luthar, 2002; Tilak, 2002; Orfield and Lee, 2005). As a consequence, this group would be more willing to support political violence as a viable political option in order to increase their economic status and improve their living conditions. At the same time, the country cases included in Round 3 of the Afrobarometer survey are those that would be considered liberalizing regimes. As Gurr (1970) and Huntington (1968) demonstrate, countries that are modernizing increase expectations among the middle class, who are typically educated; however, the economic achievements of an evolving economy are not always in line with citizens' expectations. Consequently, the more educated may support the use of political violence because they believe the government is not delivering on its promise to modernize. The results of this analysis support this

17 For marginal effects, see Appendix B.

proposition, in that I find the more educated the respondents, the more likely they are to support the use of political violence.

Findings that are Statistically Significant but Fail to Support the Hypotheses

With regards to the results, the second set of variables I would like to discuss are those that are statistically significant but fail to provide support for the stated hypotheses. The first of such variables is *Presence3*. This variable indicates the amount of time the respondent's member of Parliament, or National Assembly representative spends with his or her constituency. The findings suggest that the perceived presence of the state increases the probability that a person will support the use of political violence, which contradicts my hypothesis.

As far as personal living conditions are concerned, the results indicate that the better the respondents' living conditions, the more likely they are to support the use of political violence. Unlike the variable, *Education*, which is naturally highly correlated with an individual's living and economic conditions,[18] there is little justification to interpret this variable in support of the hypothesis. That is because the level of education for an individual confers upon that person a certain ideology and expectation that with higher levels of education comes higher economic status and improved living conditions. That is the expectation, but often that is not the case in these particular nations. However, a person's economic status and living conditions are tangible indicators that the government has delivered on its promises. At the least, higher economic status and satisfactory living conditions should indicate satisfaction with the government. Therefore, one would not expect a respondent who is living well and comfortably to support the use of political violence.

The final variable to achieve statistical significance, but contradicts the stated hypothesis, is the measure of ethnicity. This variable indicates whether a respondent feels his or her ethnic group is doing worse, the same as, or better than other ethnic groups with regards to current living conditions. The findings suggest that respondents' belief that their ethnic group is doing better than other groups increases the probability that they will support the use of political violence. One would expect only those respondents who feel their ethnic group is worse off than other groups to support the use of political violence. Therefore, it is apparent that this variable fails to support the hypothesis.

Conclusion

In this chapter, I have argued that state failure is a significant contributor of political violence in sub-Saharan African states. Out of the five dimensions of state failure, four have a significant impact on the likelihood that a citizen will support the use of political violence against the government. The findings point to the

18 Pearson correlation coefficient =.2018, p. 000.

absence of the public good of security, a corrupt and illegitimate state authority, lack of provision of essential public goods, and the inability to protect private property as the major components of state failure that increase the probability of political violence. The unexpected exception to this is the failure of this analysis to find support for the assertion that with ungoverned territory there is the absence of the state. The belief is that without the presence of the government, there is the potential for non-state actors to organize themselves in these spaces and engage in illegal and dangerous activities without having to contend with the interference from the central government. These non-state actors can be citizens who have organized themselves into militia organizations,[19] or non-citizens who have crossed into that state.[20] Yet, regardless of where these groups come from, and whom they are comprised of, the main argument remains that the absence of the government is a significant precursor to political violence. And yet, this analysis fails to find evidence to support this argument, which represents an important avenue for future research, since I remain grounded in the notion that this feature of state failure leads to political violence.

Table 2.5 Hypotheses supported by the Logistical Regression analysis

Hypotheses	**Variable and Concept Measured**
Absence of the public good of security	Security2—Personally attacked
State authority	Corrupt1—The President/Prime Minister is corrupt Corrupt3—The Local Councillor is corrupt Corrupt5—The Local Government is corrupt
State legitimacy	Legitimate2—The ease with which citizens can remove ineffective leaders
Provision of public goods	Goods2—Government provides education Goods3—Government provides healthcare
Protection of private property	Property—Illegal seizure of private property
Controls	Gender Education—Respondent's highest level of education

19 Examples of this include Examples of this include the Lord's Resistance Army (LRA) led by Joseph Kony and comprised of the Acholi ethnic group against the Ugandan state and examples of this include the Lord's Resistance Army (LRA) led by Joseph Kony and comprised of the Acholi ethnic group against the Ugandan state and the People's Liberation Movement/Army (SPLA/M) led by John Garang, and comprised of the Dinka and Nuer people of South Sudan. Both groups have been guilty of committing a number of atrocities and human rights violations against civilians.

20 Al-Qaeda, Hezbollah, the Palestinian Islamic Jihad, Hamas, the Egyptian Islamic Group, and the Abu Nidal organization have all at one point crossed into Somalia to set up operations (Linden et al., 2002).

To conclude, the findings of this chapter illustrate that in sub-Saharan Africa, where state failure is a tragic pandemic, there is evidence to suggest that individuals are likely to support political violence as a means by which to obtain tangible political, economic, and social goods. This work has important political implications because thus far, sub-Saharan Africa has not produced the level of terrorist activity that is present in the Middle East and South Asia. However, that may not always be the case. As I have demonstrated in this chapter, the conditions in failed states threaten an individual's survival, which then encourages them to obtain tangible political and economic resources through the use of violence. This phenomenon raises the question, could the failed states of sub-Saharan Africa become the next breeding ground for internationally sponsored networks of terrorism? Undoubtedly, yes, as it has already begun, but for how long will these networks find a safe haven in the region, and how deadly will this terrorist threat be to both the region and the global community? Only time can provide that answer.

Chapter 3
A Legacy of Tyranny, Tragedy and Terror: A Closer Look at Weak States, Authoritarian Rule, and Radical Religious Terrorism in the Middle East and North Africa

Introduction

The Middle East and the states that comprise the Maghreb have been plagued by enduring conflicts for the past 50 years. The region has hosted some of the bloodiest and most protracted wars in the world, namely the Israeli-Palestinian conflict, the two wars in Iraq (1991 and 2003), the civil war in Yemen (1994), the conflict in Lebanon (2007), and one of the deadliest interstate conflicts with the war between Iraq and Iran (1980–1988).

Further, insurgent and terrorist activity is also well documented in the Maghreb, most notably Sudan. Backed by the Sudanese government, in 2003 the paramilitary organization the Janjaweed began implementing a brutal campaign against the popular resistance movement, the Sudan Liberation Movement/Army (SLM/A), which is comprised of three non-Arab groups—the Masalit, Fur, and Zaghawa. The conflict between the two forces plunged the Darfur region into anarchy and led to the internal displacement of over two million forced migrants, and more than 200,000 refugees have fled to neighboring Chad. At the same time, Sudan remains on the U.S. State Department's list of states that sponsor terrorism, given that the state has provided safe haven to Hezbollah, the Palestinian Islamic Jihad, Hamas, the Egyptian Islamic Group, and the Abu Nidal organization, all well known and very dangerous terrorist organizations (Linden et al., 2002).

The Middle East and North Africa (MENA) region is a known conflict zone, rife with internal and regional conflicts, but it is also the site for some of the deadliest terror networks and attacks in the world. Thus, the prevalence of violence in the region has made the Middle East and the Maghreb the focal point for a great deal of political science research.

For years scholars have worked to understand why the Middle East and North Africa host, seemingly, an endless wave of violence. Several empirical studies have arrived at relevant theories that find the lack of democracy, the presence of religious radicalism, and intractable barriers to modernization are at the root of the conflicts (Martin, 1987; Huntington, 1991; Sorli, Gleditsch, and Strand, 2005; Piazza, 2006, 2007; Newman, 2007; Tikusis, 2009). Building upon this body of research, I explore these arguments but from a different perspective of the existing studies. Instead of tackling democracy, modernization, and religious radicalism as discrete concepts, I examine the impact these factors have on the trend to political violence in this region as components of state failure.

Next to sub-Saharan Africa and Asia, the Middle East and North Africa are comprised of the highest percentage of weak and failed states in the world. I argue that the theories that have been explored thus far as root causes of the political violence in the Middle East and North Africa are simply symptoms of all fragile states (Howard and Morris, 2013). Therefore, analyses of the causes of terrorism and political violence in the Middle East and the Maghreb should first begin with an examination of the dysfunction of the state.

Using data from the Arabarometer survey (2008), I argue that the conditions of state failure force individuals to resort to terrorism and political violence in the Middle East and North Africa as a means by which to obtain tangible political, economic, and social goods, and force strategic political concessions. Therefore, as a main assertion of this text, I contend that promoting democracy, modernization, and religious freedom on an individual basis are noble and useful pursuits, but addressing these factors in a broader context by promoting state building in the region is the first step toward addressing the systematic violence.

Terrorism and State Failure in the Middle East and North Africa

In this chapter, I evaluate the relationship between state failure and the prevalence of political violence, terrorism, and insurgent activity in the Middle East and the Maghreb in an effort to illustrate that it is the process of state failure that explains why the region is plagued by political violence, and not simply the grievance-based issues of a lack of democracy and economic development, which then fuel religious radicalism.

The root causes of terrorism and political violence cannot be fully explained by existing research, which cites the factors of economic decline, religious radicalism, and levels of frustration because of the absence of democracy, as antecedent conditions (Martin, 1987; Huntington, 1991; Sorli, Gleditsch, and Strand, 2005; Piazza, 2006, 2007; Newman, 2007; Tikusis, 2009). I argue that this body of research falls short because it ignores the critical features of state failure, which have the potential to drive an individual to commit acts of political violence and terrorism.

States that have failed experience tremendous upheaval and the consequences of this phenomenon are severe and have long-term implications for society. In failed states where there is the absence of a functioning political system and the basic tenets of security and order, citizens of these nation states are potentially more vulnerable to the radical agenda of terrorist groups. The conditions of state fragility in this region have provided extremist groups with material for propaganda, which has facilitated their recruitment efforts and legitimized their acts of terrorism among the populace (Piazza, 2006; Krueger and Maleckova, 2003; Howard, 2010a). Thus, I argue there is the potential for extremist groups to gain popular support for the use of political violence during such a tenuous period.

As discussed at the opening of this study, next to sub-Saharan Africa and Asia, the Middle East and North Africa is a region plagued by failed states (see Table 3.1 and Table 3.2). While Figure 3.1 and Figure 3.2 further illustrate the prevalence of state collapse in the region and the relationship it shares with incidents of terrorism.

I argue that at the root of the relationship between state failure and terrorism is the absence of the state in ungoverned territory, and from the lack of a state presence in many regions of the state, other symptoms of state failure emerge, as well as political violence.

Like many of the states in sub-Saharan Africa, the Middle East and North Africa have vast stretches of ungoverned territory (Kahler, 2002; Rabasa et al., 2007), and ungoverned territory is "linked to the incubation of terrorism where the central government is unable to project its power in substantial regions of the country controlled by insurgents, regional actors, [or terrorists]" (Piazza, 2007, p. 526). Within the Middle East and North Africa, the nations of Yemen, Saudi Arabia, Algeria, and Lebanon, have all hosted terrorist groups such as al-Qaeda, Hamas, the FLN, and Hezbollah within their tribal territories and remote regions of the state where the influence of the government is marginal, if not completely absent.

Table 3.1 The 2008 Index of State Weakness rankings for the Middle East and North Africa

Country	Ranking	Quintile
Iraq	4	Bottom Quintile
Sudan	6	Bottom Quintile
Yemen**	30	2nd Quintile
Mauritania	37	2nd Quintile
Algeria**	57	3rd Quintile
Syria	59	3rd Quintile
Iran	66	3rd Quintile
Egypt	78	3rd Quintile
Libya	86	4th Quintile
Lebanon**	93	4th Quintile
Morocco**	96	4th Quintile
Turkey	98	4th Quintile
Tunisia	112	4th Quintile
Jordan**	118	5th Quintile (The Highest)
Oman	128	5th Quintile (The Highest)

Note: Rankings based upon a total of 141 countries. Country cases in the Arabarometer survey are denoted by **.

Table 3.2 The 2011 Failed State Index rankings for the Middle East and North Africa

Country	Ranking	Quintile
Sudan	3	Alert
Iraq	6	Alert
Yemen**	18	Alert
Lebanon**	29	Alert
Iran	38	Alert
Egypt	43	Warning
Mauritania	46	Warning
Israel/West Bank**	58	Warning
Algeria**	73	Warning
Turkey	85	Warning
Jordan**	86	Warning
Saudi Arabia	89	Warning
Morocco**	93	Warning
Libya	112	Warning
Tunisia	121	Warning
Kuwait**	125	Warning

Note: Rankings based upon a total of 177 countries. Country cases in the Arabarometer survey are denoted by **.

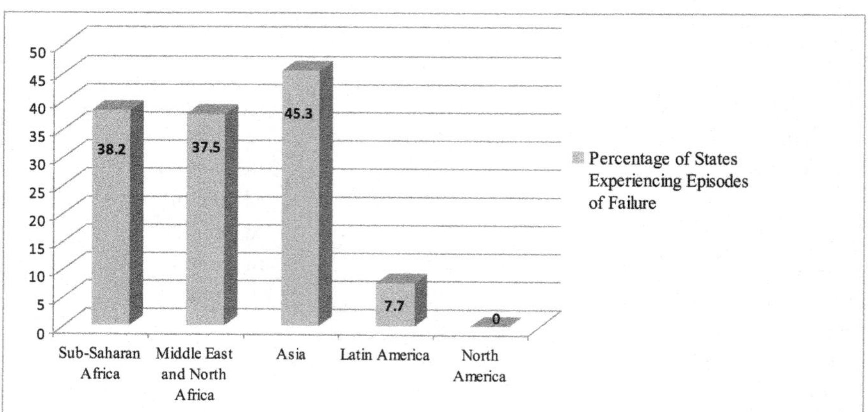

Figure 3.1 Percentage of states experiencing episodes of failure by region, 1998–2003

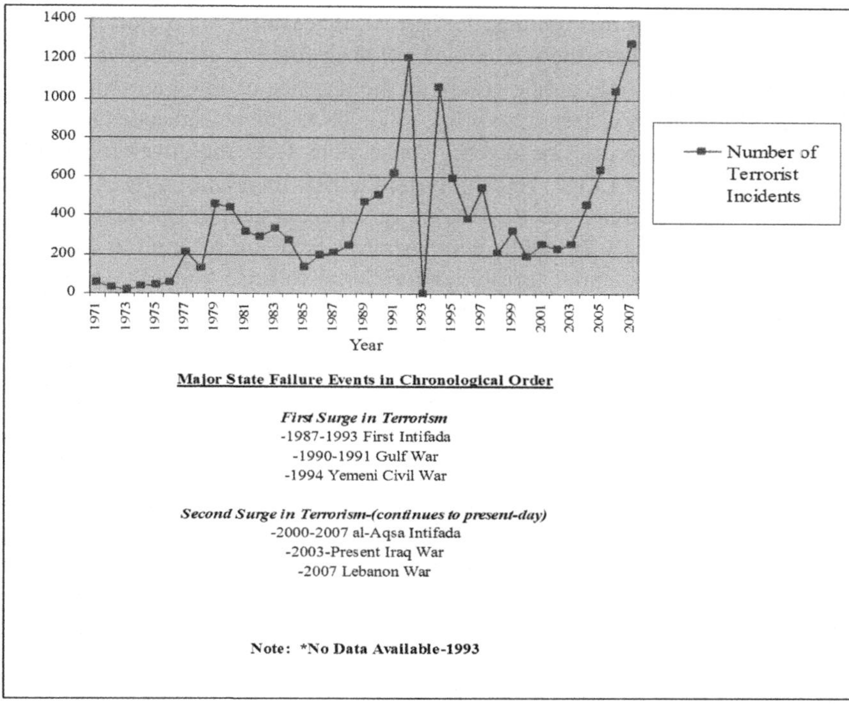

Figure 3.2 Number of reported terrorist incidents and major events of state failure in the Middle East and the Maghreb, 1977–2007[1,2]

Beyond the absence of government in ungoverned territory, the Middle East and North Africa are also plagued by other critical features of state failure: a lack of security, an illegitimate and corrupt state authority, and the inability of the states' governments to provide public goods and services to substantial segments of the population. Together, these factors represent the conditions of state failure.

1 What is important about Figure 3.2 is that two surges of terrorism are evident. The first began around 1985 and sharply increased throughout the first Palestinian Intifada through the Gulf War and then the civil war in Yemen. The Arab-Israeli Conflict, which is at the nexus of the security concerns in the region, prompted a decrease in the violence with the Oslo Peace Process of 1993–2000 and the Camp David Negotiations in 2000, but with the breakdown in negotiation talks, followed by former Israeli Prime Minister Sharon's visit to the Temple Mount, the second Intifada began that led to the second surge of political violence that has steadily increased with the war in Lebanon and the war in Iraq.

2 At the time of this writing, the Iraq War was ongoing, but since the time of this writing and prior to publication, American troops have withdrawn from Iraq (December 2011) bringing an end to this armed conflict, although political violence and terrorism continues.

Further, at the time of this writing, the current upheaval in the region represents a classic example of how these conditions of state fragility can deprive ordinary citizens of basic, tangible public goods. In the absence of these aforementioned public goods, ordinary citizens, not prone to violence, can be persuaded to engage in such acts given their desire to force concessions from the government. With regards to the cases of Libya, Yemen, Syria, Tunisia, Iran, and Egypt, in the face of state fragility, citizens are demanding an open system of government and economic opportunities, and while demonstrators have not resorted to violence,[3] there is always the potential for political violence to arise given the repressive responses of the regimes in power to the demands of the protesters.

Beyond the conditions of state fragility just discussed, there are three additional factors, which although not specifically unique to the region, their prevalence in the Middle East and North Africa have often been cited as the major root causes of the political violence in the region, and I examine them in this chapter alongside my own argument of state failure.

Consequently, I explore the impact the factors of authoritarianism, lack of economic development, and the dominance of religious radicalism have on individual support for political violence. I argue that within the Middle East and North Africa they function as intervening factors with regards to the relationship between political violence and state failure. As I pointed out at the opening of this chapter, the failure of earlier works was not that they examined these factors as key contributors to terrorism in the region, but that they failed to assess the collective influence these conditions have on terrorism within the context of state failure. I explore this relationship in greater detail in the following section. However, it is important to understand that there are cultural considerations and circumstances within the Middle East and North Africa that make the convergence of these variables so crucial to our understanding of state failure in this region, and why they have had such a key impact on ideological support for terrorism, more so than in any other region in the world.

Middle East Exceptionalism—The Prevalence of Authoritarianism, Lack of Economic Development and Religious Radicalism

The Absence of Democracy/Authoritarian Rule

The Middle East and North Africa is a region dominated by authoritarian systems of governance. Of the 24 states that make up the Middle East and the Maghreb, only Israel and Turkey represent traditional democratic states. Huntington points to the region as one that is most resistant to democratic ideals, which is evident given that the region has yet to experience a wave of democratization (1991; Sorli,

3 This was written in the spring of 2011. Since then, violence has erupted in Libya, Yemen, Egypt and Syria.

Gleditsch, and Strand, 2005). Huntington, along with other scholars, have argued that the absence of democracy in the Middle East and North Africa can be attributed to a complex set of factors—the most notable being the salient nature of Islam (1991; Martin, 1987; Lewis, 1987; Kedourie, 1994; Sorli, Gleditsch, and Strand, 2005; Piazza, 2007).

In a multivariate cross-sectional analysis, Fish finds that Islam shares a strong relationship with autocracy and attributes this finding to the subordinate role of women in Middle Eastern and North African society (2004; Sorli, Gleditsch, and Strand, 2005). As such, the prevailing thought is that the subordination of women in society fuels the necessity of authoritarian rule, because without it, women would be equal participants in the political system, which runs counter to the cultural traditions of the region. In contrast, Donno and Russett find that, in general, Arab states are more likely to be authoritarian than Islamic states (2004). Thus, debate remains as to whether or not the prevalence of autocratic systems of governance in the region is because of Arab culture or because Islam is the dominant religion in these countries. Nevertheless, regardless of whether or not Islam or Arabism is the driver of authoritarianism, the prominence of autocracy in the Middle East has long been considered a root cause of the conflicts in the region (Martin, 1987; Lewis, 1987; Kedourie, 1994; Kramer, 1996; Aarts, 1999; Rubin, 2002) mainly because in these types of states "grievances are not addressed or they are allowed to fester … [T]he nature of nondemocratic regimes retards the public virtues of political moderation and compromises, which are necessary ingredients of nonviolent political expression" (Piazza, 2007, p. 522). Despite the complex and much debated relationship between authoritarianism and political instability, there is evidence to support the assertion that authoritarian rule breeds conflict. However, the relationship between authoritarianism and terrorism is not as clearly defined, as it is lacks evidential support in the current body of research.

Existing studies have found little evidence to suggest that the absence of democracy and the presence of authoritarian rule encourage terrorism (Schmid, 1992; Charters 1994; Eubank and Weinberg, 1994, 1998, 2001; Eyerman, 1998; Li, 2005). Several studies have even found that democracies are actually more conducive to terrorist activities than authoritarian states (Schmid 1992; Charters 1994; Eubank and Weinberg, 1994, 1998, 2001). Thus, a major challenge for this analysis is to illustrate that the features of authoritarian rule that foster conflict also foster political violence, specifically terrorism. It is logical to assume there is a relationship between terrorism and autocratic forms of governance, given the strength of the relationship between violent conflict and autocracy. The fact that existing studies have not been able to establish this relationship highlights the weaknesses of these analyses and the data used. By utilizing survey data, this text diverges from existing approaches by identifying the repressive components of authoritarian states within the context of state weakness that foster individual opinions and attitudes that could then lead to political violence. This approach will reveal that autocratic systems of governance are at the root of terrorism when examined as a function of state weakness.

Absence of Economic Development

Economic development and diversity has largely been absent in the Middle East and North Africa. With an economy driven primarily by dependence upon natural resources (largely oil), foreign aid, and remittances, industrial development has lagged behind in this region (Sorli, Gleditsch, and Strand, 2005). The role that oil dependence plays in the relationship between terrorism and state failure in the MENA region is a crucial one. While some scholars point to resource scarcity as a major contributor to conflict (Homer-Dixon, 1999), a great deal of research has found empirical support for the role that resource abundance plays in generating and sustaining conflict (Collier, 1999; Collier and Hoeffler, 2002; Le Billion 2001). Further, rentier-state theory supports this assertion, and research has found that states dependent upon one or a few natural resources have slow economic growth and are more likely to be based upon authoritarian political regimes than states that are resource poor and/or have diverse economies (Beblawi and Luciani, 1987; Sachs and Warner, 1995).

The lack of economic development in the Middle East and North Africa has often been considered the main factor at the root of the violence in the region (Windsor, 2003; Piazza, 2006; Krueger and Maleckova, 2003). Lacking an inclusive economic system, the region has fostered grievances among the ideological youth who are able-bodied and educated, but are unable to find employment (Piazza, 2006; Krueger and Maleckova, 2003). I argue that the ranks of terrorist organizations are filled with this disenfranchised and disillusioned segment of the population. Thus, the lack of economic development in the region has not only crippled these states, making them perpetually weak, and driven many of the unemployed youth to terrorist organizations, but it has also allowed for something far worse to emerge. The lack of economic development has provided extremist groups with material for propaganda, which has facilitated their recruitment efforts, legitimized their acts of terrorism, and fostered an ideology based upon religious radicalism.

Religious Radicalism

Inarguably, radical Islam has its roots in the creation and militarization of Israel. Scholars assert that it was the conclusion of the Six Day War in 1967 when radical Islam and the fundamentalist organizations driving these ideologies began to gain popularity (Chasdi, 1999, 2002; Khashan, 1997; Martin, 1987). The defeat of the Arab nations by Israel in six days infused the region with a sense of humiliation and a sense of hopelessness.[4] With the failure of radical socialism in the 1950s and 1960s, along with the pan-Arabism movements, the people of the Middle East and North Africa were in many ways desperate to escape the perceived dominance of Western ideals and values, and find a political, economic, and social movement unique to the culture and dominant religion of the region that they could look to as successful.

4 Streeter, Sabin. (2005). *The Road to 9/11.* UK: Kundhardt Productions (film).

What the radical Islamist movements did was supplement, or in many cases, supplant the government as the provider of economic and social goods, which, in the end, conferred political power to these groups as well. Consequently, drawing upon a large membership base of the educated unemployed who have been frustrated with the political and economic situation in the region, the Muslim Brotherhood, Fatah, Hamas, along with other radical Islamic groups, have been able to successfully promote and implement their agenda of violence.

As discussed at the opening of this chapter, this study diverges from previous works by not simply looking at the individual impact of specific factors on the occurrence of political violence and terrorism. In the case of religious radicalism, I argue that there is nothing about the religion of Islam that accounts for the emergence of popular support for radical ideologies, or terrorism, for that matter. Instead, it is the climate of state failure that has created this multidimensional vacuum whereby authoritarian regimes have arisen, economic development has been stunted, and Islam has been horribly mutilated by radical, extremist theology. Consequently, I continue to assert that state failure remains at the root of political violence, extremism, and terrorism in the region.

The Main Hypotheses—State Failure

The main hypothesis, which guides this entire text, is that an environment of state failure fosters political violence. In the case of the Middle East and North Africa, certain mitigating factors are unique to the region and have arisen in response to state failure. Thus, beyond the features of state failure outlined in the preceding chapter, I examine three additional factors, which I argue are both unique and central to state weakness in the Middle East and North Africa.

Prevalence of Autocracy

H6: Given the presence of autocratic governance citizens of these states are more likely to support the use of political violence

Lack of Economic Development

H7: When citizens perceive their state as one that lags behind in economic development, they are more likely to support the use of political violence

Religious Radicalism

H8: Given the prevalence and acceptance of widespread radical religious ideology, citizens exposed to these ideals in their states are more likely to support the use of political violence

I hypothesize that, in addition to the lack of the public good of security, the absence of the state, a weak state authority, and the inadequate provision of public goods within the Middle East and North Africa, the dominance of autocratic regimes in the region, a lack of economic development, and the presence of religious radicalism have emerged in response to state failure. As I demonstrate in the statistical models, these factors work together to create a climate of instability in the region, and as a result, this situation encourages citizens to support the use of political violence as a means to achieve political and economic concessions from the state.

Data and Methodology

Data

The data for this analysis come from the Arabarometer survey that collects data from seven Middle Eastern and North African countries, with between 750 and 1,300 respondents of voting age for each state. In each country case, face-to-face interviews were the mode of data collection.

In Algeria, Morocco, and Kuwait, an area probability sample was employed, whereby quotas for age, education, and gender were based upon the most recent census. In Jordan, a sample of 100 clusters was randomly selected from the master sample, which was then organized according to the number of families and geographic location of the families in order to ensure adequate representation. In Lebanon, a nationally representative sample was drawn from a master sampling frame developed by *Statistics Lebanon* (Arabarometer, 2009). In Yemen, a nationally representative sample was also drawn, but in multiple stages from 21 Yemeni governorates proportional to the population in each governorate. Finally, in Palestine, a three-stage cluster sampling method was utilized based upon the most recent national census.

Description of the Variables

Dependent Variable 1—Political Violence

Two dependent variables measure the concept of support for political violence. Together, these variables capture individuals' attitudes regarding the use of political violence as a legitimate tool to threaten the state.

The first measure of political violence is based upon the following question in the Arabarometer survey:

> Question (Variable=Violence1a-Violence1e): Do you think the following operations are terrorist operations or not?

Operations	Terrorist	Not Terrorist	Have Not Heard of Them	Don't Know [Do Not Read]	Decline to Answer
1. Amman Hotel Explosions 2. Egyptian Explosions (Sharm al Sheikh/Dahab) 3. London Underground Explosions 4. Madrid Train Explosions 5. Casablanca (Morocco) Explosions	1	2	3	8	9

In order to estimate the model, I set the value "1" to zero, value "2" to one, and code the remaining values as Missing Data for each incident. The reason why I remove these values is because I am only interested in those respondents who favor the use of violence in relation to those who do not. I do not know the motivations of respondents who do not have an answer, have not heard of the incidents, or have declined to answer, so this information is not useful to me.

Given this study's definition of political violence, the incidents listed above represent such acts, thus, my reasoning for coding the variable in this manner is because if a respondent does not consider these events acts of political violence or terrorism, then I infer it is because they support these actions. The transformation of the variable allows me to determine which dimensions of state failure increase the likelihood that individuals support the use of political violence. The value "1" indicates the respondent believes the incidents cited were not acts of political violence or terrorism, and thus, sanctions the use of this type of violence, whereas the value "0" indicates the respondent believes the incidents cited were acts of political violence or terrorism, and does not support the use of this type of violence.

Dependent Variable 2—Political Violence

The second measure of political violence is based upon the following question in the Arabarometer survey:

> Question (Variable=Violence3): Do you agree that armed groups are justified in attacking *civilians* in Iraq in order to resist the American occupation?
>
> Value Labels: 1=Strongly Agree, 2=Agree, 3=Disagree, 4=Strongly Disagree, 8=Can't Choose/Do Not Read, 9=Decline to Answer

In order to estimate the model, I set the values "1" and "2" to one, values "3" and "4" to zero, and code the remaining values as Missing Data. It is widely accepted that the use of armed violence against civilians in order to make a political statement or force certain concessions from the government is considered an act of terrorism. Therefore, this variable, more so than the other dependent variable, represents a clear indication of whether or not the respondent sanctions the use of this type of violence. The transformation of this variable leaves me with a proxy measure of support for political violence, whereby if the respondents agree with this statement, it is inferred that they support the use of acts of political violence, and if they do not agree with this statement, it is inferred that they do not sanction the use of political violence.

Before turning to a discussion of the explanatory variable, two points must be made about the proxy measures for political violence. First, at no point do these measures indicate whether a respondent supports the use of political violence against their own government; actually, quite the opposite, as the second question mentions terrorist acts against the American occupation of Iraq. Therefore, it is entirely likely that some of the respondents may support the use of political violence against the United States, but not against their own state. I acknowledge the flaws that come with using these variables as measures of political violence against a respondent's home state, which raises my second point.

The literature on political violence in the Middle East and North Africa finds that negative attitudes toward the West, particularly the United States, are often correlated with dissatisfaction with one's own government. "A continued sense of humiliation through covert and direct foreign support for repressive regimes as well as direct foreign intervention has left many [in the Middle East and North Africa] disillusioned with their own governments, as well as those of the major Western powers" (Sorli, Gleditsch, and Strand, 2005, p. 148). I argue that support for the use of violence against the United States, or any other state in the Middle East or North African region, could suggest support for the use of political violence against a respondent's own state.

Table 3.3 and Figure 3.3 provide support for this argument. The Pearson Correlation analysis reveals that there is a strong correlation between the two measures of political violence. Although the coefficient results for the variable which measures terrorist violence against the United States reports weaker relationships with the other constructs, the relationships still remain statistically significant.

The findings in Table 3.3 and Figure 3.3 support my assertion that negative attitudes toward the West are also correlated with dissatisfaction with one's own government. Therefore, for the purposes of this study, regardless of the region where the terrorist incident took place, the notion that individuals sanction the use of this type of violence should infer they support the use of political violence in general, and thus there is a strong probability they also support the use of this type of violence against their own state.

Table 3.3 Pearson Correlation for measures of political violence

Variables	1	2	3	4	5	6	7
1. Amman Hotel Explosions	—	—	—	—	—	—	—
2. Egyptian Explosions (Sharm al Sheikh/Dahab)	.6704***	—	—	—	—	—	—
3. London Underground Explosions	.4559***	.5811***	—	—	—	—	—
4. Madrid Train Explosions	.4677***	.5712***	.9125***	—	—	—	—
5. Casablanca (Morocco) Explosions	.6305***	.7085***	.6525***	.6692***	—	—	—
6. Armed groups are justified in attacking civilians in Iraq in order to resist the American occupation	.1045***	.1054***	.0935***	.0993***	.1015***	.1668***	—

Note: *** p < .01 for two-tailed test.

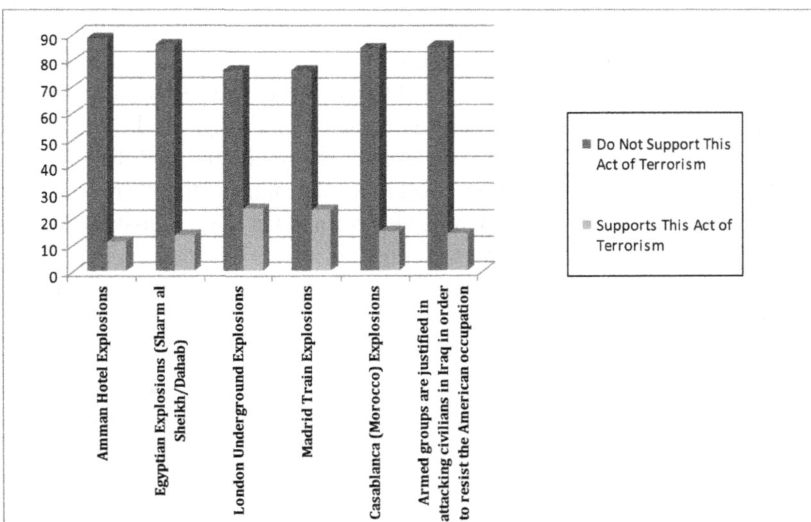

Figure 3.3 Percentage of respondents who support the use of political violence

Explanatory Variables

The public good of security

The first explanatory variable is based upon a single measure of the public good of security and captures individuals' opinions regarding how secure they feel. I argue that if feelings of personal insecurity are great, the more likely individuals are to support the use of political violence against the state that has failed in protecting them.

The measure for the public good of security is based upon the following question in the Arabarometer survey:

> Question 1 (Variable=Security1): Generally speaking, how safe is living in this (city/town/village)?
>
> Value Labels: 1=Very Safe, 2=Safe, 3=Unsafe, 4=Very Unsafe, 8=Can't Choose, 9=Declined to Answer

In order to estimate the model, I code the values of "8" and "9" as Missing Data for both variables. By removing these values, I am left with a scale that indicates an increase in perceived insecurity. Given the measurement of this explanatory variable, a positive coefficient indicates that a higher level of perceived insecurity increases the likelihood that a respondent will support the use of political violence.

The presence of the state

The second explanatory variable, the presence of the state, is based upon a single measure with five dimensions. Together, the dimensions of this variable capture individuals' opinions regarding the ease with which they can contact and receive services from the government. I argue that the more visible and accessible the government, the more likely the state is present. Similarly, the less visible and the less accessible the government, the greater the likelihood that the state is not present in the respondent's region, which would suggest there are pockets of ungoverned territory and where there is ungoverned territory, non-state actors are provided the opportunity and a place to organize.

The measures for the presence of the state are based upon the following questions in the Arabarometer survey:

> Question 1 (Variable=Presence1-Presence5): Based on your experience, how easy or difficult is it to obtain the following administrative or social services from the government?

Service	Very Easy	Easy	Difficult	Very Difficult	Never Tried	Can't Choose	Decline to Answer
1. An identity document (birth certificate, driver's license, passport)							
1. Registering a child in primary school in the public system							
2. Medical treatment at a nearby clinic	1	2	3	4	5	8	9
3. Help from the police when you need it							
4. Access to individuals or institutions to file a complaint when your rights are violated							

In order to estimate the model, I code the values of "8" and "9" as Missing Data for the three variables. By removing these values, I am left with a scale that indicates an increase in the perceived absence of the state. I recode the variables so that the scale is inverted, whereby, "5=never tried" becomes zero, "very difficult=1," "difficult=2," "easy=3," "very easy=4." I invert the scale because I do not wish to drop the value "5=never tried." In some cases, upper class individuals with the means to obtain these services from privatized sources would not rely upon the government for the provision of these services. Therefore, it is not that the government is not present and accessible, but that these individuals go elsewhere. At the same time, individuals of a lower economic status may need these services, but are apathetic toward the government and its ability to provide them with these services. Because I do not know the motivations behind an individual's reasons for not attempting to obtain these services from the government, I cannot remove the value. If I did, I would lose information. After recoding this variable, I am now left with a scale that indicates the perceived presence of the state. Given the measurement of this variable and my hypothesis, a negative coefficient indicates that the perceived *absence* of the state increases the likelihood that a respondent will support the use of political violence.

The state authority

The third explanatory variable, state authority, is based upon three measures. Together, these measures capture individuals' opinions regarding their trust in the government and their belief that the government is legitimate. I argue that if the state authority is perceived as corrupt and untrustworthy, it is difficult for the state to convince citizens to adhere to the laws and institutional rules set forth by the government. Thus, the absence of state authority encourages citizens to support the use of political violence as a means of rejecting the corrupt and illegitimate government. The measures of state authority are based upon the following questions in the Arabarometer survey:

Question 1 (Variable=Trust1-Trust5): For each institution, please tell me how much trust you have in them. Is it a great deal of trust, quite a lot of trust, not very much trust, or none at all?

Institution	A Great Deal of Trust	Quite a Lot of Trust	Not Very Much Trust	None at All	Don't Know	Decline to Answer
1. Prime Minister						
1. The Courts						
2. Parliament	1	2	3	4	8	9
3. The Police						
4. Political Parties						

In order to estimate the model, I code the values of "8" and "9" as Missing Data. By removing these values, I am left with a scale that indicates an increase in the perceived lack of trust in the government officials that represent the state. Given the measurement of these independent variables and my hypothesis, a positive coefficient indicates that the perceived lack of trust in the government increases the likelihood that a respondent will support the use of political violence.

Question 2 (Variable=Legitimate1): On the whole, how would you rate the freeness and fairness of the last national election held in [country name]? Was it:

Value Labels: 1=Completely free and fair, 2=Free and fair, but with minor problems, 3=Free and fair, but with major problems, 4=Not free or fair, 8=Can't Choose, 9=Decline to Answer

Question 3 (Variable=Corrupt1): Here are some statements that describe how widespread corruption and bribe taking are in all sectors of [country name]. Which of the following statements reflects your own opinion the best?

Value Labels: 1=Hardly anyone is involved in corruption or bribery, 2=Not a lot of officials are corrupt, 3=Most officials are corrupt, 4=Almost everyone is corrupt, 8=I don't know, 9=Decline to Answer

In order to estimate the model, I code the values of "8" and "9" as Missing Data for the variables, *Legitimate1* and *Corrupt1*. By removing these values, I am left with a scale that indicates an increase in the perceived presence of corruption among elected officials (*Corrupt1)* and the lack of government legitimacy (*Legitimate1)*. Given the measurement of these independent variables and my hypothesis, a positive coefficient indicates that perceived government corruption and lack of government legitimacy increases the likelihood that a respondent will support the use of political violence.

The provision of public goods

The fourth explanatory variable, the provision of public goods, is based upon a single proxy measure that captures individuals' opinions regarding the state's ability to provide citizens with essential public goods and social services. I argue that a state that cannot and/or does not provide public goods and services will be perceived as weak by its citizens, who are then more likely to resort to other means of obtaining these essential goods, the main alternative being political violence. In support of the hypothesis, a state that does not provide essential public services to its citizens encourages them to support the use of political violence as a method of gaining access to these goods and services.

The measure for the provision of public goods is based upon the following question in the Arabarometer survey:

> Question 1 (Variable=Goods1): Do you agree with the following statement: The government does all it can to provide citizens with all services.
>
> Value Labels: 1=Strongly disagree, 2=Disagree, 3=Agree, 4=Strongly Agree, 8=Can't Choose, 9=Decline to Answer

In order to estimate the model, I code the values of "8" and "9" as Missing Data. By removing these values, I am left with a scale that indicates the increasing ability of the government to provide citizens with necessary public services. Given the measurement of this variable and my hypothesis, a negative coefficient indicates that the perceived inability of the government to provide citizens with public goods and services increases the likelihood that a respondent will support the use of political violence.

Prevalence of autocracy

The fifth explanatory variable, the prevalence of autocracy in the region, is based upon two related proxy measures that capture individuals' opinions regarding their belief that authoritarianism is the most important problem facing their country. I argue that individuals who report that the prevalence of authoritarianism in their country is the most important problem (or second most important problem) facing their state are likely to maintain negative attitudes regarding the repressive institutions of their authoritarian states. Therefore, those individuals who consider authoritarianism a major problem in their state are more likely to support the use of violence against the state than those individuals who do not consider authoritarianism a major problem facing their nation.

The measure for the prevalence of autocracy is based upon the following questions in the Arabarometer survey:

> Question 1 (Variable=Autocracy1): In your opinion, which of the following is the most important problem facing [country name] today?
>
> Value Labels: 1=Economic situation, 2=Corruption, 3=*Authoritarianism*, 4=Ending the U.S. Occupation in Iraq, 5=The Arab-Israeli Conflict, 8=I Don't Know, 9=Decline to Answer
>
> Question 1 (Variable=Autocracy2): In your opinion, which of the following is the *second* most important problem facing [country name] today?
>
> Value Labels: 1=Economic situation, 2=Corruption, 3=*Authoritarianism*, 4=Ending the U.S. Occupation in Iraq, 5=The Arab-Israeli Conflict, 8=I Don't Know, 9=Decline to Answer

In order to estimate the model, I recode value label "3=Authoritarianism" to one, all other values to zero, and the values of "8" and "9" as Missing Data. The new coding structure leaves me with a dichotomous measure, which allows me to isolate those individuals who consider authoritarianism a major problem in their state from those who do not. Given the measurement of this variable and my hypothesis, a positive coefficient indicates that those individuals who consider authoritarianism to be a major problem in their country are more likely to support the use of political violence.

Lack of economic development

The sixth explanatory variable, the lack of economic development in the region, is based upon two proxy measures that capture individuals' opinions regarding their belief that the lack of economic development is the most important problem facing their country and that economic conditions in their country are poor.

The measure for the lack of economic development is based upon the following questions in the Arabarometer survey:

> Question 1 (Variable=EconDev1): In your opinion, which of the following is the most important problem facing [country name] today?
>
> Value Labels: 1=*Economic situation,* 2=Corruption, 3=Authoritarianism, 4=Ending the U.S. Occupation in Iraq, 5=The Arab-Israeli Conflict, 8=I Don't Know, 9=Decline to Answer

Question 1 (Variable=EconDev2): How would you rate the current overall economic condition of [country name] today?

Value Labels: 1=Very good, 2=Good, 3=Bad, 4=Very Bad, 8=Don't Know, 9=Decline to Answer

For the variable, *EconDev1*, I maintain the original coding for the value label "1=Economic Situation." I recode all the other values and set them to zero, and the values of "8" and "9," I code as Missing Data. The new coding structure leaves me with a dichotomous measure that allows me to isolate those individuals who consider the economic situation in their country to be a major problem. Given the measurement of this variable and my hypothesis, a positive coefficient indicates those individuals who consider the economic situation to be the most important problem facing their country are more likely to support the use of political violence.

For the variable, *EconDev2,* I code the values of "8" and "9" as Missing Data. By removing these values, I am left with a scale that indicates the increasing dissatisfaction with the economic situation in one's state. Given the measurement of this variable and my hypothesis, a positive coefficient indicates that the perceived inability of the government to properly manage the economic situation in an individual's country increases the likelihood that a respondent will support the use of political violence.

Religious radicalism

As outlined in the theoretical arguments discussed at the opening of this work, and the findings from earlier research, the dominance of radical Islamic ideologies have contributed to several of the intra-state conflicts in the region. Therefore, the seventh explanatory variable, the presence of religious radicalism in the region, is based upon two proxy measures that are intended to capture extreme interpretations of religious doctrine.

I argue that radical Islamic views alone are not enough to explain the political violence in the Middle East and North Africa, which is why in addition to estimating this variable as an independent factor in the model, I also interact it with the measures for authoritarianism and lack of economic development. I assert that radical Islam has only managed to flourish because of the lack of political and economic development in the region. I expect to find that those individuals, who consider authoritarianism and the lack of economic development to be major problems in their state, will also hold radical Islamic ideologies. With a repressive political climate and poor economic conditions, terrorists are able to manipulate extreme religious fervor, and thus, are also able to successfully promote support for the use of political violence against the state.

The measure for religious radicalism is based upon the following questions in the Arabarometer survey:

Question 1 (Variable=Religion1): In your opinion, how important is the following principle as a guide for making laws in your country: The government should implement *only* laws of the Sharia.

Value Labels: 1=Strongly Agree, 2=Agree, 3=Disagree, 4=Strongly Disagree, 8=I Don't Know, 9=Decline to Answer

Question 2 (Variable=Religion2): Today, as in the past, Muslim scholars and jurists sometimes disagree about the proper interpretation of Islam in response to present day issues. For the following statement, please indicate whether you strongly agree, agree, disagree, or strongly disagree with the interpretation of Islam that is presented: If a Muslim converts to another religion, he must be punished by execution.

Value Labels: 1=Strongly Agree, 2=Agree, 3=Disagree, 4=Strongly Disagree, 8=I Don't Know, 9=Decline to Answer

In order to estimate the model, I code the values of "8" and "9" as Missing Data. By removing these values, I am left with a scale that indicates a decrease in support for radical Islamic ideals as the scale moves higher. My reasoning for selecting the measure that is embodied by the variable *Religion1* is based upon my knowledge of the countries in the sample and the contemporary interpretations of Sharia Law.

Derived from the Qur'an and the life of the Prophet Muhammad, the Sharia sets forth a code of moral conduct for followers of Islam. Traditionally, there are four main schools of Sharia Law, the Hanbali, which is the most conservative, and the Hanifi, the most liberal. Sharia Law has been adopted in various forms across Islamic states, with Saudi Arabia adhering to the strictest form, while Malaysia has adopted a more liberal tradition. However, the general consensus regarding Sharia Law illustrates the justification for including this variable in the model. Strict adherence to Sharia Law represents an extreme interpretation of Islam. But regardless of school of thought, whether liberal or conservative, there is documented support for the assertion that those individuals who believe in incorporating *only* Sharia Laws, a religious set of beliefs governing moral propriety, into the laws that govern the greater society represent a radical interpretation of Islam and its role in modern society (Brown 1996; Dien 2004; Darwish and Nelson 2008).

Regarding the variable *Religion2,* the justification for including this variable in the analysis is far more obvious. Punishment by execution is an extreme one—one typically reserved for crimes involving murder. The rationale behind this measure is that an individual who supports such a position, because one converts to another religion, would in many cases be considered an individual of radical thought.

Therefore, given the measurement of these variables and my hypothesis, a negative coefficient indicates that the stronger the support for radical Islamic ideologies the greater the likelihood that a respondent will support the use of political violence.

Controls

I operationalize a series of control variables that capture the socioeconomic conditions of the respondents. These include the variables, level of education, employment status, age, and gender. These variables serve as appropriate indicators of an individual's socioeconomic position within that country, and are included in the model to control for their influence on the relationship between the selected independent conditions and political violence. See Appendix E for a description of the control variables and their measurement.

Table 3.4 List of variable names and description of the concepts measured

Variable Name	Indicator Concept
Violence1a-Violence1e	Measures Political Violence *Indicates the respondent does not believe the following are terrorist attacks:* *-Amman Hotel Explosions* *-Egyptian Explosions* *-London Underground Explosions* *-Madrid Train Explosions* *-Casablanca Explosions*
Violence2	Measures Political Violence *Indicates respondents believe armed groups are justified in attacking civilians in Iraq in order to resist the American occupation*
Security1	How safe they feel
Presence1-Presence5	The ease or difficulty with which citizens may obtain the following services from the government: *-Identity document* *-Registering a child for public school* *-Medical treatment at a nearby clinic* *-Help from the police when needed* *-Access to government in order to file a complaint when rights are violated*
Trust1	Measures State Authority *Do they trust the Prime Minister*
Trust2	Measures State Authority *Do they trust the Courts*
Trust3	Measures State Authority *Do they trust the Parliament*

Table 3.4 *Concluded*

Variable Name	**Indicator Concept**
Trust4	Measures State Authority *Do they trust the Police*
Trust5	Measures State Authority *Do they trust the Political Parties*
Legitimate1	Measures State Authority *Indicates how they would rate the freeness and fairness of the last national election.*
Corrupt1	Measures State Authority *Indicates there is widespread corruption in all sectors of the respondent's country.*
Goods1	The government does all it can to provide social services
Autocracy1	Authoritarianism is the most important problem facing their state
Autocracy2	Authoritarianism is the second most important problem facing their state
EconDev1	The economic situation in the respondent's nations is the most important problem facing their state
EconDev2	The current overall economic condition in their state is bad.
Religion1	The government should implement only laws of Sharia
Religion2	If a Muslim converts to another religion, he must be punished by execution
Education	Respondent's highest level of education
Gender	Gender
Employment	Respondent's employment status
Age	Respondent's age

Model

I conduct cross-sectional analysis using logistical regression in order to determine which dimensions of state failure increase the probability that an individual will support the use of political violence in the selected country cases. In order to test my assumptions I estimate three logit models. The first model captures respondents' support for the use of political violence and includes the variables that I identify as features of state failure in the preceding chapter as well as in this one (See Figure 3.4). The second model indicates respondents' support for the use of political violence and includes the variables that I identify as features of state failure, along with the three variables, prevalence of autocracy, lack of economic development, and the presence of religious radicalism (See Figure 3.5). The third logit model I estimate (See Figure 3.6) is similar to the logit model in Figure 3.5; the only difference is that the model in Figure 3.6 includes the interactions between religious radicalism, authoritarianism, and economic development.

Logit Models

$$Model1 = h\left(\frac{p_i(violence)}{1-p_i(violence)}\right) = \beta_0 + \beta_1 Security + \beta_2 StatePresence + \beta_3 StateAuthority + \beta_4 StateLegitimacy + \beta_5 PublicServices + \beta_6 Employment + \beta_7 Education + \beta_8 Age + \beta_9 Gender + e$$

Figure 3.4 Traditional state failure model

Note: I must omit the measure *protection of private property* because of the lack of available data for this measure in the Arabarometer survey.

$$Model2 = h\left(\frac{p_i(violence)}{1-p_i(violence)}\right) = \beta_0 + \beta_1 Security + \beta_2 StatePresence + \beta_3 StateAuthority + \beta_4 StateLegitimacy + \beta_5 PublicServices + \beta_6 Authoritarianism + \beta_7 Religion + \beta_8 EconDev + \beta_9 Employment + \beta_{10} Education + \beta_{11} Age + \beta_{12} Gender + e$$

Figure 3.5 Traditional state failure model with measures specific to Middle East and North Africa—authoritarianism, religious radicalism, economic development

$$Model3 = h\left(\frac{p_i(violence)}{1-p_i(violence)}\right) = \beta_0 + \beta_1 Security + \beta_2 StatePresence + \beta_3 StateAuthority + \beta_4 StateLegitimacy + \beta_5 PublicServices + \beta_6 Authoritarianism + \beta_7 Religion + \beta_8 EconDev + \beta_9 Employment + \beta_{10} Education + \beta_{11} Age + \beta_{12} Gender + \beta_{13} Authoritarianism * Religion + \beta_{14} Religion * EconDev + \beta_{15} Authoritarianism * EconDev + e$$

Figure 3.6 Model of state failure with measures specific to Middle East and North Africa—authoritarianism, religious radicalism, economic development including interactions

Findings

Statistical Results

In Table 3.5, I report the binary logit estimates for the model that indicates the probability that a respondent will support the use of political violence. This is the Traditional State Failure Model, and within it I operationalize a series of standard variables, which I argue are conditions that are present in situations of state failure worldwide, but more importantly, I assert these factors have an overwhelming influence on an individual's decision to support or engage in political violence.

Table 3.5 Binary logit estimates of support for political violence—traditional state failure model

Variable	Violence1a—Amman	Violence1b—Egypt	Violence1c—London	Violence1d—Madrid	Violence1e—Casablanca	Violence2	Violence3
Security1	.357** (.140)	.429*** (.140)	.244** (.115)	.125 (.117)	.205 (.152)	.166** (.084)	-.052 (.117)
Presence1	.111 (.101)	-.017 (.097)	.027 (.078)	.063 (.079)	.001 (.109)	.005 (.051)	-.178** (.072)
Presence2	.165** (.083)	-.012 (.076)	.060 (.061)	.024 (.061)	-.004 (.086)	.042 (.040)	-.062 (.058)
Presence3	.297** (.099)	.356*** (.097)	.199** (.075)	.197** (.076)	.230 (.105)	-.003 (.049)	.156 (.070)
Presence4	-.219** (.088)	-.118 (.088)	.035 (.068)	.034 (.069)	.016 (.097)	.101** (.049)	.017 (.070)
Presence5	.089 (.100)	-.092 (.099)	-.142** (.073)	-.146** (.074)	-.073 (.100)	-.003 (.050)	.017** (.070)
Trust1	.085 (.109)	.131 (.106)	-.001 (.081)	-.047 (.084)	-.077 (.116)	.207*** (.057)	.177** (.078)
Trust2	.148 (.118)	-.062 (.113)	.010 (.089)	-.013 (.094)	-.248** (.124)	-.335*** (.063)	.013 (.090)
Trust3	.349** (.117)	.074 (.106)	.256** (.085)	.319*** (.086)	.127 (.117)	.128** (.054)	.016 (.076)
Trust4	.437*** (.111)	.593*** (.111)	-.082 (.084)	-.017 (.086)	.428*** (.116)	-.037 (.058)	-.145* (.084)
Trust5	-.208** (.108)	-.223** (.102)	.001 (.081)	-.191** (.081)	-.129 (.110)	-.184*** (.054)	.302*** (.073)
Legitimate1	.392*** (.091)	-200** (.087)	.231*** (.071)	.239*** (.071)	.464*** (.099)	.073 (.048)	-.011 (.067)
Corrupt1	-.042 (.132)	.107 (.132)	.104 .101	.197* (.101)	-.052 (.137)	-.072 (.067)	.228** (.079)

Goods1	-.213** (.096)	-.195** (.099)	-.304*** (.081)	-.272*** (.081)	-.150 (.111)	-.047 (.057)	-.248** (.079)
Autocracy1	—	—	—	—	—	—	—
Autocracy2	—	—	—	—	—	—	—
EconDev1	—	—	—	—	—	—	—
EconDev2	—	—	—	—	—	—	—
Religion1	—	—	—	—	—	—	—
Religion2	—	—	—	—	—	—	—
Gender	.223 (.189)	.025 (.191)	-.589*** (.159)	-.239 (.157)	-.108 (.209)	-.177 (.111)	-.376 (.158)
Age	-.008 (.009)	-.009 (.008)	-.014** (.006)	-.016** (.006)	.012 (.008)	-.009** (.004)	.003 (.005)
Education	.248*** (.064)	.095 (.062)	.178*** (.051)	.152** (.051)	.208** (.067)	-.084** (.035)	-.030 (.050)
Employment	.258 (.064)	.462** (.214)	-.338** (.158)	-.259 (.161)	.253 (.225)	-.068 (.114)	-.515*** (.157)
Interactions							
Autocracy1*EconDev1	—	—	—	—	—	—	—
Autocracy1*EconDev2	—	—	—	—	—	—	—
Autocracy1*Religion2	—	—	—	—	—	—	—
Religion2*EconDev1	—	—	—	—	—	—	—
Religion2*EconDev2	—	—	—	—	—	—	—
Constant	-8.24*** (.880)	-5.96*** (.823)	-3.63*** (.642)	-3.27*** (.640)	-5.97*** (.888)	.883** (.419)	-.597 (.569)
Observations	2325	2283	2172	2109	1999	1765	1810
Pseudo R^2	.1757	.1196	.1689	.0639	.0792	.0466	.0633
LR χ^2	200.98	131.78	103.23	93.19	73.23	114.10	94.95
Prob> χ^2	.000	.000	.000	.000	.000	.000	.000

Note: *** $p < .01$ for two-tailed test; ** $p < .05$ for two-tailed test; * $p < 0.1$ for two-tailed test; standard errors in parentheses.

The results of the model in Table 3.5 are consistent with our understanding of the relationship between state failure and political violence. The findings suggest the variables that measure the absence of the public good of security, the absence of the state, the perceived absence of the legitimacy of the state authority among citizens, the lack of trust citizens have in the state authority, and the lack of essential public goods all have an influence on a citizen's decision to support the use of terrorism.

The control variables, age, education, and employment also play a role in this relationship. The findings suggest that younger adults are more likely to support the use of political violence than older adults. However, as far as gender is concerned, the findings are weak. Gender is only significant in one equation, and in that one, the findings reveal that men are more likely to support political violence than women. Also, in the majority of the logit equations, the variable education reveals that those individuals with higher education are more likely to support the use of political violence than the less educated. The findings are mixed, however, for employment. In one equation, those individuals who are not employed are more likely to support political violence, whereas, in two other equations, those who are employed are more likely to support the use of political violence. Coupled with the results for the variable education, I am inclined to believe that the educated and employed feel this way for similar reasons that I expressed in the preceding chapter. In countries that are in the process of modernizing, there is sometimes an expectation for rapid economic growth which is not consistent with the reality of the economic climate in that country. This is especially true for the Middle East and North Africa, where efforts to modernize have been stagnant and have lagged behind other regions. The educated and the employed are more likely to have access to a breadth of media sources and information, and thus, may be disgruntled with their governments, knowing their earning potential could possibly be higher in a more economically developed nation.

The findings of the Traditional State Failure Model are consistent with the hypothesis that the conditions of state failure are often so severe that they compel individuals to develop alternative mechanisms for obtaining economic and political goods, and these alternatives sometimes manifest themselves in the form of terrorism and political violence.

In Table 3.6, I report the binary logit estimates for the model that indicates the probability a respondent will support the use of political violence. This model differs from the model in Table 3.5 in that it incorporates the variables economic development, autocracy, and religious radicalism, which I argue play a unique role in the relationship between state failure and political violence in the Middle East and North Africa.

The results of the model in Table 3.6 suggest that the traditional model of state failure remains significant even after the inclusion of additional measures. The findings reveal that the variables that measure the absence of the public good of security, the absence of the state, the perceived absence of the legitimacy of the state authority, the lack of trust citizens have in the state authority, and the inadequate provision of essential public goods all have an influence on a citizen's decision to support the use of terrorism.

With regard to the variables economic development, the presence of an autocratic government, and religious radicalism, that I include in the model, given my argument that these factors are unique to the Middle East and North Africa, the only measure to consistently achieve both statistical and substantive significance is the measure of religious radicalism. The findings indicate that religious radicalism is a strong predictor of support for political violence. This finding is not surprising, given the existing literature; however, it does contradict my hypothesis and my belief that radical Islam alone cannot explain an individual's support for political violence. The results suggest otherwise, and I will delve deeper into this finding in the conclusion of this chapter. In addition to religious radicalism, the model does reveal only weak support, at best, for the measure lack of economic development. The variable *EconDev1* is only substantively and statistically significant in one equation, and while it is statistically significant in a second equation, the interpretation of the coefficient contradicts the hypothesis. Thus, from those results, I am convinced that with regards to the Middle East and North Africa, the lack of economic development alone is not enough to convince individuals to turn to political violence. I will expand upon this in greater detail with a discussion of the model in Table 3.7.

While the variable autocracy is not significant in the model, and there is only marginal support for economic development, I remain convinced that these variables are still important to the discussion of the relationship between state failure and political violence. However, as I discussed at the beginning of this chapter, I believe these factors are intricately tied to one another, and thus, as we have seen in this model, they have little individual influence on support for political violence. As we will see with the statistical model in Table 3.7, these factors have a greater impact on support for political violence when examined collectively.

Finally, the control variables, gender, age, education, and employment, once again have a significant impact on support for political violence. The findings suggest that men and young adults are more likely to support political violence. As far as employment is concerned, individuals who are not employed are more likely to support the use of political violence. And finally, respondents with increasing levels of education are more likely to support the use of political violence. The findings for education and employment differ somewhat, however, from the results in Table 3.5. I argue that the model in Table 3.5 is a general model of state failure, applicable to the majority of cases of state failure around the world. But with the model in Table 3.6, and given the inclusion of factors that are specific to the region of the Middle East and North Africa, I am convinced that we are seeing findings that are also specific to the region. The region has a substantial proportion of young males who are educated but are unemployed and the literature suggests this group is most easily swayed by the propaganda and radical ideologies used by terrorist groups to recruit this segment of the population, because they are dissatisfied with their lack of employment, despite their educational achievements (Urdal, 2006, 2008; Urdal and Hoelscher, 2009; Urdal and Malmberg, 2008; Martin, 1987; Schmid, 1992; Piazza, 2006; Krueger and Maleckova, 2003).

Table 3.6 Binary logit estimates of support for political violence—traditional state failure model with measures specific to Middle East and North Africa—authoritarianism, religious radicalism, economic development

Variable	Violence1a-Amman	Violence1b-Egypt	Violence1c-London	Violence1d-Madrid	Violence1e-Casablanca	Violence2	Violence3
Security1	.227 (.157)	.352** (.166)	.302** (.132)	.184 (.134)	.158 (.171)	.105 (.091)	-.058 (.124)
Presence1	.079 (.112)	.035 (.118)	.019 (.093)	.112 (.095)	-.053 (.122)	-.112* (.058)	-.168** (.078)
Presence2	.103 (.091)	-.069 (.088)	.042 (.070)	.025 (.070)	-.086 (.092)	.046 (.044)	-.051 (.061)
Presence3	.146 (.114)	.091 (.118)	-.013 (.088)	-.011 (.089)	.088 (.122)	-.055 (.055)	.154 (.075)
Presence4	-.178* (.099)	-.155 (.106)	-.048 (.077)	-.082 (.078)	.012 (.109)	.082 (.055)	-.025 (.075)
Presence5	.005 (.115)	-.041 (.123)	-.131 (.087)	-.085 (.087)	-.153 (.118)	.001 (.055)	.210 (.072)
Trust1	.035 (.128)	.161 (.132)	.021 (.098)	-.097 (.099)	-.042 (.134)	.180** (.062)	.144* (.084)
Trust2	.364** (.137)	.056 (.136)	.129 (.104)	.082 (.109)	-.100 (.142)	-.304*** (.070)	.025 (.096)
Trust3	.137 (.136)	-.196 (.132)	.188* (.103)	.278** (.104)	-.045 (.138)	.122** (.059)	.034 (.079)
Trust4	.439*** (.126)	.681*** (.130)	-.056 (.098)	-.004 (.102)	.434*** (.132)	-.020 (.064)	-.130 (.089)
Trust5	.001 (.126)	.026 (.125)	-.032 (.094)	-.162* (.095)	-.124 (.124)	-.158** (.059)	-.331*** (.077)
Legitimate1	.303** (.109)	.037 (.108)	.057 (.084)	.056 (.085)	.331** (.115)	.006 (.053)	.002 (.071)
Corrupt1	.161 (.151)	.357** (.158)	.286** (.115)	.381*** (.116)	.099 (.156)	-.029 (.075)	.168* (.096)
Goods1	-.055 (.110)	.126 (.120)	-.153 (.094)	-.094 (.096)	.015 (.130)	.014 (.065)	-.180** (.087)

Autocracy1	.099 (.509)	-.045 (.485)	.394 (.361)	.019 (.391)	.455 (.467)	-.544** (.232)	-.215 (.343)
Autocracy2	-.115 (.412)	.307 (.365)	-.114 (.294)	-.477 (.321)	-.343 (.449)	-.595*** (.172)	-.196 (.235)
EconDev1	.701*** (.219)	-.106 (.215)	.254 (.174)	.215 (.177)	.152 (.228)	-.314** (.117)	.012 (.155)
EconDev2	-.255* (.144)	-.279* (.150)	-.309** (.109)	-.260** (.110)	-.199 (.150)	.060 (.073)	-.022 (.092)
Religion1	-.496*** (.127)	-.405** (.134)	-.545*** (.103)	-.653*** (.106)	-.351** (.136)	-.237*** (.067)	-.023 (.092)
Religion2	-.407*** (.105)	-.683*** (.121)	-.500 (.085)	-.373*** (.084)	-.676*** (.122)	-.247*** (.062)	-.082 (.078)
Gender	-.034 (.216)	-.017 (.222)	-.781*** (.182)	-.376** (.179)	-.214 (.234)	-.113 (.120)	-.383** (.165)
Age	.006 (.010)	.004 (.009)	-.004 (.007)	-.010 (.008)	.029** (.009)	-.008* (.004)	.004 (.006)
Education	.337*** (.073)	.129* (.072)	.221*** (.058)	.203*** (.059)	.225** (.075)	-.042 (.039)	-.030 (.054)
Employment	.225 (.237)	.377 (.247)	-.331* (.181)	-.231 (.186)	.373 (.255)	.034 (.123)	-.450** (.164)
Interactions							
Autocracy1*EconDev1	—	—	—	—	—	—	—
Autocracy1*EconDev2	—	—	—	—	—	—	—
Autocracy1*Religion2	—	—	—	—	—	—	—
Religion2*EconDev1	—	—	—	—	—	—	—
Religion2*EconDev2	—	—	—	—	—	—	—
Constant	-6.94*** (1.09)	-4.34*** (1.08)	-.953 (.815)	-.956 (.832)	-3.40** (1.08)	2.39*** (.499)	-.173 (.652)
Observations	1990	1958	1861	1809	1730	1571	1606
Pseudo R^2	.2638	.2391	.1831	.1753	.1895	.0785	.0677
LR	265.91	223.56	238.67	220.55	155.24	170.99	93.12
Prob>	.000	.000	.000	.000	.000	.000	.000

Note: *** $p < .01$ for two-tailed test; ** $p < .05$ for two-tailed test; * $p < 0.1$ for two-tailed test; standard errors in parentheses.

Table 3.7 Binary logit estimates of support for political violence—traditional state failure model with measures specific to Middle East and North Africa—authoritarianism, religious radicalism, economic development, and interaction terms

Variable	Violence1a-Amman	Violence1b-Egypt	Violence1c-London	Violence1d-Madrid	Violence1e-Casablanca	Violence2	Violence3
Security1	.235 (.159)	.354** (.168)	.307** (.133)	.187 (.134)	.142 (.173)	.075 (.092)	-.043 (.125)
Presence1	.078 (.111)	.037 (.118)	.020 (.093)	.104 (.095)	-.045 (.123)	-.123** (.058)	-.177** (.079)
Presence2	.090 (.091)	-.107 (.089)	.040 (.070)	.032 (.070)	-.105 (.094)	.052 (.044)	-.042 (.062)
Presence3	.143 (.116)	.095 (.119)	-.013 (.089)	-.018 (.090)	.102 (.123)	-.046 (.056)	.158 (.076)
Presence4	-.177* (.100)	-.092 (.108)	-.049 (.078)	-.086 (.079)	.013 (.111)	.081 (.055)	-.024 (.076)
Presence5	-.005 (.117)	-.037 (.124)	-.131 (.088)	-.078 (.088)	-.139 (.119)	.002 (.056)	.191 (.074)
Trust1	.044 (.129)	.158 (.132)	.022 (.098)	-.098 (.099)	-.034 (.135)	.185** (.063)	.158* (.084)
Trust2	.355** (.135)	.046 (.134)	.132 (.105)	.088 (.109)	-.123 (.143)	-.334 (.071)	.026 (.096)
Trust3	.129 (.135)	-.205 (.132)	.188* (.103)	.280** (.105)	-.049 (.139)	.121** (.059)	.016 (.080)
Trust4	.437*** (.126)	.656*** (.130)	-.065 (.099)	-.008 (.103)	.419** (.134)	-.015 (.064)	-.143 (.091)
Trust5	-.014 (.126)	-.005 (.128)	-.035 (.095)	-.152 (.096)	-.126 (.126)	-.152** (.060)	-.348 (.079)
Legitimate1	.305** (.110)	.021 (.109)	.053 (.085)	.064 (.086)	.321** (.117)	.005 (.053)	.004 (.072)
Corrupt1	.177 (.152)	.376** (.156)	.293** (.116)	.379*** (.116)	.136 (.155)	-.002 (.075)	.173* (.097)
Goods1	-.050 (.110)	.133 (.122)	-.156* (.095)	-.102 (.096)	.025 (.132)	.006 (.066)	-.157* (.089)
Autocracy1	-2.24** (1.04)	-.697 (.801)	.368 (.563)	-.483 (.652)	-.088 (.892)	-.187 (.344)	-.191*** (.591)

Autocracy2	-1.36 (.919)	.098 (.668)	-.109 (.563)	-1.22* (.698)	-.984 (.965)	-.691** (.326)	-1.41** (.500)
EconDev1	.510 (.339)	-.158 (.389)	.171 (.274)	.088 (.268)	.067 (.397)	-.175 (.142)	-.025 (.200)
EconDev2	-.372** (.179)	-.684*** (.185)	-.337** (.138)	-.235* (.139)	-.415** (.192)	.003 (.085)	-.305** (.110)
Religion1	-.490*** (.133)	-.286** (.139)	-.529*** (.107)	-.657*** (.110)	-.274** (.141)	-.201** (.069)	.032 (.093)
Religion2	-.168 (.170)	-.243 (.169)	-.385** (.125)	-.304** (.126)	-.375** (.171)	-.343*** (.039)	.202* (.110)
Gender	-.014 (.220)	.026 (.228)	-.783*** (.182)	-.367** (.179)	-.184 (.236)	-.109 (.121)	-.391** (.168)
Age	.006 (.010)	.005 (.010)	-.004 (.007)	-.009 (.008)	.028** (.009)	-.009** (.004)	.004 (.006)
Education	.356*** (.076)	.121* (.073)	.222*** (.058)	.207*** (.059)	.212** (.075)	-.034 (.039)	-.045 (.054)
Employment	.283 (.242)	.398 (.252)	-.325* (.182)	-.229 (.186)	.415* (.256)	.003 (.124)	-.141** (.168)
Interactions							
Autocracy1*EconDev1	-3.00** (1.24)	-.862 (.831)	-.059 (.596)	.512 (.669)	.167 (.937)	.792** (.355)	-.771 (.530)
Autocracy1*EconDev2	1.95** (.853)	.163 (.658)	-.541 (.490)	-.210 (.546)	-.781 (.720)	-.450 (.309)	1.69** (..495)
Autocracy1*Religion2	1.76** (.819)	.754 (.675)	.457 (.497)	.927* (.575)	1.23 (.831)	-.359 (.320)	1.36** (.457)
Religion2*EconDev1	.540 (.396)	.199 (.434)	.149 (.311)	.146 (.311)	.147 (.443)	-.791*** (.216)	.199 (.277)
Religion2*EconDev2	.268 (.371)	1.47*** (.380)	.237 (.284)	-.024 (.293)	.909** (.390)	.569** (.233)	.924** (.281)
Constant	-7.39*** (1.13)	-4.70*** (1.13)	-1.21 (.846)	-1.18 (.861)	-3.87*** (1.13)	2.81*** (.540)	-.393 (.703)
Observations	1990	1958	1861	1809	1730	1571	1606
Pseudo R^2	.2802	.2602	.1858	.1788	.2014	.0889	.0941
LR χ^2	282.41	243.29	242.13	224.91	164.95	193.64	129.36
Prob> χ^2	.000	.000	.000	.000	.000	.000	.000

Note: *** $p < .01$ for two-tailed test; ** $p < .05$ for two-tailed test; * $p < 0.1$ for two-tailed test; standard errors in parentheses.

In Table 3.7, I report the binary logit estimates for the model that indicates the probability a respondent will support the use of political violence. This model differs from the models in Table 3.5 and Table 3.6 in that it incorporates the interactions between the variables economic development, autocracy, and religious radicalism.

First, the findings reveal that the traditional model of state failure remains stable in this equation. The variables that measure the absence of the public good of security, the absence of the state, the perceived absence of the legitimacy of the state authority, the lack of trust citizens have in the state authority, and the inadequate provision of essential public goods all have an influence on a citizen's decision to support the use of political violence. The substantive interpretation of the control variables also remains consistent. Young males who are educated, but not employed, are more likely to support the use of political violence. Also, out of the three factors that I argue are unique to the Middle East and North Africa, the only measure to achieve both statistical and substantive significance is the measure of religious radicalism. The dominance of this variable in the two models and across the equations suggests that religious radicalism is a salient factor in predicting support for terrorism.

Turning now to the interactions between economic development, autocracy, and religious radicalism—the findings are very telling. Whereas with the model in Table 3.6, where the variables autocracy and economic development appear to have no impact on support for political violence, the results in Table 3.7 reveal that these factors have a significant influence on a respondent's decision to support the use of political violence. The findings suggest that the interaction between the presence of autocracy and a lack of economic development has an influence on the decision to support the use of political violence. The same is true for the interaction between the presence of autocracy and the presence of religious radicalism; this interaction term has a significant impact on one's decision to support the use of political violence. Now the interaction between the presence of religious radicalism and the lack of economic development is the most consistent across all equations and indicates this relationship has a significant influence on one's decision to support the use of political violence. The findings in Table 3.7 are consistent with the hypotheses in that the factors of economic development, autocracy, and religious radicalism have a stronger predictive influence on the support for political violence when examined together as interaction terms than when they are incorporated into the model as individual variables.

Conclusion

The Middle East and North Africa have been at the center of international politics for the past 60 years. With the creation of Israel and subsequent wars, the Iranian revolution, oppressive authoritarian regimes, and the existence of dangerous terrorist networks and activity, the region has been the source of much scholarly discourse and debate. What has emerged from this is a breadth of research on the Middle East and North Africa, and the root causes of the violence in the region. I have drawn upon the foundation of these studies in this chapter, but at the same time, I have also worked to fill in the gaps that still remain. One such gap is the absence of research on the relationship between state failure in the region and political violence. As this study has demonstrated, weak states create a socio-political climate that fosters support for political violence. However, beyond that finding, this study has also arrived at conclusions regarding existing theories of violence in the Middle East and North Africa that have important implications for future research.

The results of the Traditional Model of State Failure are consistent with the overarching hypothesis for this text. With the exception of the measure protection of private property, which was omitted from this analysis because of lack of data, the remaining measures of state failure are significant predictors of individual support for political violence. The findings reveal that the presence of the state, the absence of the public good of security, the measures of state authority—which include trust in government, the legitimacy of the state, and the perceived corruptness of the state authority—all appear to have a strong impact on the decision-making process of individuals to support the use of political violence. At the same time, the measures that capture the concept of inadequate provision of public goods are also extremely important to the decision-making process of individual support for political violence.

The findings from the model of state failure estimated in this chapter suggest that regardless of the region, certain conditions of state failure remain salient to individuals and have a strong influence on their decision to support political violence. Yet despite the findings, one important point must be made. Unlike the models estimated in the preceding chapter, where the dependent variable simply asks if the respondent supports political violence, the Arabarometer data has no such broad measure; therefore, I was forced to use proxy variables. These variables represented important indicators of the willingness of individuals to condone the use of political violence by asking them if they believed certain well-documented terrorist attacks were in fact terrorist attacks to them. The expectation was that those individuals who did not consider these events to be terrorist attacks were more likely to believe that political violence against the state is permissible, based upon what could only be perceived as a predisposition to condone radical violent behavior. The results reveal a general consensus among the respondents, in the sense that the geographic location of the terrorist attack (Europe vs. MENA) led to expected cultural delineations. For example, the public good of security was not important to the decision-making process of a respondent if the incident took place outside of MENA. In other words, the results reveal that certain state failure conditions were more important to respondents given the location of the terrorist incident. As I indicated, this was expected. One would not expect a respondent to feel the absence of the public good of security is important to them when it concerns a terrorist incident in Madrid; however, the lack of the public good of security does become important to them when the incident takes place in a country within their region, because the effects of such an incident are far more tangible to them. Yet, despite some of the discrepancies between the estimated equations and the geographic locations of the attacks, the findings of the model reveal that state failure conditions are salient contributors to individual support for the use of political violence.

In the model of state failure, which includes those variables that are considered important to the Middle East and North Africa, the findings are generally consistent with the hypotheses. First, the traditional model of state failure remains salient. Thus, in the presence of additional variables, the conditions of state failure continue to have an impact on support for political violence. Also, the variable religious radicalism appears to be a strong predictor of support for political violence. While scholars have argued that the presence of authoritarian regimes, a lack of economic development, and the widespread prevalence of religious extremism in the region provide an explanation for the violence, I have argued otherwise. I hypothesized that as individual factors, these variables would have no significant impact on support for political violence. I asserted that the relationship between the variables as interaction terms would provide greater explanatory power. The results are generally consistent with my hypotheses, with the exception of religious radicalism. This variable proves to be a consistent predictor of support for political violence, which has forced me to reevaluate my position.

Apparently, there is something unique and enduring about religious extremism in the region that makes it such an important contributor to political violence. And yet, out of the three variables (authoritarianism, economic development, religious radicalism) included in the state failure models, this is the one that is most difficult to control for in society, if one's goal is to address the root causes of political violence and terrorism.

It appears that the presence of state failure and religious radicalism in the region is a volatile combination. In an effort to address terrorism, the international community can foster economic development and democratic ideals in the region, but what it cannot do is tell people what to believe when it comes to their religion. Thus, without addressing what is at the root of religious radicalism, the region will continue to witness political violence and export terrorists and terrorist threats to other parts of the world. This analysis stops short of investigating what is at the root of religious radicalism. I can postulate that lack of economic development and the presence of authoritarian regimes play a role, which is what I argue at the opening of this chapter. However, I do not test the assumption that these two factors could be at the root. That is something for future works to explore. However, I will say this. The causes of religious radicalism should certainly be explored and dissected in an effort to understand how this single factor represents such a significant predictor of political violence, and what can be done to address religious extremism in an already fragile region plagued by deeply rooted religious factions.

Table 3.8 Hypotheses supported by the Logistical Regression analysis

Hypotheses	Variable and Concept Measured
Absence of the Public Good of Security	Security2—Respondent feels safe
State Presence	Presence1—Identity document Presence4—Help from the police Presence5—Government access to file complaint when rights are violated
State Authority	Trust1—Trust Prime Minister Trust2—Trust the courts Trust3—Trust parliament Trust4—Trust the police Legitimate1—Free and fair national election Corrupt1—Corruption in all sectors of the state
Provision of Public Goods	Goods1—The government provides social services
Economic Development	EconDev1—Economy is most important problem facing nation
Religious Radicalism	Religion1—Sharia Law Religion2—Execution if convert to other religion
Interactions	Autocracy2*EconDev1 Autocracy2*EconDev2 Religion1*EconDev2 Autocracy1*Religion2
Controls	Gender Age Employment status—Employed or not employed Education—Respondent's highest level of education

Finally, as I argued, the interactions between authoritarianism, economic development, and religious radicalism are significant predictors of support for political violence. This finding is consistent with my understanding of the interconnected relationship between these factors. Together they all function to create a climate in the region that is ripe for terrorism and political violence, and the results illustrate this. In addition, the control measures also reveal that young men who are educated but not employed are more likely to support violence, which is consistent with the literature on terrorism.

In conclusion, state failure undoubtedly has a devastating impact on any state, but in the region of the Middle East and North Africa, where there is a lack of economic development, a prevalence of authoritarian regimes, and pervasive religious radicalism, the conditions of state failure have further crippled the region and positioned it as an enduring frontier for terrorism and political violence.

Chapter 4
Crouching Tiger, Hidden Dragon No More: The Emerging Crisis of Collapsed States and Extremist Terrorism in Southeast and South Asia

Introduction

The network of states in Southeast[1] and South Asia[2] are not strangers to the corrosive system of state failure and collapse and the presence of terrorism. Within Southeast Asia alone, nine of the ten states are considered failing based upon the 2011 Failed State Index and the 2008 Index of State Weakness; and insurgent movements, terrorist organizations, and ethno-religious separatist movements that are present in the region represent significant security challenges to these fragile states.

A closer look at Southeast Asia reveals that in the southern region of Thailand, the Malay Muslim separatist movement rages on after over five decades of a complex ethno-religious conflict. While Indonesia must contend with one of Southeast Asia's most organized and deadliest terrorist threats, the Jemaah Islamiyah (JI); and in the Philippines, the small state is plagued by a complex security challenge in that it is faced with a separatist movement, violent Islamic radicalism, and a communist insurgency.

The states that comprise South Asia seem to fare no better. The current political climate within Afghanistan, India, Bangladesh, Pakistan, and Sri Lanka is well known; thus, these fragile states, which represent over half of the eight states in the South Asia region, are embroiled in steady conflict, armed challenges from non-state actors, and must contend with both insurgent groups and terrorist threats from within and across state borders.

Given the current state of conflict and the presence of state failure in Southeast and South Asia, this chapter examines the role this phenomenon (state failure) plays in fostering individual support for political violence and terrorism.

1 The states that comprise Southeast Asia include Indonesia, Malaysia, the Philippines, Singapore, Thailand, Brunei, Myanmar (Burma), Cambodia, Laos, and Vietnam.

2 The states that comprise South Asia include Afghanistan, Bangladesh, Bhutan, India, the Maldives, Nepal, Pakistan, and Sri Lanka.

Similar to the earlier chapters, I utilize barometer survey data to evaluate this relationship between state failure and support for political violence.

What is unique about Southeast and South Asia is that the international community did not really begin to take notice of the insurgent and terrorist activities in the region until the War on Terror began after the 9/11 attacks. However, this type of violence has flourished for many decades in these regions, and I argue this has largely been due to the fragility of the states that comprise Southeast and South Asia. As I discussed earlier in this work, failing and failed states attract these types of groups because rule of law is weak there. And yet, as we have seen in the preceding chapters, individuals are also inclined to support these groups because of the perception that they will provide the public goods that the state fails to—once again making failing and failed states attractive to terrorists and insurgents.

The major goal of this work is to demonstrate that regardless of certain distinguishing factors, such as the historical development and contemporary features of the state, the region where a state is located, and its predominant culture, ethnicity, or religion, state failure functions as a compelling motive for individual support of political violence and terrorism.

Argument

As in previous chapters, the major argument of this study is that the features of state failure foster support for political violence. This dynamic is certainly evident in the regions of Southeast and South Asia, which have been embroiled in a number of conflicts because of ethnic factions and lagging economic development. However, in stark contrast to sub-Saharan Africa and the Middle East, there has been tangible evidence that Southeast and South Asia have worked to move in the direction of building sustainable political and economic institutions, and yet, armed conflicts continue, which poses serious obstacles to the continued growth of the fragile states in these regions.

Terrorism, Political Violence and State Failure in South Asia

South Asia is a region of great promise, and with India leading the way as the region's hegemonic state, there is clear evidence that opportunities for economic growth continue, and over time, the potential for widespread economic development is a viable reality. However, before the states in South Asia can even begin to reap the benefits of modernization and economic development, they must first overcome the political turmoil and instability that plagues the region.

India is currently a nation suffering from a confusing identity crisis. While it boasts the world's fifth largest economy,[3] it ranks 134 out of 182 on the 2010 Human Development Index, largely because of ongoing armed challenges to the government and continued economic disparities among the state's upper and lower classes. Despite the tremendous progress of India, it remains embroiled in conflict with Pakistan, China, and the terrorist forces in Jammu and Kashmir over the Northwestern territory, even as separatist movements in the Northeastern region of India, and the Maoist insurgency in the interior and Eastern region threaten to divide the nation.

The protracted nature of the conflict in Jammu and Kashmir[4] is an intricate and multifaceted one that boils down to the basic tenet of ethno-religious divisions and control over territory. India's position is that Kashmir is an integral component of India. However, with the exception of the Jammu region, which is the only majority Hindu state in the Kashmir region, the rest of the territory is Muslim, and thus this is the argument which Pakistan makes for the inclusion of the region within Pakistan's territory. However, another dynamic remains, and that is the strong presence of Kashmiri independence groups who, over the years, have implemented a series of terrorist attacks against both Pakistan and India and within Kashmir itself in an effort to highlight their position that Kashmir should be independent of both India and Pakistan. What is important about this conflict is that it continues today and has led to the destabilization of not just Kashmir, but India, Pakistan, and Afghanistan as well. Kashmiri insurgents are using ungoverned territory within Afghanistan to train new recruits, while also recruiting Afghan youth to their ranks. With this dynamic in place, it poses many problems to the entire region, but most notably to India and its future prospects for continued economic growth.

While the dispute over Kashmir has been a continual source of contention for the growing state, India is also facing tremendous internal upheaval. Within the Northeastern region, the Naga tribe has used violence for the past three decades to force India to support the creation of a greater Nagaland—an autonomous state along ethnic lines. Since 1979, approximately 25,000 people have died in Nagaland, and the separatist conflict has affected the majority of the states in the region. As a result, other ethnic groups in the region have begun to organize and challenge the Indian state for territorial autonomy.

Although smaller in scale when compared to the violence and casualties attributed to the conflicts in Kashmir and the Northeastern region of India, the Maoist Naxal movement has led to the deaths of more than 6,000 people, with the majority of these casualties taking place in recent years. The problem with the resurgence of the Naxal movement is that unlike the other two conflicts that seek

3 2009 CIA The World Factbook. https://www.cia.gov/library/publications/the-world-factbook/rankorder/2001rank.html. Accessed March 21, 2010.

4 Conflict within the region can be traced back to 1947 with the onset of the Indo-Pakistani War.

the secession of territory—and the belief that the conflicts could be resolved if this should ever happen— the Naxal movement is driven by a basic desire for control over the government and it is not going away. Therefore, the Indian government has found itself embroiled in an ideological conflict with an insurgent group that seeks state power, which is steadily gaining momentum. The Naxalite movement presents one of the greatest threats to the Indian state, while it must also address the territorial conflicts in Kashmir and Nagaland.

As far as progress in the region, India has undoubtedly made the greatest strides, even though it struggles to address features of state failure, such as the absence of security, a lack of state authority, the absence of the state in ungoverned territory, and the lack of provision of critical public goods, which are at the root of the conflicts in the state. The enduring nature of the conflicts in India, coupled with the widespread poverty that remains in its undeveloped areas, as well as a host of terrorist attacks that have emerged in protest of the Indian government's handling of the major conflicts I just outlined, represent the main reasons why India continues to be viewed as a fragile state, one that is developing but still has many internal and external obstacles to overcome before it can ever reach its full potential.

I opened the discussion with India because it represents one of the more successful states in South Asia, with regards to economic development and an open political system, despite the challenges it faces. And yet, while the region boasts one of the world economy's leading states, it also boasts one of the world's most tragically failed states in contemporary history.

Afghanistan has unfortunately been the victim of the world's major powers, first with Great Britain, and then later serving as one of many Cold War battlegrounds between the Soviet Union and the United States, until the collapse of the Soviet Union. The Saur Revolution of 1978 epitomized the Cold War tensions between the two super powers, and eventually became the major catalyst for the Soviet invasion of Afghanistan. As a result of the Saur Revolution, Afghanistan entered into a period of violent political turmoil, which sparked what has basically been a 30-year civil war where rival warlords and non-state actors have continuously vied for power within the failed state at one point or another. Supported by the *mujahidin* (Islamic Warriors), a guerilla opposition force that gained popularity during the Saur Revolution, the Taliban eventually emerged as the dominant regime, and at its height controlled approximately 95 percent of the country. As a result of the Taliban's oppressive rule, efforts to modernize within Afghanistan were brutally derailed, plunging the country into anarchic chaos, leaving it so ravaged and impoverished that it currently ranks 155 out of 169 countries on the 2010 Human Development Index, and based upon data from the IMF, at the time of this writing it is one of the ten poorest countries in the world.

Afghanistan has never truly enjoyed a period of peace and stability. As a result, it has witnessed one of the most protracted refugee crises in contemporary history. At the height of the war with the Soviet Union, and the subsequent revolution and civil war, approximately five million Afghans were refugees abroad, a number that climbed as high as 7.5 million after the U.S. led Coalition Forces occupied the nation following the September 11th attacks. Further, while some 2.1 million Afghan refugees are still living abroad—many in refugee camps, neighboring Pakistan, and other states, such as Iran and Russia—that number has steadily risen with the renewed United Nations Coalition efforts that began in 2009 under President Obama.

What is important to note about Afghanistan, at least with respect to this analysis, is that Afghanistan remains one of the worst failed states in history, and will probably remain a failed state for a long time to come. Afghanistan continues to suffer from weak central governance and a weak economy. These two are intricately linked in the case of Afghanistan as estimates suggest that 25 billion dollars in international aid have been pumped into the state, and yet only three-fifths of it has been spent on boosting the economy. Government corruption, a lack of legitimate political institutions, and the absence of a comprehensive state authority have been blamed for the failures of the central government. This perceived impotency of the central government has thus contributed to the emboldened presence of the insurgency, driven by longstanding groups that engage in terrorist activity, such as the Taliban and the Haqqani Network, as well as the Jund al-Sham, which emerged in Afghanistan around 1999. The unfortunate implication of Afghanistan's failure as a state is that it represents a classic case of study for this analysis when it comes to examining the relationship between state collapse and support for political violence.

A discussion of state failure and political violence in South Asia would not be complete without an examination of Sri Lanka, a nation that during the height of the Tamil Tigers insurgency, witnessed some of the deadliest terrorist attacks in modern history. Currently, Sri Lanka ranks at 91 on the Human Development Index and remains a failing state on both the Index of State Weakness and the Failed State Index, despite the recent end to the civil war. Consequently, Sri Lanka continues to exist in a tenuous position as it struggles to recover from many decades of war and works to subdue tensions that could plunge the nation back into conflict.

Undoubtedly the most successful and enduring armed challenge to Sri Lanka's Sinhalese government has come in the form of the Tamil Tigers. The Liberation Tigers of Tamil Eelam (LTTE) is a secessionist armed insurgent group within Sri Lanka that has used terrorism to further its separatist agenda. Sri Lanka gained its independence in 1948 from Great Britain and almost immediately, tensions between the Tamils and the ethnic majority, the Sinhalese, emerged. During the colonial period, the Tamils enjoyed many privileges, equal to that of the Sinhalese, if not better. Many Sinhalese regarded the Tamil minority as a privileged group under imperial rule and came to resent their preferential treatment by the British. For the most part, however, the Tamils shared economic, social, and cultural power with the Sinhalese, even though the political arena was primarily dominated by the British until independence (Wickramasinghe, 2006), after which the Sinhalese majority gained political power, and the Tamil minority became a marginalized group. One of the first tactics used by the Sinhalese was the government program of land reform. The Sinhalese sought land 'colonization' or agricultural settlements in the interior of Sri Lanka, which meant several thousand Sinhalese peasants were now living and working on land the Tamils considered their traditional homelands. What this government program did was change the ethnic character of the majority Tamil region, creating tension between the Tamils and Sinhalese.

Beyond the government land program, the Tamil anger was also incited when the Sinhalese government declared that Sri Lanka would adopt one national language, instead of the pre-existing two. Sinhala became the official language of the state, thus ensuring Tamil would no longer be spoken in schools, official government places, and commercial businesses. The Tamil minority saw this action as one of many that would come, where the Sinhalese would gradually do away with any cultural imprint the Tamil had on the country.

By the early 1970s, the Sinhalese government was experiencing strong opposition; interestingly enough, it did not come from the Tamils, but rather from a leftist Sinhalese faction that would later organize itself into the Sinhalese Sri Lankan People's Liberation Front, or Janatha Vimukthi Peramuna (JVP). Although it tried unsuccessfully to overthrow the government in 1971 and then again between 1987 and 1989, the JVP did succeed in bringing a spirit of Marxist ideals to the nation, and at one point the group enjoyed a period of political legitimacy. At the same time, the JVP ushered in a period of visceral political turmoil in Sri Lanka that weakened the government. Thus, while the Sri Lankan government was struggling to maintain legitimacy, the Tamil nationalist movement was steadily making strides in recruiting support and growing stronger daily. In the midst of political turmoil, the LTTE was born and in 1983 with the Tamil Tigers' attack on the military that killed 13 soldiers, and the subsequent brutal retaliation of the government that killed an estimated 3000 ethnic Tamils, the civil war began (Wickramasinghe, 2006).

The civil war between the Tamils and the Sinhalese government continued for 25 years, bringing about thousands of casualties and ravaging the entire nation. And while the civil war was finally brought to an end in May 2009, there continue to be instances of small-scale violence between the government and the Tamils. Therefore, despite the peace agreement, it remains to be seen if the nation can overcome the conditions of state failure that persist in the fledgling state.

The Tamil Tigers still remain the biggest threat to Sri Lankan security, in more ways than initially obvious. Sri Lanka is still heavily dependent upon foreign assistance, and it remains to be seen if the Sri Lankan economy has the ability to sustain itself once this assistance disappears. Also, according to the 2010 Index of Economic Freedom, Sri Lanka's economic freedom score is 54.6, which makes its economy the 120th freest in the index. What is important about its ranking is that its score is 1.4 points lower than its score from the previous year, and reflects deterioration in four of the ten economic freedoms measured by the index. Also, Sri Lanka is ranked 23rd out of 41 countries in the Asia–Pacific region, and its overall score on the index is lower than the global average. At the same time,

Sri Lanka has experienced steady GDP growth over the past three years, and as of 2010 its economy was ranked 67 out of 185 countries according to data from the World Bank.[5] These economic figures demonstrate that Sri Lanka's economy is growing, albeit slowly. What that means for the government is that if the Tamil minority begins to enjoy the benefits of this economic growth, the ingrained hostilities will hopefully soon diminish over time, as long as political freedoms remain in place for this group. However, if the failing Sri Lankan state continues to languish in its current position, the resurgence of the Tamil movement is very likely, given that many Tamils will likely believe that the end of the civil war brought about no positive benefits for the ethnic minority.

Several scholars have hypothesized about such a phenomenon taking place within Sri Lanka in the next few years (Winslow and Woost, 2004; Rotberg et. al., 1999; Allen, 1999; Clarence, 2007; Cox, 2009; McGilvray, 2008; Peebles, 2006; Wilson, 1988). Sri Lanka is in a fragile place. With the end of decades-long civil war, the still majority Sinhalese government must now live up to its promises and move the country forward, and that includes promoting economic and political equality for the marginalized Tamils. If this does not happen, and the status quo continues, the LTTE will utilize the bleak conditions within the fragile state to once again promote their separatist agenda and recruit the next generation of Tamil Tigers to challenge the Sri Lankan government.

Terrorism, Political Violence and State Failure in Southeast Asia

It is apparent that the region of South Asia is a diverse one, with both its successes and failures. Most notably, it has given rise to India, a nation that may struggle with pockets of internal conflict and trans-border terrorist threats, but at the same time is an important economic player on the global stage. And yet, the region has also given rise to one of the most tragically failed states with Afghanistan, as well as one of the deadliest terrorist organizations in the world (the LTTE) that has utilized suicide bombing more than any terrorist group in modern history (Arena and Arrigo, 2006; Art and Richardson, 2007; Bjorgo, 2005; Gambetta, 2005; Heiberg et al., 2007).

Similar to South Asia, Southeast Asia is comprised of a broad spectrum of nations within various stages of their evolution as contemporary states. The main difference is that the region does not have a country such as India, where it is advancing in one area, and at a very high level, while it struggles in the socio-political sector. Instead, within Southeast Asia, there are only two types of states: those that are *stable,* and those that are *failing*—where they are not failed states, but they are not stable either. An example of the former can be seen with Singapore and Brunei, which are both developed states that maintain high levels

5 2009 World Bank—World Development Indicators. http://data.worldbank.org/indicator. Accessed March 24, 2010.

of human development and strong economies (CIA World Factbook, 2008; IMF, 2009). And yet, the region must also contend with the failing states of Cambodia, Laos, Myanmar (Burma), and the Philippines, which are struggling to develop economically and are facing internal political upheavals.

Despite that failing states exist in Southeast Asia, the conditions within the region are not as easily comparable to the situation in South Asia, mainly because the fragile states in Southeast Asia—to be plain—are not as bad off as those of South Asia. Terrorism and political violence are certainly present in Southeast Asia, which became glaringly apparent after September 11, 2001, when the United States enlisted the support of Indonesia, Malaysia, the Philippines, Singapore, and Thailand to crack down on the Jemaah Islamiyah presence in their countries, a prominent Pan Asian terrorist network with extensive ties to al-Qaeda.

What is important about Southeast Asia and evaluating the relationship between state failure and political violence is that while the levels of state failure in no way approach the severe conditions of failure in sub-Saharan Africa, or even South Asia, the region provides an ideal case for analysis. Terrorism emerged and grew in Southeast Asia during a time when governments in the region were unwilling to acknowledge the right of minority self determination (Chalk et al., 2009). The fear of many Southeast Asian post-colonial governments was that if they gave in to ethno-nationalist separatist demands that eventually secessionist movements would become the norm, thus undermining the basic concept of state sovereignty envisioned by these newly independent states (Acharya, 1993; Christie, 1995; Findlay, 1996; Nathan 1997). As a result of the intractability of the Southeast Asian governments, radical Islamic movements were able to gain a strong foothold in the region toward the end of the twentieth century.

However, beyond the inflexibility of the governments in Southeast Asia, the emergence of extremist Islamic movements in the 1990s can also be attributed to the confluence of several simultaneous factors. Most notably was the reaction to the negative implications of globalization, which has been particularly associated with the United States. Globalization in Southeast Asia often brings to mind sweatshops and abusive and predatory practices by foreign corporations. Beyond negative reactions toward globalization, there was also the frustration with the repressive secularist governments that I discussed in the section above, but what I did not touch upon was how the radical Islamist movement was able to associate the authoritarianism of the governments and the inherent problems of globalization with the corrupt characteristics of a secular state. The rhetoric used by the extremist Islamic movements was effective in generating support for a pan-Islamic Southeast Asia among its supporters. Adding to this combustible situation was the reaction of Muslims in Southeast Asia—particularly Indonesia, which is home to the largest Muslim population in the world—to the Israeli occupation of the West Bank and Gaza, coupled with the simultaneous immigration of seasoned terrorist veterans from Afghanistan into the region. The convergence of these factors was key to the emergence of a radical Islamic terrorist movement in Southeast Asia during the nineties.

Like the Middle East, terrorism in Southeast Asia emerged in response to authoritarian rule and a struggling economy. However, *unlike* the Middle East, Southeast Asia has transformed into a region with rapidly modernizing economies and more open political systems, and yet, even with this progress, and despite brutal crackdowns on terrorist groups in the region, the serious threat of terrorism still looms over the region like a heavy cloud. As recent as July 2009, the simultaneous hotel bombings in Jakarta rocked the region, and have once again given rise to speculation that despite the many advancements taking place in Southeast Asia, conditions of state fragility remain prevalent, which explains the continued presence of terrorists groups such as Jemaah Islamiyah throughout Southeast Asia, along with the Abu Sayyaf and the Moro Islamic Liberation Front (MILF) in the western and southern regions of the Philippines, and to a lesser extent, the Muslim insurgency in Southern Thailand.

As I have stated, the classic conditions of state failure witnessed in sub-Saharan Africa are not readily visible in Southeast Asia, nor is the extremism of religious ideology and repressive governance as prevalent in Southeast Asia as is found in the Middle East—at least not at first glance. Although political violence has waned in recent months, neither the threat nor the presence of terrorist networks have disappeared from Southeast Asia, and that is because at the root of the violence in the region are the conditions of state failure—a weak state authority, the absence of the state, and the inadequate provision of public goods.

Therefore, as I conclude this section, I reemphasize the argument of this chapter, which is the major theme of this work, and that is the notion that conditions of state failure compel individuals to support the use of political violence and terrorism. The Jemaah Islamiyah network was able to mobilize Pan-Southeast Asian support for its terrorist agenda because Muslims throughout the region faced economic and political marginalization and discrimination. This type of phenomenon meant that many Muslims were not provided with essential public goods, despite the increasing economic prosperity of these nations. In addition, other features of state failure were evident in the region, compounding the growing unrest among Muslims in the region. Probably the most important component of state failure to have an impact on the emergence of political violence in the region was that pockets of Southeast Asia lacked the presence of the state, which allowed Jemaah Islamiyah and other terrorist groups to train and organize attacks. One instance of this was in Indonesia right after the fall of the Suharto regime in 1998. Jemaah Islamiyah benefited tremendously from the political instability in Indonesia at the time. With Jakarta unable to maintain control over Indonesia's outer islands, Jemaah Islamiyah was "provided with critical opportunities to recruit, train, and fund local mujahedeen fighters to participate in the sectarian conflict, in which hundreds died" (Vaughn et al., 2005, p. 5).

Before moving into a discussion of the hypotheses, one final note must be made regarding the major argument of this chapter. As I highlighted in the previous section, several components of state failure were present in Southeast Asia throughout the nineties into the twenty-first century, which led to the emergence of terrorism in the region. However, I also want to point out that despite the economic and political progress of the region, the root causes of political violence have not been eradicated from Southeast Asia. Muslims are still discriminated against throughout the region, and there remain stretches of ungoverned territory in Thailand, the Philippines, and Indonesia where insurgent and terrorist groups continue to exist. Also, while Jemaah Islamiyah and other terrorist groups have been weakened by the persistent and coordinated efforts of the international community and Southeast Asian governments, they have not succeeded in eliminating the threat of terrorism. As long as these groups exist, along with the root causes that prompted the first cycle of terrorism in the region, it is highly likely Southeast Asia will continue to bear witness to acts of political violence for many years to come.

Hypotheses

By now it is clear, the overarching hypothesis of this work is that state weakness and failure have a direct impact on a citizen's decision to support the use of political violence against the state. In this chapter, I test the hypothesis that is the foundation for this work. At the same time, my expectations from the analysis of Southeast Asia and South Asia are somewhat mixed.

In the past two chapters there was clear evidence of institutional weakness within the states of sub-Saharan Africa, as well as the states of the Middle East and the Maghreb. Thus, establishing the causal impact of state failure on political violence was a logical one. However, in the case of Southeast Asia and South Asia, the linear relationship is less explicit. This is because out of all of the regions examined in this text, Southeast Asia and South Asia (as a whole) have proven to be the least susceptible to the consequences of state failure. That is not to say the conditions of state failure are not present in these regions, because the fact that the majority of the states in these regions are on the Failed State Index (See Table 4.1) and the Index of State Weakness (See Table 4.2) suggests there are systematic failures within the state structures of many of these nations. At the same time, however, states such as Thailand, Indonesia, and India have managed to overcome some of these inherent obstacles to establish dynamic economies.

Therefore, given the dichotomy of economic success within the fragile states of Southeast and South Asia, I expect the results of the analysis to reflect this contradiction. Further, in light of the available data and the sample of country cases within the dataset—which I will discuss in the following section—I expect to observe some systematic variation in the findings from this analysis.

Table 4.1 The 2008 Index of State Weakness rankings for South Asia and Southeast Asia

Country	Ranking	Quintile
Afghanistan	2	Bottom Quintile
Burma (Myanmar)	17	Bottom Quintile
Nepal	22	Bottom Quintile
Pakistan	33	2nd Quintile
Cambodia	34	2nd Quintile
Laos	45	2nd Quintile
Bangladesh	48	2nd Quintile
Sri Lanka	56	2nd Quintile
Philippines**	58	3rd Quintile
India	67	3rd Quintile
Indonesia**	77	3rd Quintile
Thailand**	79	3rd Quintile
Vietnam**	83	3rd Quintile
Bhutan	94	4th Quintile
Maldives	100	4th Quintile
Malaysia**	124	5th Quintile (The Highest)

Note: Rankings based upon a total of 141 countries. Country cases in the Asian Barometer survey are denoted by **.

Table 4.2 The 2011 Failed State Index rankings for South Asia and Southeast Asia

Country	Ranking	Quintile
Afghanistan	7	Alert
Pakistan	10	Alert
Burma (Myanmar)	13	Alert
Bangladesh	18	Alert
Sri Lanka	22	Alert
Nepal	25	Alert
Laos	44	Warning
Bhutan	48	Warning
Cambodia	49	Warning
Philippines**	53	Warning
Indonesia**	61	Warning
Thailand**	79	Warning
Maldives	82	Warning
India	87	Warning
Vietnam**	94	Warning
Malaysia**	115	Warning
Brunei	118	Warning

Note: Rankings based upon a total of 177 countries. Country cases in the Asian Barometer survey are denoted by **.

Data and Methodology

Data

The data for this analysis come from the Asian Barometer Survey-Wave Two, which collects data from 13 Asian countries between the years of 2006–2008, with between 800 to 3,200 respondents of voting age from each state. For the purpose of this analysis, country cases outside of the regions of South Asia and Southeast Asia were excluded. Therefore, data are only analyzed from the following states: the Philippines, Thailand, Malaysia, Indonesia, Vietnam, and Cambodia.[6,7]

In each country case, face-to-face interviews were the mode of data collection. In Thailand, the sampling plan for the study consisted of two-stage cluster sampling, plus systematic sampling of the final populations (Asian Barometer, 2009). The sampling method yielded a total of 1,546 respondents of voting age. In the Philippines, multi-stage probability sampling (proportional to population size) was used in the selection of sample frames. This method yielded a total of 1,200 respondents. At the time of this writing, detailed information on the sampling procedures for the remaining countries is not available. However, the sampling methods of the researchers is based upon national probability samples to establish the sampling frame, while face-to-face interviews and a standard survey instrument were utilized in each case. Consequently, the efforts of the researchers yielded 1,598 respondents in Indonesia, 1,200 respondents in Vietnam, 1,218 respondents in Malaysia, and 1,598 respondents in Indonesia.

Before moving on to a discussion of the variables, it is important to note some of the weaknesses of the data, the most notable being that the worst of the failed states in the regions of South Asia and Southeast Asia are not included in the Asian Barometer survey. Thus, there is certainly a bias toward more stable states in the dataset, which I expect will have an impact on the findings. Unfortunately, this study is limited by the availability of data, which I make an effort to address and control for in my analysis.

Description of the Variables[8]

Dependent Variable—Political Violence

The dependent variable operationalized in this chapter represents a measure of political violence. Its purpose is to capture individuals' attitudes regarding the use

6 Unfortunately, and despite that data have been collected on this region by the barometer project, South Asia is not represented in this wave of the Asian Barometer survey, nor have these data been made publicly available at the time of this writing.

7 Singapore was removed from the analysis due to the state's position as a stable state.

8 I exclude the measure protection of private property, because of the absence of this measure in the Asian Barometer survey.

of and support for political violence as a legitimate tool to obtain goods or political concessions from the state. The measure for political violence is based upon the following question in the Asian Barometer survey:

> Question (Variable=Violence): Evaluate the following statement:
>
> A: Used force or violence for a political cause
>
> Value Labels: 1=Once, 2=More Than Once, 3=Never, 4=Can't Choose, 5=Decline To Answer

To estimate the model, I set the values "1" and "2" to one, value "3" to zero, and code the remaining values as Missing Data. I choose to code the variable in this way because I am primarily interested in those respondents who support the use of violence, or in this case, have used political violence in relation to those who neither support it nor have used it. I do not know the motivations of respondents who are unable to select a response, or decline to answer, so despite what drives their responses, (i.e. fear of being discovered by the government, their family, etc.) given the lack of information, these response categories are not useful to me, and do not provide me with any explanatory information. Thus, the coding of the variable allows me to determine which dimensions of state failure increase the likelihood that individuals will support or use political violence. Therefore, the value "1" indicates the respondent is more likely to support the use of political violence, whereas the value "0" indicates the respondent is less likely to support the use of political violence.

Explanatory Variables

The public good of security

The measure for the public good of security is based upon two variables. Together, these variables indicate respondents' opinions regarding how secure they feel in their state.

The measures for the public good of security are based upon the following questions in the Asian Barometer survey:

> Question 1 (Variable=Security1): Generally speaking, how safe is living in this city/town/village?
>
> Value Labels: 1=Very Safe, 2=Safe, 3=Unsafe, 4=Very Unsafe, 7=Don't Understand the Question, 8=Can't Choose, 9=Decline to Answer

In order to estimate the model, I code the values of "7," "8," and "9" as Missing Data. By removing these values, I am left with a scale that indicates an increase in perceived insecurity. For the ease of interpretation, I recode the values so that the new scale indicates an increase in perceived security. Thus, "0"=Very Unsafe, "1"=Unsafe, "2"=Safe, and "3"=Very Safe. Given the transformation of this explanatory variable, a negative coefficient indicates that perceived insecurity increases the likelihood that a respondent will more readily engage in the use of political violence.

> Question 2 (Variable=Security2): Have you been a victim of physical violence?
>
> Value Labels: 0=Not Applicable, 1=No, 2=Yes, 8=Can't Choose, 9=Decline to Answer

In order to estimate the model, I code the values of "0," "8," and "9" as Missing Data. By removing these values, I am left with a dichotomous variable that functions as an indicator of perceived physical insecurity. For the ease of interpretation, I recode the values so that "0"=No, and "1"=Yes. Therefore, a positive coefficient indicates that a victim of physical violence is more likely to engage in the use of political violence against the state.

The presence of the state

The second measure represents the perceived presence of the state. As with the models in the previous chapters, the argument is that political violence flourishes in the absence of the state. The measure for the presence of the state is based upon two variables. Together, these variables indicate respondents' opinions regarding the presence and visibility of their state officials, which I argue is a direct indicator of the state presence throughout the country.

The measures for the presence of the state are based upon the following questions in the Asian Barometer survey:

> Question 1 (Variable=Presence1): Contacted government (administrative) official
>
> Value Labels: 1=Once, 2=More Than Once, 3=Never, 8=Can't Choose, 9=Decline to Answer
>
> Question 2 (Variable=Presence2): Contacted elected officials or legislative representatives at any level
>
> Value Labels: 1=Once, 2=More Than Once, 3=Never, 8=Can't Choose, 9=Decline to Answer

In order to estimate the model, I code the values of "8" and "9" as Missing Data for both questions. By removing these values, I am left with a scale that indicates an increase in the perceived absence of the state. For the ease of interpretation, I recode the values so that the new scale indicates an increase in the perceived presence of the state. Thus, "0"=Never, "1"=Once, "2"=More Than Once. Given the transformation of the explanatory variable, a negative coefficient indicates that the perceived absence of the state increases the likelihood that a respondent will engage in the use of political violence.

The state authority

The third explanatory variable, state authority, is based upon seven measures of this dimension. Together, these measures capture individuals' opinions regarding the legitimacy of the government and its elected officials, the level of corruption present among their elected officials and in their government, and the level of trust they hold in their government and elected officials.

The measure for the dimension of state authority that captures trust in government is based upon the following questions in the Asian Barometer survey:

> Question 1 (Variable=Trust1): Trust in Prime Minister or President
>
> Value Labels: 1=None at All, 2=Not Very Much Trust, 3=Quite a Lot of Trust, 4=A Great Deal of Trust, 7=Don't Understand the Question, 8=Can't Choose, 9=Decline to Answer
>
> Question 2 (Variable=Trust2): Trust in the National Government
>
> Value Labels: 1=None at All, 2=Not Very Much Trust, 3=Quite a Lot of Trust, 4=A Great Deal of Trust, 7=Don't Understand the Question, 8=Can't Choose, 9=Decline to Answer
>
> Question 3 (Variable=Trust3): Trust in Parliament
>
> Value Labels: 1=None at All, 2=Not Very Much Trust, 3=Quite a Lot of Trust, 4=A Great Deal of Trust, 7=Don't Understand the Question, 8=Can't Choose, 9=Decline to Answer
>
> Question 4 (Variable=Trust4): Trust in Local Government
>
> Value Labels: 1=None at All, 2=Not Very Much Trust, 3=Quite a Lot of Trust, 4=A Great Deal of Trust, 7=Don't Understand the Question, 8=Can't Choose, 9=Decline to Answer

In order to estimate the model, I code the values of "7," "8," and "9" as Missing Data. By removing these values, I am left with a scale that indicates an increase in perceived trust in the government. For the ease of interpretation, I maintain the original coding structure. Thus, "1"=None at All, "2"=Not Very Much Trust, "3"=Quite a Lot of Trust, and "4"=A Great Deal of Trust. Given the structure of this explanatory variable, a negative coefficient indicates that a lack of trust in the government increases the probability that a respondent will engage in the use of political violence.

In this section, I discuss the second measure of state authority, which indicates a respondent's perception of the legitimacy of their government. The measure for the dimensions of state authority that capture the legitimacy of the state is based upon the following question in the Asian Barometer survey:

> Question 1 (Variable=Legitimate): On the whole, how would you rate the freeness and fairness of the last national election?
>
> Value Labels: 0=Not Applicable, 1=Completely Free and Fair, 2=Free and Fair, but with minor problems, 3=Free and Fair, but with Major Problems, 4=Not Free or Fair, 8=Can't Choose, 9=Decline to Answer

In order to estimate the model, I code the values of "0," "8," and "9" as Missing Data. By removing these values, I am left with a scale that reports the perceived lack of legitimacy of the government. For the ease of interpretation, I recode the values so that "0"=Not Free or Fair, "1"=Free and Fair, but with Major Problems, "2"=Free and Fair, but with Minor Problems, and "3"=Completely Free and Fair. Given the transformation of the variable, a negative coefficient indicates that respondents' perception of the government as one that is not legitimate increases the probability that they will engage in the use of political violence against the state.

In this section, I discuss the third measure of state authority, which indicates a respondent's perception of corruption within their government.

The measure for the dimension of state authority that denotes corruption is based upon the following questions in the Asian Barometer survey:

> Question 1 (Variable=Corrupt1): How widespread do you think corruption and bribe taking are in your local/municipal government?
>
> Value Labels: 1=Almost Everyone is Corrupt, 2=Most Officials are Corrupt, 3=Not a Lot of Officials are Corrupt, 4=Hardly Anyone is Involved, 8=Can't Choose, 9=Decline to Answer
>
> Question 2 (Variable=Corrupt2): How widespread do you think corruption and bribe taking are in the national government?
>
> Value Labels: 1=Almost Everyone is Corrupt, 2=Most Officials are Corrupt, 3=Not a Lot of Officials are Corrupt, 4=Hardly Anyone is Involved, 8=Can't Choose, 9=Decline to Answer

In order to estimate the model, I code the values of "8" and "9" as Missing Data. By removing these values, I am left with a scale that reports the perceived absence of corruption in the government. For the ease of interpretation, I recode the values so that "1"=Hardly Anyone is Involved, "2"=Not A Lot of Officials are Corrupt, "3"=Most Officials are Corrupt, and "4"=Almost Everyone is Corrupt. Given the transformation of the variable, a positive coefficient indicates that the perceived presence of corruption in the government increases the probability that a respondent will engage in the use of political violence.

The provision of public goods

The fourth explanatory variable, the provision of public goods, is based upon three measures of this dimension. Together, these measures represent individuals' perceptions regarding the state's ability to provide its citizens with essential public goods.

The measures for the provision of public goods are based upon the following questions in the Asian Barometer survey:

> Question 1 (Variable=Goods1): How easy is it to obtain: A place in public primary school for a child
>
> Value Labels: 0=Not Applicable, 1=Very Difficult, 2=Difficult, 3=Easy, 4=Very Easy, 5=Never Try, 8=Can't Choose, 9=Decline to Answer
>
> Question 2 (Variable=Goods2): How easy is it to obtain: Medical treatment at a nearby clinic
>
> Value Labels: 0=Not Applicable, 1=Very Difficult, 2=Difficult, 3=Easy, 4=Very Easy, 5=Never Try, 8=Can't Choose, 9=Decline to Answer
>
> Question 3 (Variable=Goods3): How easy is it to obtain: Help from the police when you need it
>
> Value Labels: 0=Not Applicable, 1=Very Difficult, 2=Difficult, 3=Easy, 4=Very Easy, 5=Never Try, 8=Can't Choose, 9=Decline to Answer

In order to estimate the model, I code the values of "0," "8," and "9" as Missing Data for all three variables. And instead of dropping value "5," which indicates citizens have never tried to obtain certain public goods from the government, I recode it as "0." I do this because I do not know if the respondent is well off, and thus does not need to obtain certain public goods from the government, or if the respondent is impoverished, and while they may need these services, they may be apathetic toward the government and its ability to provide them with these goods. Since I do not know the motivations of the respondents who selected "5," I cannot drop this value. After recoding this variable, I am left with a scale that indicates the increasing ease with which a respondent can obtain certain public goods from the government. Thus, "0"=Never Try, "1"=Very Difficult, "2"=Difficult,

"3"=Easy, and "4" Very Easy. Given the measurement of this variable and my hypothesis, a negative coefficient indicates that the perceived inability of the government to provide the public goods of education, medical treatment, and a local security force increases the likelihood that a respondent will engage in acts of political violence.

Control Variables

I utilize a series of control variables that measure the socioeconomic conditions of the respondents. Thus, the variables level of education, personal economic status, the respondent's age, gender, and whether the respondent lives in an urban or rural area are included in the model. See Appendix G for a description of the control variables and their measurement.

Table 4.3 List of variable names and description of the concepts measured

Variable Name	Indicator Concept
Violence	Measures Political Violence
Security1	Victim of a Physical Attack
Security2	Their city/town/village is unsafe
Presence1	Contacted administrative government official
Presence2	Contacted government and legislative officials at any level
Trust1	Trust in the Prime Minister or President
Trust2	Trust in the National Government
Trust3	Trust in Parliament
Trust4	Trust in Local Government
Corrupt1	The local/municipal level of government is corrupt
Corrupt2	The National Government is corrupt
Legitimate1	The last national election was both free and fair
Goods1	It is easy to obtain public education for a child from the government
Goods2	It is easy to obtain medical treatment from a nearby clinic
Goods3	It is easy to get help from the police when you need it
Education	Respondent's highest level of education
Gender	Gender
Age	Age
PersEcon	Respondent's current economic level
Urban	Respondent is from an urban or rural area

Model

I conduct cross-sectional analysis using logistical regression in order to determine which dimensions of state failure increase the probability that an individual will engage in political violence in the selected country cases. In order to test my assumptions I estimate a logit model that indicates the respondents' probability of engaging in acts of political violence.

Logit Model

$$Model1 = h\left(\frac{p_i(violence)}{1 - p_i(violence)}\right) = \beta_0 + \beta_1 Security + \beta_2 StatePresence + \beta_3 StateAuthority + \beta_4 StateLegitimacy +$$
$$\beta_5 SPublic\ \ Goods + \beta_6 Education + \beta_7 Gender + \beta_8 PersEcon + \beta_9 Ethnic + \beta_0\ Urban + e$$

Figure 4.1 Traditional state failure model

Note: I must omit the measure *protection of private property* because of the absence of this measure in the Asian Barometer survey.

Findings

Statistical Results

Table 4.4 Binary logit estimates of support for political violence

Variable	Restricted Model	Full Model
Security1	.699 (.445)	.685 (.453)
Security2	-.185 (.188)	-.180 (.193)
Presence1	.393** (.147)	.484** (.155)
Presence2	.578*** (.142)	.455** (.154)
Trust1	-.273 (.205)	-.210 (.214)
Trust2	-.099 (.228)	-.187 (.236)
Trust3	.483** (.208)	.503** (.228)
Trust4	-.403** (.185)	-.425** (.191)
Corrupt1	.482** (.194)	.526** (.203)

Table 4.4 ***Concluded***

Variable	Restricted Model	Full Model
Corrupt2	-.355* (.198)	-.401* (.209)
Legitimate1	-.110 (.147)	-.077 (.157)
Goods1	-.038 (.125)	-.070 (.131)
Goods2	-.391** (.144)	-.375** (.151)
Goods3	.239* (.125)	.247* (.128)
Age	—	.001 (.009)
Gender	—	.480* (.262)
EconStatus	—	.207 (.159)
Education	—	-.037 (.067)
Urban	—	.012 (.093)
Constant	-4.26*** (.981)	-4.72*** (1.27)
Observations	4699	3404
Pseudo R^2	.0974	.1072
LR χ^2	70.06	68.10
Prob> χ^2	.000	.000

Note: *** p < .01 for two-tailed test; ** p < .05 for two-tailed test; *p < 0.1 for two-tailed test; standard errors in parentheses.

Findings that are Statistically Significant and Support the Hypotheses

In Table 4.4, I report the binary logit estimates[9] for the model that tests the probability that a respondent will participate in an act of political violence. In the first column, I present the estimates for the model, excluding the control variables. While in the second column, I present the full model that contains both the explanatory variables of interest as well as the control variables. Given that the findings are consistent across models, I interpret them simultaneously.

9 For marginal effects see Appendix H.

The first set of variables I discuss are those that are both statistically significant and provide support for the stated hypotheses. The first of such variables is *Trust4*. This is one of three measures for the concept of state authority and this particular variable measures whether the respondent has trust in the local government. The findings suggest that the less trust citizens have in their local level of government the greater the probability that they will support or engage in the use of political violence. With regard to the second measure of the concept of state authority, the variable *Corrupt1* measures the perception of corruption by the respondent at the local level of government. The findings suggest that a higher level of perceived corruption at the local level of government the greater the probability that a person will support or engage in the use of political violence.

Turning now to the provision of public goods, the findings suggest that the more difficult it is for respondents to receive the public good of medical treatment, i.e., health care from the government, the more supportive they are of using or engaging in political violence as a political tool.

Finally, I turn to interpreting the control variable, *Gender*. Given the measurement of the variable, the findings are consistent with our understanding of the role gender plays in support for terrorist activity. The results indicate that men are much more likely to support the use of political violence or engage in it than women.

Findings that are Statistically Significant but Fail to Support the Hypotheses

With regards to the results, the second set of variables I would like to discuss are those that are statistically significant but fail to provide support for the stated hypotheses. The first of such variables is *Trust3*. This variable measures the level of trust respondents place in their parliament. The findings suggest that the greater the level of trust respondents have in their parliament the greater the probability that they will support or engage in the use of political violence, which contradicts our hypothesis.

The variable *Corrupt2* measures the perception of corruption by the respondent at the national level of government; the findings suggest that a lower level of perceived corruption at the national level of government the greater the probability that a person will support or engage in the use of political violence. This finding is inconsistent with our stated hypothesis that the greater the level of corruption the more likely a respondent will support the use of political violence.

As for the variable *PGood3,* which captures how well the state does at providing the essential public good help from the police when they need it, the results indicate that the ease with which respondents can obtain assistance from the police, the more likely they are to support the use of political violence. This finding fails to support the hypothesis.

The final measure to achieve statistical significance, but contradicts the stated hypothesis, are the variables that measure the concept of the presence of the state. The variables indicate that the respondents have contacted their government (administrative) official and/or have contacted their elected official or legislative representative at any level of government. The findings suggest that ease with which individuals can access their government officials the greater the probability that they will support or engage in the use of political violence. One would expect only those respondents who feel their government is absent from their lives, and thus the presence of the state is minimal, to support the use of political violence. Therefore, it is apparent that this variable fails to support the hypothesis.

Findings that are Not Statistically Significant and Fail to Support the Hypotheses

While there are several variables in both models that fail to achieve either statistical or substantive significance,[10] the only measure I will discuss is public good of security. In the models, two variables measure the concept of the public good of security. These variables include *Security1*, which indicates whether a person has been physically attacked, and *Security2*, which indicates whether or not a person feels unsafe in his community. What concerns me about these findings is that the literature regarding the relationship between the absence of security and support for political violence is abundant and consistent in the assertion that the absence of security in a state is an important contributor to political violence. Also, in previous chapters, this measure consistently had an impact on the dependent variable, political violence, and was typically the strongest of all the state failure variables. Therefore, that neither one of these variables is significant in any way is troubling.

At this point in the chapter, I would enter into a discussion of the findings and their greater significance in my concluding section. However, given the weak findings in the model, I want to probe deeper into the relationship between state failure and political violence within the context of Southeast and South Asia. Although I remain convinced that in Southeast Asia and South Asia the conditions of state failure contribute to individual support for political violence, I acknowledge that the statistical model does not conclusively support this. I believe that this is largely due to the complexities of the states within these regions, and that in many ways they do not possess the most obvious features of a failed state—that is until one looks closer at the violence and poverty present in these states that exist beyond the major capitals and urban financial centers.

Regarding the weak results, I also wonder if there are other factors at play, such as how representative the sample is to the population of interest—which are individuals who have been exposed to political violence in some capacity. There may also be cultural factors to consider, and how citizens of the states within these regions perceive the authority of their governments, and the appropriateness of criticism toward their elected officials and institutions of governance. I will never fully understand why

10 The variables that fail to achieve both statistical and substantive significance include, Trust1=Trust in the Prime Minister, Trust2=Trust in the National Government, Security1=Has Been Physically Attacked, Security2=Unsafe in their Community, Legitimate=Government Elections Are Free And Fair, PGood1=Public Good of Education, and the control variables Age, Education, Economic Status, and Lives in an Urban or Rural Area.

the statistical results fail to support the hypotheses; however, in the next section I evaluate the descriptive statistics of the Asian Barometer data, as well as data from the Global Terrorism Database, the U.S. Department of State's "Patterns of Global Terrorism" project, the MIPT Terrorism Knowledge Database, and the State Failure Task Force/Political Instability Task Force Dataset to better frame the argument—that while the statistical results are weak, *at best*, that the relationship between state failure and political violence in Southeast Asia and South Asia is just as salient in these regions as it is in sub-Saharan Africa, the Maghreb and the Middle East.

A Closer Look at State Failure and Political Violence in Southeast and South Asia

In order to understand the weaknesses of the statistical model, I must gain deeper insight into the nature of the Asian Barometer data. A closer look at the dependent variable reveals one of the reasons why there were serious problems with the model. In Figure 4.2, I present the figures for those individuals in the survey who support the use of political violence, compared to those individuals who do not. As was the case in preceding chapters, the majority of respondents do not support the use of political violence. However, with the Afrobarometer and Arabarometer surveys, there were enough respondents in the dataset who supported political violence for me to estimate a statistical model. In the case of the Asian Barometer survey, only 1.3 percent of the respondents support the use of political violence. Such a small number makes it extremely difficult for me to draw inferences from the findings of my statistical model.

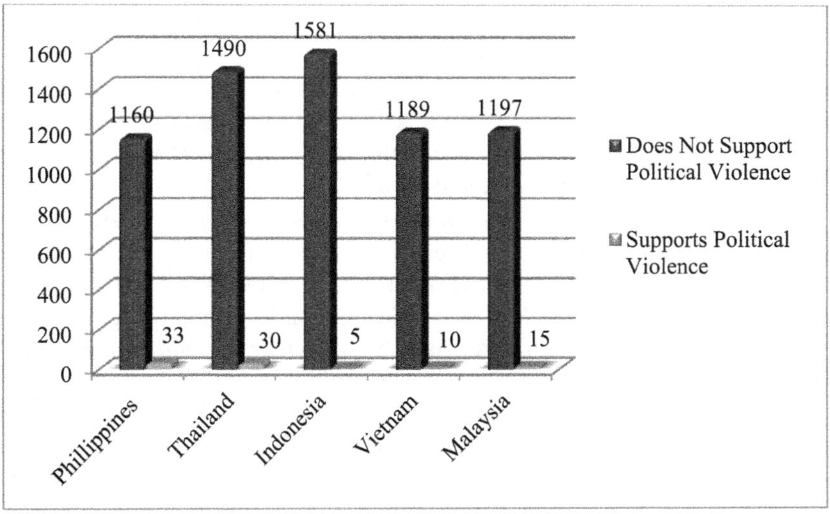

Figure 4.2 Number of respondents who support the use of political violence by country (2006–2008)

When I looked at Figure 4.2, the first question I asked myself was why are there so few respondents in the Asian Barometer survey who support political violence when compared to the other barometer surveys? To be honest, I really cannot answer that question definitively. As I hinted at in the preceding section, individuals may not feel comfortable expressing their true views to a stranger (the interviewer), given the cultural and political climate of their state. At the same time, other members of a respondent's family may have been present during the interview, which may have made the respondent uncomfortable, thus making them less forthcoming with the interviewer regarding their true opinions. Within the survey, there is a question for the interviewer that asks if others were present during the interview. Approximately 51 percent of the respondents in the sample completed their interview with another person in the room, compared to the Afrobarometer where 40 percent of the respondents had another person present during their interview, which means 60 percent (the majority of the sample) did not have another person present.[11] In the Asian Barometer survey, over half of the sample was administered a survey while another person was present, which has serious implications regarding the validity of the responses obtained. Therefore, one could assume that with the Asian Barometer survey, of those individuals sampled, there are likely more respondents who have engaged in political violence, as the survey question asks, but were reluctant to admit this in the presence of others.

Although there are flaws in the methodology of the Asian Barometer survey, I would like to point out the sample was constructed based upon a probability sample of the population; thus, for the most part it is representative of the population. With that said, one could make the assumption that the responses from the surveys simply represent the attitudes of the general populace, and to infer there is a larger community of support for political violence within the surveyed regions would be an overstatement. I acknowledge this. I would argue further that supporters and participants of political violence are a small subset of the population and that for the most part, the greater populace does not support acts of terrorism and political violence. This is a logical assumption given that violence presents a security threat to a community and disrupts civil order, the administration of necessary public goods, and the economic foundation of a state.

Therefore, it runs counter to one's needs for basic survival that an individual would support political violence. And yet, what if the state represents a security threat to the community through oppressive and repressive governance, fails to provide public goods, and there is a lack of economic opportunity for many segments of the population? It would stand to reason that these individuals *would* support political violence, and even if they do not necessarily participate, they may be more likely to condone acts of terrorism, especially if these acts are directed against the state. This scenario would likely be the case for marginalized groups such as the Malay Muslims in Thailand and other Muslims in the region, particularly the Philippines.

11 The Arabarometer and Latinobarometer surveys do not have this question in their questionnaire.

As I discussed earlier in this chapter, overwhelmingly the political violence in the region is the result of ethno-religious tensions (See Appendix I) and perpetrated by those individuals excluded from the politicial and economic processes within the state. Therefore, while most citizens in most states do not support and engage in the use of political violence, and actually disapprove of it, marginalized populations with tangible grievances would be the exception, and while I have no evidence to suggest otherwise, I wonder if maybe the Asian Barometer survey has somehow undersampled this group.

Whether or not the Asian Barometer survey has missed a critical subset of the population in their sampling efforts is not the greater concern, nor are the limitations of the data or statistical models. The greater problem is that the statistical findings would have one believe there is a weak relationship between the conditions of state failure and individual support for political violence; however, other sources of data suggest this is not an accurate assumption.

In Table 4.5, data from the State Failure Task Force Project/Political Instability Task Force and the Department of State's *Pattern of Global Terrorism* project reveal that from 1998 to 2003, of the regions with the greatest number of episodes of state failure, Asia had the highest along with the second highest number of terrorist incidents. It was unusual to me that Latin America would have the highest number of terrorist incidents in the world during that time period, more so than Asia and the Middle East. Table 4.6 reveals why that is the case. While Colombia is the only state from the region of Latin America on the list of the top 20 states in the world with the greatest number of terrorist incidents, Colombia is ranked number three, and prior to 2003, when the war in Iraq began, Colombia was ranked second, behind the West Bank.

The data in Table 4.5 end in 2003, while the data in Table 4.6 are from 2000–2006, which includes the war in Iraq, when incidents in that state rocketed within 12 months. Thus, Table 4.5 does not illustrate that terrorism in Latin America is driven by a single state. However, Table 4.6 reveals that the regions of Southeast Asia and South Asia are major sites of terrorism in the world. Out of 20 states, Southeast Asia and South Asia make up almost half of the states with the greatest number of incidents of terrorism in the world, with nine states on the list—more than any other region.

The figures presented in Tables 4.5 and 4.6 suggest that there is a strong correlation between the conditions of state failure and incidents of terrorism. With the highest percentage of episodes of state failure, Asia also has the second highest rate of terrorism in the world. The Asian Barometer data are unable to capture this phenomenon or the strength of this relationship. However, I return to the Asian Barometer survey to test the strength of the relationship between state failure and political violence, because as we have seen, the data are not robust enough to conduct logistical regression analysis, but correlation analysis may reveal support for this relationship. Nevertheless, I do realize I will be unable to establish causal inferences from my findings, which represents a serious limitation.

Table 4.5 Percentage of states experiencing episodes of failure and incidents of terrorism by region, 1998–2003

Region	Percentage of States Experiencing Episodes of Failure	Total Number of Terrorist Incidents
Sub-Saharan Africa	38.2	174*
Middle East and North Africa**	37.5	208
Asia	**45.3**	**561**
Latin America	7.7***	692
Western Europe	2.7	222
North America	0.0	6

Notes: * As I pointed out in Chapter 2, the U.S. State Department does not report incidents of terrorism in the region not sponsored by international groups such as Al-Qaeda, so domestic groups like the RUF are excluded; thus, this number is grossly underestimated.
** Does not include data from Iraq.
*** This number is grossly underestimated given the measurement errors of the State Failure Task Force/Political Instability Task Force. See Howard (2010b). *The Tragedy of Failure*.
Source: Piazza, 2007; Percentage of states experiencing at least one state failure, State Failure Task Force, Consolidated State Failure Events, http://cidcm.umd.edu/stfail.
Number of international terrorist incidents, United States Department of State, "Patterns of Global Terrorism, 2003. http://www.state.gov/s/ct/rls/pgtrpt/2003/33777.htm.

The results of the Pearson Correlation analysis for the measures of state failure and political violence support my argument that while the data are not robust enough to conduct logistical regression, correlation analysis reveals there is a relationship between these two factors. Out of the list of variables, only three do not share a statistically significant correlation with political violence. These variables include trust in parliament, obtaining the good of public education, and obtaining help from the police. That these variables are not correlated with political violence are not especially troubling since none of them are substantively significant in the logit model. However, the findings do raise some concerns only because the variables obtaining the public good of education and obtaining help from the police are statistically significant in the logit model, although they contradict the hypothesis. While not unheard of, it is unusual for a variable to have a causal impact on another variable (even if it is contradictory to the hypothesis), but then not share a statistically significant *correlation* with the same variable.

Despite that, what remains important is the correlation analysis reveals that many of the measures of state failure share a statistically significant relationship with political violence that is consistent with the hypothesized relationship. For example, the coefficient for *Security2*, which measures how safe respondents feel in their community, is negative. Thus, as support for political violence increases, the less safe a respondent feels, and vice versa.

While the results of the correlation analysis are encouraging, there remain limitations, besides the one I already mentioned, and that is the findings cannot infer causation. The other major weakness is that the variables that capture whether a respondent has been physically attacked and both measures of the presence of the state, while statistically significant, the sign for the coefficients are inconsistent with the hypothesized relationship. Thus, a major setback for this analysis as a whole is that at no point do the statistical results support the hypothesis that the absence of the state contributes to support for political violence, which is a major assertion of this study. The implications of this weakness in the analysis will be discussed in the conclusion of this chapter.

Table 4.6 Global incidences of terrorism by country and region, 2000–2006

Rank	States	Number of Incidents	Region
# 1	Iraq	4,606	Middle East
# 2	West Bank	1,927	Middle East
# 3	Colombia	1,135	Latin America
# 4	Spain	732	W. Europe
# 5	**Thailand**	**619**	**SE Asia**
# 6	**Afghanistan**	**591**	**South Asia**
# 7	**India**	**509**	**South Asia**
# 8	**Pakistan**	**504**	**South Asia**
# 9	Turkey	477	Eurasia
# 10	Israel	463	Middle East
# 11	France	446	W. Europe
# 12	Nepal	379	South Asia
# 13	Russia	284	E. Europe
# 14	Greece	230	E. Europe
# 15	**Philippines**	**213**	**SE Asia**
# 16	**Indonesia**	**197**	**SE Asia**
# 17	**Sri Lanka**	**131**	**South Asia**
# 18	Italy	125	S. Europe
# 19	**Bangladesh**	**111**	**South Asia**
# 20	United States	98	N. America

Source: MIPT Terrorism Knowledge Database, http://www.terrorisminfo.mipt.org/incidentcalendar.asp. Accessed April 23, 2010: compiled by author.

Note: Total of 94 countries and 14,934 attacks. Countries ranking 21–94 are not listed in table.

Table 4.7 Pearson correlation for measures of state failure and political violence

Variables	Correlation Coefficient and Statistical Significance of Relationship Between Measures of State Failure and Political Violence
1. Political Violence	—
2. Trust in the Prime Minister	-.0339**
3. Trust in the National Government	-.0376**
4. Trust in Parliament	-.0178
5. Trust in Local Government	-.0476***
6. Physically Attacked	-.0369**
7. Feel Safe in Community	.0328*
8. Free and Fair Elections	-.0207*
9. Corruption at Local Level	.0325**
10. Corruption at National Level	.0230*
11. Public Education	-.0079
12. Medical Treatment	-.0298**
13. Help from the Police	.0085
14. Contact Administrative Government Official	.0597***
15. Contact Any Elected Official	.0689***

Note: *** $p < .01$ for two-tailed test; ** $p < .05$ for two-tailed test; * $p < 0.1$ for two-tailed test.

Yet despite some of the limitations of the correlation analysis, overall, the results support the data presented in the preceding descriptive tables and provide evidence to support the argument that the conditions of state failure share a relationship with support for political violence.

Conclusion

At first glance, Southeast Asia and South Asia are regions comprised of economically and politically viable states. The statistical findings of this analysis would largely support this (See Table 4.8 and Table 4.9). And yet, while that is true in many ways, given that these regions are undoubtedly experiencing enviable economic growth, a closer look reveals these two regions are plagued by internal problems not readily visible.

Southeast and South Asia have the highest percentage of state failure episodes in the world, and the second highest incidence of terrorist attacks (See Table 4.5). Further, out of the top 20 states across the globe with the greatest number of terrorist attacks, nearly half of this list comprises states from either Southeast

Asia or South Asia (See Table 4.6). Statistics such as these suggest that while the regions of Southeast Asia and South Asia are making strides to develop economically, they are still plagued by conditions of state failure and subsequent incidents of political violence.

As I have discussed throughout this chapter, Southeast Asia and South Asia are regions that have been longtime sponsors of terrorism and international terrorist groups. However, it wasn't until September 11 when the international community began to take notice, that groups such as the JI were caught harboring al-Qaeda terrorists recently flushed out of Afghanistan. In recent years, terrorists have been active in the region with deadly attacks in Mumbai, Bali, Jakarta, and throughout Afghanistan and Pakistan. These incidents have kept international attention focused on the region, but unfortunately, beyond some progress in Indonesia, Afghanistan, and Pakistan, global efforts have not gone far enough in removing the terrorist threat from these regions.

The greater implication of the lack of a strong government presence in many states within these regions is that networks of terrorism still exist, which allows them to recruit members, plan attacks, and implement operations throughout Southeast and South Asia. An example of this can be found in the growing presence of terrorist groups in Cambodia. Much like sub-Saharan Africa, Cambodia has long been a safe haven for terrorists without much activity, but there is always the possibility that this will change.

Table 4.8 Hypotheses supported by the Logistical Regression analysis

Hypotheses	Variables and Concept Measured
State Authority	Trust4—Trust in Local Government Corrupt1—Corruption at Local Level
Provision of Public Goods	PGood2—Public Good of Medical Treatment
Control Measure—Gender	Gender—Men Support Political Violence

Table 4.9 Hypotheses supported by the Correlation analysis

Hypotheses	Variables and Concept Measured
State Authority	Trust1—Trust in Prime Minister Trust2—Trust in National Government Trust4—Trust in Local Government Corrupt1—Corruption at Local Level Corrupt2—Corruption at National Level
State Legitimacy	Legitimate—Free and Fair Elections
Public Good of Security	Security2—Feel Unsafe in Community
Provision of Public Goods	PGood2—Public Good of Medical Treatment

Note: Control variables were not statistically significant.

A Cambodian journalist concluded that "the country was a convenient base from which to launder money, buy arms, forge documents, and perform any number of other tasks crucial to the smooth running of illegal activities" (Chalk et al., 2009, p. 200). Given Cambodia's porous sea borders, illegal arms dealers, drug traffickers, and terrorists have all been able to effectively utilize the fragile state for their operations. For example, in 2003, the mastermind behind the October 2002 bombing in Bali, Riduan Isamuddin (aka Hambali) was able to circumvent immigration into Cambodia and rent a home in the city Phnom Penh, despite that he was wanted by Indonesian officials (Chalk et al., 2009). The absence of a strong state presence and the lack of security, both features of state failure, are evident in Cambodia, which increases the likelihood that support for political violence is already brewing in the state.

Some speculate that this is in fact the case, as religious extremists from the Middle East and Malaysia, who are connected to JI, have begun migrating to Cambodia where they have worked to implement a comprehensive strategy of 're-Islamizing' Cambodia's minority Cham and Malay populations (Chalk et al., 2009).

Will there soon be an active presence of terrorist groups and terrorist activity in Cambodia? Will Cambodia soon look like Indonesia or even Pakistan? There is certainly evidence to suggest this. I am convinced that as the global community continues to turn up the heat on international networks of terrorism in states such as Afghanistan and Pakistan, these groups will seek out other failing and failed states in the region as havens where they will continue to organize and recruit, beyond the close scrutiny of the global community. Thus, I argue that like sub-Saharan Africa, the states in South Asia, but particularly those in Southeast Asia, are at the greatest risk. These regions are on the cusp of economic development, and yet, they still remain in a fragile place with the potential for crisis, given that they continue to be plagued by the conditions of state fragility and the seeds of political violence.

Chapter 5
The Delayed Reign of the Latin King: Why Drug Lords, Rebels and Terrorism Will Forever Plague Latin America's Frail States

Introduction

Latin America[1] is comprised of a network of weak states, some hovering on the brink of absolute collapse (Colombia and Guatemala), while many others enjoy a measure of security, even if economic and state fragility remain predominant concerns. Thus, while the region as a whole would generally be viewed as peaceful, Latin America still would not be considered a region of stable states.

This is because of a number of factors stemming from the post-Cold War era and the role the United States has played in the region. Unlike the regions of sub-Saharan Africa and Southeast/South Asia, which have faced security challenges because of ethnic rivalries and religious conflict, Latin America is a region of religious homogeneity, and while it does suffer from racial and ethnic inequality, with the marginalization of many of the indigenous populations, state fragility in Latin America does not stem from some variant of ethno-religious conflict. Instead, Latin America shares many similarities with the Middle East and North Africa in how it has evolved into a region comprised of weak and failing states.

Like the Middle East and North Africa, Latin America has a long and complex relationship with the United States. A pawn in the politics of the Cold War, the fall of the Soviet Union brought an almost abrupt end to the Marxist revolutionary movements that were instrumental in removing the military juntas and dictators who wielded power in the region by replacing them with democratically elected leaders (Hakim, 2000). Consequently, with new leadership, a series of economic reforms were soon implemented. However, with inequitable free trade agreements between Latin America and the United States, coupled with a stagnant economy, the region saw little in the way of economic prosperity. As a result, black market economies, such as drug and human trafficking, have flourished along with guerilla groups, cartels, and paramilitary operations that have replaced the military dictatorships as the primary security threats to the region.

---

1 For the purposes of this research, Latin America refers to the Americas region south of the United States, which also includes Anglophone and Francophone countries of the Caribbean because of the shared economic history of these countries.

Having to contend with weak institutions, corrupt political leaders, and the explosion of drug trafficking and subsequent violence, several states within Latin America have completely collapsed—Haiti; exist on the brink of failure—Colombia and Mexico; or they remain in a precarious position of instability—Guatemala, Nicaragua, and the entire Andean region in South America. The collapse of these states will undoubtedly have a far-reaching impact on its neighbors, many of which are also structurally weak as they continue to struggle with addressing slow economic growth and competing political factions.

The main concerns for a region such as Latin America is that it is undergoing the process of economic transformation, but this has been stalled by the presence of violent paramilitary groups, drug cartels, and rebel organizations that threaten the governments within the region and hamper the development of mechanisms to ensure stability and security. As a consequence, citizens within Latin America have been affected by a culture of pervasive violence, the prevalence of drugs, and stagnant economic growth. The combination of these factors have undoubtedly shaped public opinion regarding the fragility of the states in which Latin Americans live, but has this climate of insecurity also influenced support for political violence?

I argue that in Latin America the causal relationship between the presence of state failure and support for political violence is more nuanced than in any other region examined thus far. That is because the violence in Latin America is a multifaceted conflict with multiple players, driven by the drug trade, competition over territory, and who exercises a monopoly over the violence. Unlike most violent extremist groups who maintain a core ideology and utilize submarket economies to fund their operations, the insurgent groups in Latin America that emerged during the Cold War have evolved from this model. Most notably, the FARC is no longer a social movement grounded in Marxist ideology, instead, it is now a multimillion dollar drug trafficking organization that 'claims' to provide protection to citizens from right wing paramilitary groups, such as the United Self-Defense Forces of Colombia (AUC), and even the Colombian government. Consequently, Latin American states must deal with several contending actors including terrorist organizations, drug cartels, paramilitaries, *and* rebel groups.

A majority of the states in Latin America suffer from corrupt leadership where the legitimacy of the government is challenged by these aforementioned non-state actors. It is well known that corruption exists at all levels of the Mexican government, from the local police force to national authorities, many of whom are guilty of taking bribes from drug cartels. In Colombia, however, in an attempt to exercise a measure of authority, the government has often supported one group against the other—as is the case with the government's backing of paramilitaries against the guerilla groups—even though it is at the expense of Colombian citizens who are often caught in the middle of the conflict. Thus, the presence of paramilitary groups, guerilla organizations, and the active violence of Latin American governments against their own people complicate the dynamic witnessed in preceding chapters. As a result of this mired relationship, I expect the results of the analysis in this chapter to reveal a similarly complex finding.

Despite the complexities of the political violence in Latin America, I remain true to the argument that I outlined at the opening of this work: that failed states threaten an individual's survival, which ultimately drives them to obtain tangible political and economic resources through the use of political violence. In the case of Latin America, respondents may not report actively engaging in political violence, given the absence of ideologically driven groups who represent an alternative to the corrupt and illegitimate state. However, I do expect the analysis to reveal respondent dissatisfaction toward the state, and that this attitude will manifest itself in the survey questions that report using violence to displace the current leadership. Therefore, in spite of the intervening factors in Latin America, the driving mechanisms for individual support for political violence remain identical to all other regions examined in this text—and that is a climate of state failure.

Violence and State Failure in Latin America

State Failure, the Drug Trade and Violent Actors

Compared to other regions, particularly Africa and the Middle East, scholars would argue that Latin America remains a relatively safe place to live in the developing world (Koonings and Kruit, 2004). That the *severity* of violence is not comparable to other regions of the world is not up for dispute. What is important to understand about Latin America is that while violence may not be particularly severe, "widespread societal violence has become a general feature in modern [Latin American] society" (Koonings and Kruit, 2004, p. 188). This is evidenced by the massive movement of forced migrants within the region that at the time of this writing is exceeded only by the Democratic Republic of the Congo and Sudan. In 2010 alone, the percentage of forced migrants within Haiti increased by 38 percent; while in Colombia, it is estimated more than three million people have been internally displaced because of the ever-present violence that claims the lives of close to five thousand people every year (Chesterman, Ignatieff, and Thakur, 2005; UNHCR Global Trends, 2010).

Colombia is by far the most critical state in the region simply because of its strategic location and that it leads the world in the production of cocaine. Bordered by Brazil, Peru, Ecuador, Venezuela, and Panama, Colombia is literally the gateway between Central and South America and dominates the trafficking and flow of drugs in and out of South America. Because of this, the crisis in Colombia affects not only the people of that state, but the entire region, as has been the case over the past decade. "The effects of the conflict are spilling across the five adjacent borders. There is social unrest in Ecuador as workers see their wages being undercut by the [Colombian] refugees; rising insecurity along the borders of Ecuador and Venezuela, as Colombian guerrillas and paramilitaries extend their practices of criminal extortion there; [and finally] there are the reports of trafficking between the FARC and the Venezuelan army" (Chesterman, Ignatieff, and Thakur,

2005, p. 104). While the crisis emerging from the South American region is indeed a critical concern, the implications of the turmoil in the region extend far beyond.

Cocaine traffickers from Colombia depend upon an integrated network of smuggling routes that extend throughout the Caribbean islands of Haiti and the Dominican Republic, to Mexico, and into the United States. It is control over the latter route, from Mexico into the U.S. that has sparked the wave of drug cartel violence in Mexico, which has further exacerbated the crisis of instability in that state (Jacobson, 2006).

It would seem that the state weakness in Latin America stems from the proliferation of drugs, but such an assumption is misleading. That Latin America has capitalized on drug production and trade, from which violence has emerged, is merely a symptom of state fragility. Based upon the classic Westphalian model of the nation-state, Latin America, like sub-Saharan Africa, has always fallen short of this ideal. Internal struggles for power by political elites in the early 1900s gave way to revolutionaries of the fifties and sixties, which led to democratically elected leaders who have since failed at their promises of economic equality, only to be displaced by paramilitaries and drug cartels of the '90s and today. Further, "states such as Bolivia, Ecuador, Peru, and Venezuela can be said to be suffering legitimation crises, with poor governance indicators, disastrously low citizen approval of political parties and leaders, and conflicts over scarce resources between the central authority and newly decentralized regions" (Chesterman, Ignatieff, and Thakur, 2005, p. 105).

In the absence of state building, Latin America represents a classic example of this cycle of violence, which I discuss at the opening of this entire work. The actors may change, but the root cause of the political violence in Latin America can always trace its origins back to endemic state weakness. Coupled with the institutionalization of organized crime, this dynamic has created challenges for the fledgling democracies in Latin America. As a result of the poor management of state and economic affairs by weak and corrupt governments, the legitimacy of the state has been compromised, and with it the ability of the state to challenge the numerous non-state actors who effectively utilize violence to achieve their strategic goals.

Internationally Sponsored Terrorism in Latin America

In the aftermath of September 11, while the United States primarily focused its counterterrorism efforts on the Middle East and North African region, it also began to scrutinize other pockets of the world, which had long been safe havens for terrorists groups. Given the close proximity of Latin American and Caribbean nations, concerns regarding terrorist threats from this region were raised. Yet, what U.S. officials discovered was that the threat of internationally sponsored terrorism in the Western Hemisphere was comparatively low in relation to other regions of the world, and this remains so. At the same time, while terrorist organizations may not be as pervasive in Latin America as they are in other regions, they are present and it is the relationship these groups have with other violent non-state actors that represents yet another challenge to the fragile states of this region.

As far as internationally sponsored terrorism is concerned, the tri-border region of Brazil, Paraguay, and Argentina is probably the most active spot within Latin America. "[The tri-border region] has long been characterized as a regional hub for Hezbollah and Hamas fundraising activities, but it is also used for arms and drug trafficking, contraband smuggling, document and currency fraud, money laundering, and the manufacture and movement of pirated goods," (Patterns of Global Terrorism Report, 2003; Country Reports on Terrorism, 2009). Further, it was reported that Hezbollah was responsible for two bombings in Buenos Aires, which claimed the lives of 126 people and injured more than 150; the 1992 bombing of the Israeli Embassy; and the 1994 bombing of the Argentine-Israeli Mutual Association. However, beyond these attacks in Argentina, accounts of a deeply entrenched terrorist presence remain uncorroborated, just as it has not been confirmed that internationally sponsored terrorist threats are active in the region. Again, with the exception of reports that the Cuban government provided safe haven to as many as 20 Basque ETA terrorists from Spain, most accounts of terrorism in the region do not involve internationally sponsored terrorist networks.

Despite the apparent lack of an immediate security threat from internationally sponsored terrorist networks in the region, it does not in any way suggest there is an absence of terrorism or political violence in Latin America. Domestic terrorist groups and violent political actors have long been a threat to Latin America, and in recent years, these organizations have grown more violent and aggressive with struggles for power and money. As a result of the violence, the already fragile states of Latin America have been severely weakened, which has raised credible security concerns for the people living in this region.

Conflict and Political Violence in Latin America

Within Latin America, authoritarian leaders, ineffectual democracies, and inequalities within society have been the antecedent conditions of internal conflict. At the root of many of the rebel movements that emerged in the 1950s and flourished until the '70s were class and ethnic grievances. These rebel groups were mainly comprised of the rural and urban poor whose specific demands from the government were grounded in the redistribution of land and wealth. Compounded by the presence of repressive leaders and unstable governments, that Latin America would give rise to a number of bloody civil wars, guerilla movements, coups d'état, and terrorism is no surprise. However, like many of the conflicts that emerged during the era of the Cold War, when the Cold War ended, several of the Marxist movements could no longer mobilize their base of support and the seeds of dissent fizzled as the conflicts abruptly came to an end. This was glaringly apparent in El Salvador. After 12 years of civil war, the government of El Salvador and the multi-group guerillas—now the FMLN (Farabundo Martí National Liberation Front)—brokered a peace agreement in 1991 and the FMLN was institutionalized into the political landscape of El Salvador as a legitimate political party, despite that the main goals of the left wing movement remain unachieved and the root causes of the conflict remain unresolved, which include agrarian reform and high rates of rural unemployment.

What took place in El Salvador also occurred in many other Latin American countries during the nineties, including Nicaragua and Guatemala. Despite the absence of true agrarian reform and economic redistribution, conflict ceased and many formal guerilla groups became legitimate political parties. However, the FARC of Colombia and Peru's Sendero Luminoso (The Shining Path),[2] have managed to transform themselves from rebels and guerillas into outright terrorists, bringing with them a wave of internal conflict fueled by resources from the illegal drug trade, which has outlived the Cold War and proven resilient (Solimano, 2004).

During the nineties, with the movement toward democracy in Latin America, many were optimistic that the "strongest insurgent force on the continent" (Ortiz, 2001, p. 127) would peacefully channel its social demands into the emerging democratic political structure to better achieve its ideological objectives. However, that was not what happened. The guerillas of the Revolutionary Armed Forces of Colombia (FARC) have done anything but weaken and go away peacefully. Quite the opposite. The FARC abandoned the characteristics associated with many of the armed insurgents that emerged between the fifties and the seventies, and instead adapted new strategic priorities. The result has been, at least in the case of the FARC and the National Liberation Army (ELN), that guerillas have not disappeared from Latin America as originally predicted. Further, these remaining organizations are far worse than their predecessors. Where they were once driven by political power that existed just beneath the façade of ideological grievances, these groups are now explicitly driven by greed and control over territory for the sole purpose of maintaining a stronghold in the illegal drug trade.

Outside of the FARC and the ELN, the government of Colombia must also contend with the United Self-Defense Forces of Colombia (AUC), a rightist paramilitary organization. Among these three groups, elected government officials are often targeted for attack; subsequently, many civilians find themselves innocent victims of the violence. Beyond the attacks upon the government and its representatives, all three groups engage in civilian massacres, political assassinations, political kidnappings, and the forced recruitment of minors. As a consequence, the violence that has erupted between these groups has led to substantial forced migration, the largest in the region. An estimated four to five million Colombians, or one in ten of the country's population, are reportedly now living abroad (Semana, 2003) and its internally displaced population (IDP) numbers more than three million.

Colombia is undoubtedly a unique case within Latin America, but as this chapter has touched upon, the *entire* region still faces armed challenges, domestic conflicts, drug cartels, and gang violence, as well as the presence of deadly

2 Although since 2003 the Shining Path has experienced a notable decline.

insurgent groups. Peru still must contend with the presence of the Shining Path, and drug gangs still have a very strong presence in El Salvador, Nicaragua, and along the U.S.-Mexico border. In variant forms, steady patterns of violence have existed in Latin America for several decades and this continues today, to which I assert that the enduring presence of conflict has undoubtedly had a definitive impact on citizens and their public opinion regarding the state and political violence.

The Main Hypothesis—State Failure

As I have discussed in the sections leading up to this, and as evidenced by the statistics (See Table 5.1 and Table 5.2) reported by the Index of State Weakness (2008) and the Failed State Index (2011), Latin America is not a region rife with a mass of crumbling states all set to tumble and collapse. Instead, Latin America is comprised of states that have been institutionally weak since their inception and remain so to this day. What keeps Latin America from mirroring sub-Saharan Africa, or even the Middle East, is that it has managed to create a resilient economy, which is stable even if there has been the absence of sustained growth. Similarly, the democratic institutions of Latin America have created a semblance of government transparency, even if these governments suffer from corruption. Viewed from the blurry lens of other regions discussed in this work, the situation in Latin America really doesn't look like state failure at all—except when one actually examines the conditions of, well, *state failure.*

The majority states of Latin America hover in the "Warning" category of the Failed State Index for a reason—they have been unable to effectively monopolize security of either person or property; state authorities are considered ineffective, inefficient, and most importantly illegitimate; vast stretches of territory are governed by non-state actors; and there are glaring inequities in resource distribution, which means many citizens are not provided with basic public goods. Sound like the conditions for a failed state? That's because they are.

Latin America shares many similarities with the regions of Southeast and South Asia in that the dichotomy of economic development exists within the context of state fragility. Therefore, much like Southeast and South Asia, the subsequent acts of terror and political violence that emerge within the climate of state failure are not as severe as the violence observed in the Middle East or sub-Saharan Africa. That does not mean that the political violence in Latin America would not be considered acts of terror, because they are. However, the pattern of violence found in Latin America is generally low intensity and isolated to specific territorial regions within the state, which is indicative of the chronic weakness of Latin American states that have managed to do everything *but* fail.

Returning to the argument at the core of this analysis and with it, the central hypothesis, I expect the findings to reveal that a climate of state failure, or in the case of Latin America, state fragility, has an influence on popular support for political violence directed *against* the state. With that in mind, however, I do not anticipate the results to reveal that respondents actually support the existing groups such as the drug cartels or the FARC, given the absence of ideologically driven groups coupled with the brutal human rights abuses perpetrated by cartels and drug gangs, guerillas, and the paramilitaries against the average citizen of Latin America. Instead, I expect the results to illustrate dissatisfaction with the state and its inability to manage and eliminate the security threats created by these non-state actors.

Although one can only suppose that if a terrorist organization driven less by economic incentives and more by a substantive ideology began to organize in the region, the phenomenon we've witnessed in the Middle East, Africa, and particularly South Asia could certainly emerge in Latin America, *especially* if these groups provided tangible economic goods and offered an alternative to the status quo.[3]

Table 5.1 The 2008 Index of State Weakness rankings for Latin America

Country	Ranking	Quintile
Haiti	12	Bottom Quintile
Colombia**	47	2nd Quintile
Guatemala**	60	3rd Quintile
Cuba	62	3rd Quintile
Bolivia**	64	3rd Quintile
Honduras**	69	3rd Quintile
Venezuela**	70	3rd Quintile
Nicaragua**	72	3rd Quintile
Paraguay**	75	3rd Quintile
Ecuador**	85	4th Quintile
Guyana	87	4th Quintile
Dominican Republic**	91	4th Quintile
Peru**	92	4th Quintile
El Salvador**	95	4th Quintile
Brazil**	99	4th Quintile
Argentina**	115	5th Quintile (The Highest)
Belize**	117	5th Quintile (The Highest)
Mexico**	120	5th Quintile (The Highest)
Panama**	122	5th Quintile (The Highest)
Costa Rica**	130	5th Quintile (The Highest)
Uruguay**	132	5th Quintile (The Highest)
Chile**	139	5th Quintile (The Highest)

Note: Rankings based upon a total of 141 countries. Country cases in the Latinobarometer survey are denoted by **.

3 Status quo meaning an alternative to both the existing state authorities and the non-actors who are responsible for the security threats of the region.

Table 5.2 The 2011 Failed State Index rankings for Latin America

Country	Ranking	Quintile
Haiti	5	Critical
Colombia**	44	Warning
Bolivia**	59	Warning
Ecuador**	62	Warning
Nicaragua**	66	Warning
Guatemala**	72	Warning
Honduras**	78	Warning
Venezuela**	80	Warning
Dominican Republic**	84	Warning
Cuba	86	Warning
El Salvador**	89	Warning
Mexico**	94	Warning
Peru**	99	Warning
Guyana	100	Warning
Paraguay**	101	Warning
Suriname	105	Warning
Belize**	114	Warning
Brazil**	123	Warning
Panama**	131	Moderate
Costa Rica**	137	Moderate
Argentina**	145	Moderate
Chile**	153	Moderate
Uruguay**	154	Moderate

Note: Rankings based upon a total of 177 countries. Country cases in the Latinobarometer survey are denoted by **.

Data and Methodology

Data

The data for this analysis come from the most recent wave of the Latinobarometer data that was released in 2009. It includes data for 18 Latin American countries, which unlike other barometer studies, includes a pretty comprehensive sample of the region. Eighteen of the twenty-three countries that comprise the Latin American and Caribbean region are sampled. Of the Latin American states that are found on the Index of State Weakness and the Failed State Index, only Cuba and Haiti are absent from the Latinobarometer dataset.[4]

With the exception of Brazil and Nicaragua, where the age of adulthood is 16, the remaining countries in the dataset include data from adult respondents, 18 years and older. Various stages of probability sampling were utilized with a series of quotas employed in the final stage based upon demographic strata. This method of modified probability sampling yielded no less than 1,000 and no greater than 1,204 face-to-face interviews for each case, for a collective sample of approximately 20,204 observations from eighteen states.

It is important to note that of the Global Barometer data utilized for this entire work, the Latinobarometer in its latest venture has the most representative sample of all other barometer projects. Using census data as a guide, the Latinobarometer dataset includes distributions that are reflective of the population of that country; thus, important factors, such as respondents' gender, socioeconomic status, level of education, whether they live in an urban versus rural area, and their affiliation with a certain ethnic or indigenous population, are all taken into account in the collection of the data.

Description of the Variables

Two dependent variables are operationalized in this analysis to capture the features of support for political violence among the citizenry of Latin America.

Dependent Variable 1—Social Movements

The first measure of political violence is based upon the respondents' beliefs that social movements are necessary for society to evolve. This variable is captured by the following question in the Latinobarometer survey:

> Question (Variable=Movement): Social movements are necessary mechanisms for the development of society?
>
> Value Labels: 0=Don't know or Did not answer, 1=Strongly Agree, 2=Agree, 3=Disagree, 4=Strongly Disagree

To estimate the model I set the values "1" and "2" to one, values "3" and "4" to zero, and I code the value "0" as Missing Data. This leaves me with 18,240

---

4 Guyana and Suriname are included in Tables 5.1 and 5.2 because they are geographically a part of the Latin American region and are situated on both the Index of State Weakness and the Failed State Index, which is relevant to the analysis. However, they are excluded from the working list of Latin American states discussed in this chapter because of their widely accepted status as territories of Great Britain and the Netherlands, respectively.

observations. The transformation of the variable in this manner provides the analysis with a variable that clearly distinguishes between individuals who believe a social movement is a legitimate tool to employ in order for society to evolve and those who do not. The reasoning behind including this variable as a proxy for political violence is grounded in the work of Skocpol, Tilly, Huntington and Gurr, who characterize social revolutions as transformative processes born out of state crisis (Huntington, 1968; Gurr, 1970; Skocpol, 1979; Tilly, 1978, 2004). Along that same line of thinking, I argue that social movements are the antecedents to social revolutions. Thus, I believe respondents recognize social movements for what they are—the precursors to social revolutions, which give rise to permanently altered civic institutions. With that in mind, including this variable (social movements) as a proxy measure for political violence in the model is simply another way for me to tackle the relationship of interest, and that is state failure fosters political violence.

Dependent Variable 2—Support for Coup d'État

The second measure of political violence is a proxy variable based upon the following question in the Latinobarometer survey:

> Question (Variable=Coup): Agreement with the military removing the president if the regime violates the constitution?
>
> Value Labels: 0=Don't know or Did not answer, 1=Strongly Agree, 2=Agree, 3=Disagree, 4=Strongly Disagree

In order to estimate the model I set the values "1" and "2" to one, values "3" and "4" to zero, and I code the value "0" as Missing Data. This leaves me with 18,082 observations. The incorporation of this variable in the model is based upon the assertion that to support the deposal of the president and his/her regime is an extreme position one can take, even more extreme given that the institution to replace a democratically elected leader would be a military government. Therefore, I argue for respondents to support a military coup should imply support for the use of political violence against the state, even as I acknowledge this measure falls short of revealing support for the individuals themselves to engage in political violence. However, in the absence of such measures and data, this proxy variable serves as a strong indicator of support for the use of political violence against the state.

As in the preceding chapters, when estimating a model using multiple dependent variables, it is important to establish a contiguous relationship between the variables that serves to unify them as appropriate measures of the construct of interest, which in this case is political violence (See Figure 5.1). At the same time, while the measures share a statistically significant relationship, Table 5.3 reveals the two dependent variables are not highly correlated. The correlation results in Table 5.3 support my belief that estimating two individual models provides additional explanatory value to the analysis.

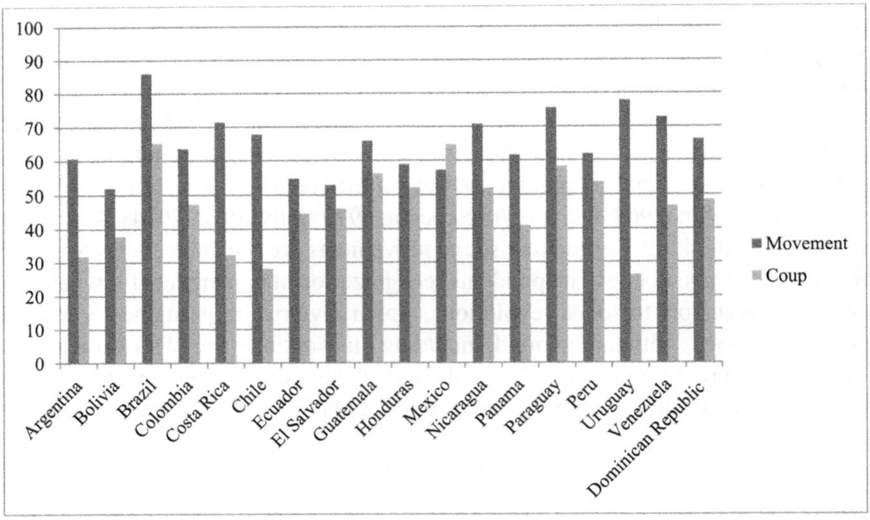

Figure 5.1 Percentage of respondents who support social movements and coup d'états (2009)

Table 5.3 Pearson Correlation for measures of political violence

Variables	Movement
1. Coup	.0129**
2. Movement	—

Note: *** p < .05 for two-tailed test; ** p < .10 for two-tailed test.

Explanatory Variables[5]

The public good of security

I utilize five variables within the Latinobarometer survey to measure perceptions of security among Latin Americans. The measures for the public good of security are derived from the following questions in the Latinobarometer survey:

> Question1 (Variable=Crime): To what extent does the guarantee that you will be protected from crime apply to you in (country)?

5 There were no adequate measures of the absence of the state in the Latinobarometer survey so this variable is excluded from the statistical analysis. However, I do address this feature of state failure in the Descriptive Statistics section following the statistical results, and once again in the Discussion section of this chapter.

Value Labels: 0=Don't know or Did not answer, 1=Completely Guaranteed, 2=Fairly Guaranteed, 3=A Little Guaranteed, 4=Not Guaranteed at All

To estimate the model, I recode the value of "0" as Missing Data. By removing this value, I am left with a scale that indicates an increase in perceived insecurity. Given the transformation of this variable, a positive coefficient suggests that perceived insecurity increases the likelihood that a respondent will more readily support the use of political violence.

Question 2 (Variable=Victim): Have you (1) or a relative (2) been assaulted, attacked, or the victim of a crime in the last twelve months?

Value Labels: 0=Did not answer, 1=Yes, You, 2=Yes, Relative, 3=No, 8=Don't know

Regarding this second explanatory measure of security, I recode values "0" and "8" as Missing Data. I then recode values "1" and "2" as "1" and value "3" as "0." After recoding these values, I am left with an indicator of perceived insecurity if the respondent or a relative of that respondent has been the victim of a violent crime in the past year. Given the transformation of this variable, a positive coefficient suggests that respondents are more willing to support political violence if they themselves, or someone close to them, have been victims of an attack.

Question 3 (Variable=CSafe): In general, how safe is living in your country?

Value Labels: 0=Did not Answer, 1=Very Safe, 2=Safe, 3=Very Unsafe, 8=Don't know

Question 4 (Variable=NSafe): In general, how safe is living in your neighborhood?

Value Labels: 0=Did Not Answer, 1=Very Safe, 2= Safe, 3=Very Unsafe, 8=Don't Know

Regarding the third and fourth explanatory variables of security, the coding structure was the same. Therefore, I recode values "0" and "8" as Missing Data. Given the transformation of these two variables, I am left with a scale that indicates an increase in perceived insecurity, whereby a positive coefficient suggests that perceived insecurity increases the likelihood that a respondent will support the use of political violence.

Question 5 (Variable=Concern): How often are you concerned that you may become victim of a violent crime?

Value Labels: 0=Did Not Answer, 1=All or Most of the Time, 2=Sometimes, 3=Occasionally, 4=Never, 8=Don't Know

In order to estimate the model I recode values "0" and "8" as Missing Data for the fifth explanatory variable. I am left with a scale that indicates an increase in perceived security. For the ease of interpretation, I recode the values so that the new scale indicates an increase in perceived insecurity. Thus, "0"=Never, "1"=Occasionally, "2"=Sometimes, and "4"=All or Most of the Time. Given the transformation of this explanatory variable, a positive coefficient indicates that perceived insecurity increases the likelihood that a respondent is more willing to support the use of political violence.

The state authority

I utilize eight variables within the Latinobarometer survey to measure perceptions of the effectiveness and legitimacy of the state authority among Latin Americans. The measures for trust in the state authority are derived from the following questions in the Latinobarometer survey:

Trust

Question 1 (Variable=Govt): How much trust would you say you have in the government?

Value Labels: 0=Did Not Answer, 1=A Lot, 2=Some, 3=Little, 4=None At All, 8=Don't Know

Question 2 (Variable=Congress): How much trust would you say you have in the national congress/parliament?

Value Labels: 0=Did Not Answer, 1=A Lot, 2=Some, 3=Little, 4=None At All, 8=Don't Know

Question 3 (Variable=Courts): How much trust would you say you have in the judiciary?

Value Labels: 0=Did Not Answer, 1=A Lot, 2=Some, 3=Little, 4=None At All, 8=Don't Know

Question 4 (Variable=Army): How much trust would you say you have in the armed forces?

Value Labels: 0=Did Not Answer, 1=A Lot, 2=Some, 3=Little, 4=None At All, 8=Don't Know

Question 5 (Variable=Admin): How much trust would you say you have in public administration?

Value Labels: 0=Did Not Answer, 1=A Lot, 2=Some, 3=Little, 4=None At All, 8=Don't Know

Question 6 (Variable=Local): How much trust would you say you have in the local government?

Value Labels: 0=Did Not Answer, 1=A Lot, 2=Some, 3=Little, 4=None At All, 8=Don't Know

The first measure of state authority is trust in the state authority, which is based upon six survey questions with the same coding structure. Therefore, in order to estimate the model I recode values "0" and "8" as Missing Data for these six measures. I am left with a scale that indicates an increase in distrust in the government and the institutions of governance. For the ease of interpretation, I recode the values so that the new scale indicates an increase in trust for the state authorities. Thus, "0"=None At All, "1"=Little, "2"=Some, and "4"=A Lot. Given the transformation of this explanatory variable, a negative coefficient indicates that declining trust in the state authority increases the likelihood that a respondent will more readily support the use of political violence.

Legitimacy

Question 7 (Variable=Rigged): Generally speaking, do you believe elections are clean in (country) or are they a fraud?

Value Labels: 0=Did Not Answer, 1=Clean, 2=Fraud, 8=Don't Know

The second measure of state authority is the legitimacy of the state and its institutions of governance, which is based upon two survey questions, the first of which measures the legitimacy of the election process in that country. In order to estimate the model I recode values "0" and "8" as Missing Data. I am left with an indicator of the legitimacy of elections in that country. For the ease of interpretation, I set value "1" to "0" and value "2" to "1"; therefore, a positive coefficient suggests that respondents are more willing to support political violence if they consider the state to be illegitimate due to fraudulent elections.

Question 8 (Variable=Corrupt): How much progress do you think there has been progress in reducing corruption in state institutions over the past two years?

Value Labels: 0=Did Not Answer, 1=Much, 2=Some, 3=Little, 4=No Progress At All, 8=Don't Know

The second survey question that addresses state legitimacy measures the progress the state has made in reducing corruption among state institutions. To estimate the model, I recode values "0" and "8" as Missing Data. Given the transformation of the variable, I am left with a scale that indicates a perceived decrease in progress made toward reducing corruption. Therefore, a positive coefficient suggests that where respondents perceive no progress has been made regarding corruption the likelihood that they will support the use of political violence increases.

The provision of public goods

I utilize six variables within the Latinobarometer survey to measure perceptions of the state's ability to provide public goods to Latin American citizens. The measures for the provision of public goods are derived from the following questions in the Latinobarometer survey:

> Question 1 (Variable=Water): Do you or any member in your family have drinking water?
>
> Value Labels: 0=Did Not Answer, 1=Yes, 2=No, 8=Don't Know
>
> Question 2 (Variable=Sewage): Do you or any member in your family have a sewage system?
>
> Value Labels: 0=Did Not Answer, 1=Yes, 2=No, 8=Don't Know
>
> Question 3 (Variable=Electric): Do you or any member in your family have electricity?
>
> Value Labels: 0=Did Not Answer, 1=Yes, 2=No, 8=Don't Know

Regarding the provision of essential public goods, the coding structure for the first three measures are the same and represent indicators of the availability of drinking water, a sewage system, and electricity. In order to estimate the model I recode values "0" and "8" as Missing Data. I am left with an indicator of the availability of these public goods in a respondent's country. For the ease of interpretation, I set value "2" to "0"; therefore, a negative coefficient suggests that respondents are more willing to support political violence given the state's inability to provide them with the public goods of drinking water, sewage, and electricity.

> Question 4 (Variable=Hospital): How satisfied are you with the way public hospitals work?
>
> Value Labels: 0=Don't Know or Did Not Answer, 1=Very Satisfied, 2=Rather Satisfied, 3=Not Very Satisfied, 4=No Satisfied At All

Question 5 (Variable=Schools): How satisfied are you with the way the public education system works?

Value Labels: 0=Don't Know or Did Not Answer, 1=Very Satisfied, 2=Rather Satisfied, 3=Not Very Satisfied, 4=No Satisfied At All

The next two variables that serve as measures for the provision of public goods are based upon the survey questions that indicate a respondent's satisfaction with the public hospital and education systems. Because the coding structure for these two measures are the same, I recode value "0" as Missing Data for both variables. I am left with a scale that represents increasing dissatisfaction with public hospitals and education. Therefore, a positive coefficient suggests that increasing dissatisfaction with these two public goods increases the likelihood that a respondent will support the use of political violence.

Question 6 (Variable=Roads): How satisfied are you with the roads and paving services where you live?

Value Labels: 0=Did Not Answer, 1=Very Satisfied, 2=Rather Satisfied, 3=Not Very Satisfied, 4=No Satisfied At All, 9=Do Not Have These Services Where You Live

The final variable that serves as a measure for the provision of public goods is based upon a survey question that indicates satisfaction with the roadway system in that country. To estimate the model I recode value "0" as Missing Data. I then set value "9" to "0," which indicates this particular service is not present where this respondent lives. With the transformation of this variable, I am left with a scale that represents increasing dissatisfaction with the roadway system in that country. Thus, a positive coefficient suggests that increasing dissatisfaction with this public good increases the likelihood that a respondent will support the use of political violence.

The protection of private property

I utilize a single variable within the Latinobarometer survey to measure perceptions of the state's ability to provide for the protection of private property. The measure for the protection of private property is derived from the following question in the Latinobarometer survey:

Question 1 (Variable=Property): To what extent does the guarantee that your private property will be protected apply to you in (country)?

Value Labels: 0=Don't know or Did Not answer, 1=Completely Guaranteed, 2=Fairly Guaranteed, 3=A Little Guaranteed, 4=Not Guaranteed at All

Table 5.4 List of variable names and description of the concepts measured

Variable Name	Indicator Concept
Movement	Measures Political Violence—Support for Social Movements
Coup	Measures Political Violence—Support for Military Coup
Crime	Protection from Crime
Victim	Victim of Violent Crime
CSafe	Country is Safe or Unsafe
NSafe	Neighborhood is Safe or Unsafe
Concern	Concerned about becoming a victim of violence
Govt	Trust in Government
Congress	Trust in National Congress/Parliament
Courts	Trust in the Judiciary System
Army	Trust in the Military
Admin	Trust in Public Administration
Local	Trust in the Local Government
Rigged	Elections are fraudulent in that country
Corrupt	Progress has been made with regards to reducing corruption in state institutions
Water	Availability of drinking water
Sewage	Availability of sewage system
Electric	Availability of electricity
Hospital	Satisfaction with public hospitals
Schools	Satisfaction with public education
Roads	Satisfaction with roadway system
Property	Protection of private property
Education	Respondent's highest level of education
Econ	Individual and family's economic situation
Salary	Salary is sufficient to cover needs
Gender	Gender
Ethnic	The respondent's ethnic or racial group affiliation
Town	Size of town respondent lives in
Age	Age of respondent
Job	Employment status
Income	Equality in income distribution
Discrim	Respondent is a part of a group that is discriminated against
Trafficking	Drug trafficking is the most important problem in that country
Druguse1	Drug use is the most important problem in that country
Gangs	Gang violence is the most important problem in that country
Viol	Violence is the most important problem in that country

Regarding the explanatory variable of protection of private property, I recode value "0" as Missing Data. Given the transformation of this variable, I am left with a scale that indicates an increasing lack of protection of one's private property, whereby a positive coefficient suggests that if respondents believe there are no guarantees from the state that their private property will be protected, the greater the likelihood that respondents will support the use of political violence.

Control Variables

Demographic control variables

I incorporate a series of control variables in the model that capture demographic features of the respondents. As is the case in the preceding chapters, I argue that it is important to control for the salient differences between the respondents that could have an impact on the results of the analysis. Therefore, I include the variables level of education, socioeconomic status, and income level, ethnicity, gender, age, employment status, and whether a respondent lives in an urban or rural area. See Appendix K for a description of the control variables and their measurement.

Specific control variables unique to Latin America

As I touched upon in the opening of this chapter, Latin America suffers from three critical factors that distinguishes the region from other regions regarding the relationship between state failure and support for political violence and they are: 1) income inequalities between the various ethnic groups, particularly the economic marginalization of the indigenous population, 2) the distinct influence the drug industry has on the populace of Latin America, and 3) the subsequent non-state actor violence that is a direct result of the drug industry. Therefore, within the model I also include variables that capture the inequities in economic and resource distribution according to ethnicity, and the impact the drug trade and drug violence have on Latin Americans. A description of these variables and their measurement can also be found in Appendix K.

Model

I conduct cross-sectional analysis using logistical regression in order to determine which dimensions of state failure increase the likelihood that an individual will support the use of political violence. To test my assumptions I estimate two logit models. The first model tests respondents' support for the use of political violence and includes the variables that I identify as the traditional features of state failure, along with the demographic control variables (See Figure 5.2). The second model captures respondents' support for the use of political violence and includes the variables that I identify as features of state failure, along with the demographic control variables and the specific control variables unique to Latin America (See Figure 5.3).

Logit Models

$$Model1 = h\left(\frac{p_i(violence)}{1 - p_i(violence)}\right) = \beta_0 + \beta_1 Security + \beta_2 StateAuthority + \beta_3 StateLegitimacy +$$
$$\beta_4 SPublic\quad Goods + \beta_5 Property + \beta_6 Education + \beta_7 Gender + \beta_8 PersEcon + \beta_9 Urban +$$
$$\beta_0\ Age + \beta_1\ Employment + e$$

Figure 5.2 State failure model of support for political violence with demographic control variables

$$Model2 = h\left(\frac{p_i(violence)}{1 - p_i(violence)}\right) = \beta_0 + \beta_1 Security + \beta_2 StateAuthority + \beta_3 StateLegitimacy +$$
$$\beta_4 SPublic\quad Goods + \beta_5 Property + \beta_6 Education + \beta_7 Gender + \beta_8 PersEcon + \beta_9 Urban +$$
$$\beta_0\ Age + \beta_1\ Employment + \beta_2\ Drugs + \beta_3\ Gangs + \beta_4\ Viol + \beta_5\ IncomeInequality +$$
$$\beta_6\ + EthnicInequality + e$$

Figure 5.3 State failure model of support for political violence including all control variables

Findings

Statistical Results

See Table 5.5.

Findings that are Statistically Significant and Support the Hypothesis for the Traditional State Failure Model

In Table 5.5, I estimate the logistical regression model for state failure. The general hypothesis upon which this model is based asserts that a climate of state failure fosters support for political violence among the populace. Given the findings, I would argue that within Latin America there is consistent support for this hypothesis. Among the five features of state failure outlined in this entire work (security, state authority, absence of the state, protection of private property, and provision of public goods) four of these features are both statistically and substantively significant. Although I must point out that because of a lack of appropriate measures, the absence of the state is omitted from the analysis, an issue I will tackle in the section following the statistical results. Nonetheless, of the four features analyzed in the model, measures of the public good of security, protection of private property, provision of public goods, and trust/legitimacy of the state authority report statistically significant values and support the stated hypothesis.

Table 5.5 Binary logit estimates of support for political violence—traditional state failure model with demographic control variables only

Variable	Movement	Coup
Crime	.029 (.021)	.0288 (.021)
Victim	-.037 (.040)	.107** (.039)
NSafe	-.021 (.031)	.012 (.030)
CSafe	.027 (.034)	.073** (.033)
Concern	.049** (.022)	.084*** (.022)
Govt	.101*** (.025)	-.177*** (.024)
Congress	.075** (.031)	-.125*** (.030)
Courts	.039 (.031)	.074** (.031)
Army	-.009 (.061)	.315*** (.024)
Admin	.057* (.033)	.012 (.032)
Local	.043 (.029)	.009 (.028)
Rigged	-.080** (.042)	.533*** (.041)
Corrupt	-.068** (.024)	.058** (.023)
Water	-.0009 (.061)	.005 (.059)
Sewage	.133** (.060)	-.020 (.046)
Electric	-.140 (.133)	.003 (.127)
Hospital	.107*** (.028)	.037 (.027)
Schools	.116*** (.035)	.018 (.028)
Roads	.081*** (.026)	-.046** (.021)
Property	-.081*** (.021)	065** (.026)
Education	.006 (.005)	-.027*** (.005)

Table 5.5 *Concluded*

Variable	Movement	Coup
Econ	.013 (.026)	.0004 (.026)
Salary	-.033 (.026)	.019 (.025)
Town	-.017* (.010)	-.066*** (.009)
Gender	-.039 (.042)	.030 (.041)
Age	-.003** (.001)	-.009*** (.001)
Job	.074 (.046)	-.039 (.046)
Constant	.685*** (.226)	-.247 (.219)
Observations	12420	12265
Pseudo R^2	.0159	.0474
LR χ^2	251.85	805.10
Prob> χ^2	.0000	.0000

Note: *** $p < .01$ for two-tailed test; ** $p < .05$ for two-tailed test; * $p < 0.1$ for two-tailed test; standard errors in parentheses.

Undoubtedly, one of the most important features of state failure is the public good of security. Among the six variables that capture this aspect, four of them are significant. The findings also suggest that individuals who have 1) been the victim of a crime or someone close to them has been a victim (*Victim*), 2) consider their country to be an unsafe place to live (*CSafe*), and 3) are concerned about being a victim of violence (*Concern*) report a higher probability of supporting or engaging in or supporting political violence. Of the four features of state failure present in the model, the absence of the public good of security is the most consistent across the two equations. This finding would suggest that the lack of personal security has a strong influence on the decision-making process of individual support for political violence.

The second feature of state failure important to this analysis is trust and legitimacy of the state authority. Of the six measures of trust in the state authority, two are significant in the model; as for the two measures of state legitimacy, both of them are statistically and substantively significant. The findings reveal that with regards to trust in the state authority, distrust in the national legislature (*Congress*) and the government in general (*Govt*) incites the strongest feelings regarding support for political violence. Similarly, individuals who believe elections are fraudulent (*Rigged*) and that the state has not made any effort to address corruption within the government (*Corrupt*) are more likely to support the use of political violence. What is most interesting—a matter I will discuss in greater detail at the end of this section—is that of the two equations estimated (*Coup, Movement*) the measures of trust in state authority are only significant in the equation where support for the military overthrowing the government (*Coup*) is the dependent variable. This would suggest that a glaring distrust in the government is an inciting factor for most people in Latin America, one that is enough to propel them to support extreme actions such as the removal of the existing government and leadership. With regards to state legitimacy, the findings suggest that a fraudulent election (*Rigged*) has the strongest impact on Latin Americans, and would compel many of the respondents to also support a military coup.

Regarding deficiencies in the provision of public goods as a feature of state failure, the model reveals that dissatisfaction with medical services (*Hospital),* the public education system (*Schools*), and the roadway system (*Roads*) are the strongest indicators of support for political violence among the six measures of public goods. This finding is consistent with the hypothesis, which is based upon the assertion that frustrations over a lack of basic public goods and services are important inciting factors.

The last feature of state failure found in this model is protection of private property. The general premise of this hypothesis is that personal property represents a tangible extension of a person. Thus, a violation of property is often considered a violation of one's person. Without the security of property, many people feel they are not secure themselves. The findings are consistent with the hypothesis and reveal that when the state fails to protect ones private property, individuals indicate support for political violence.

Finally, I turn to a discussion of the control variables included in the model. The control variables age, education, and living in a rural area appear to play a role in the relationship between state failure and political violence. The findings indicate that the less educated, the youth, and those from smaller more rural towns are more likely to support the use of political violence.

A final point I should make, which is particularly relevant to this analysis, is that of the two equations estimated, the strongest is inarguably the one where the dependent variable asks respondents if they would support a military coup if it was justified (*Coup*). Given the nature of the variable, and the destabilizing effect most coups have on a state, such an extreme position should be noted. Therefore, I think the results reveal the very point of this entire analysis—that living within a state where the conditions of state failure have become severe compels individuals to support radical measures that will bring about alternative governing structures to the existing ones within the fragile states in which they live. Based upon the statistical results, these radical measures would appear to manifest themselves in the form of political violence.

Table 5.6 Binary logit estimates of support for political violence—traditional state failure model with all control variables

Variable	Movement	Coup
Crime	.021 (.023)	.034 (.022)
Victim	-.056 (.042)	.110** (.041)
CSafe	.011 (.037)	.092** (.035)
NSafe	-.021 (.033)	-.012 (.032)
Concern	.052** (.023)	.095*** (.023)
Govt	.092*** (.026)	-.168*** (.026)
Congress	.067** (.033)	-.132*** (.032)
Courts	.051 (.033)	.091** (.032)
Army	-.013 (.025)	.315*** (.025)
Admin	.067** (.034)	.014 (.034)
Local	.031 (.030)	.016 (.029)
Rigged	-.102** (.045)	.516*** (.043)
Corrupt	-.073** (.025)	.048** (.024)
Water	-.054 (.065)	-.035 (.062)
Sewage	107* (.063)	-.002 (.049)
Electric	-.206 (.144)	.011 (.136)
Hospital	.107*** (.029)	.042 (.029)
Schools	.114*** (.037)	.021 (.029)
Roads	.078** (.028)	-.043** (.022)
Property	-.094*** (.022)	.061** (.028)
Education	.006 (.005)	-.024*** (.005)

Variable	Movement	Coup
Econ	-.013 (.028)	. 069** (.044)
Salary	-.066** (.034)	.030 (.027)
Town	-.023** (.011)	-.070*** (.010)
Gender	-.047 (.044)	.036 (.043)
Age	-.003** (.001)	-.008*** (.001)
Job	.069 (.049)	-.034 (.048)
Income	.094*** (.030)	.065** (.030)
Discrim	.096** (.054)	.0002 (.052)
Trafficking	.119** (.055)	-.093* (.052)
Viol	-.021 (.215)	-.143 (.212)
Gangs	.150 (.118)	.010 (.111)
Druguse1	.108 (.201)	.062 (.195)
Constant	.743** (.248)	-.498** (.239)
Observations	11176	11049
Pseudo R^2	.0174	.0481
LR χ^2	247.83	736.03
Prob> χ^2	.0000	.0000

Note: *** p < .01 for two-tailed test; ** p < .05 for two-tailed test; * p <0.1 for two-tailed test; standard errors in parentheses.

Findings that are Statistically Significant and Support the Hypothesis for the Traditional State Failure Model with All Control Variables

I turn now to a discussion of the model of state failure, which includes additional control variables that are unique to the region of Latin America. Marginalization of the indigenous population and discrimination along the racial/ethnic caste system in Latin America has long been a problem in the region, which is something I wanted to capture in the model. It was important to evaluate this dynamic within the context of state failure because of my belief that it would have an impact on the relationship between state failure and support for political violence against the state. The same is true for the impact the drug trade has had on the region, along with the emergence of violent gangs, paramilitaries and guerillas, and the contributing role these factors have undoubtedly played in creating an environment of instability across Latin America's fragile states. Although, I argue that it is the fragility of the Latin American state that has given rise to the drug trade and these non-state actors, which is a topic I will tackle at the conclusion of this chapter. Consequently, for the purposes of estimating the model in Table 5.6, I assert that weak states have given rise to the drug trade and violent groups, and it is this system of fragile states on the verge of failure which has allowed for the continued existence of the drug trade. Furthermore, that the drug trade has flourished in recent decades and the violence of these non-state actors involved in the drug trade has intensified has certainly had an impact on Latin Americans and their opinions regarding the failure of the state to manage and eliminate the drug trade and the groups that fuel it.

Looking at the state failure model in Table 5.6, the first point of interest is that the model remains stable despite the inclusion of additional variables. Of all the models estimated throughout this text, the state failure model of Latin America is the most consistent. With the exception of the control variable, *Econ*, for each equation, the statistical and substantive significance of the variables remains unchanged between the two models.

As for the individual variables, because the traditional model of state failure remains unchanged, I will reserve my discussion for the additional variables included in this model. There are two variables included in the model that capture the inequities in income distribution (*Income*) and discrimination (*Discrim*) in Latin America and the findings for these variables reveal that these two factors have an influence on support for political violence. Individuals who believe income inequality is a problem in their country report an increased probability of support for political violence. The same is true for those who believe they are members of a group that is discriminated against.[6]

As for the variables that measure the impact the drug trade, gangs, violent paramilitaries, and guerillas have had on Latin American support for political violence, their performance in the statistical model, in a word, is *disappointing*. The only measure that supports the hypothesis and is statistically significant is the one that indicates drug trafficking is a major concern to respondents (*Trafficking*) and it is only an important factor in the equation where the dependent variable is *Movement*, or participation in a social movement to bring about political change. My initial reaction to these findings is that neither drugs nor the violence of non-state actors are compelling enough factors to drive someone to support

6 At one point, I included an interaction term between the two variables in the model, but its inclusion did not change the results nor did it provide any substantive information to the analysis, so I removed it from the final model.

political violence against the state, which is something I will address in the discussion section towards the end of this chapter.

A Deeper Look at State Failure in Latin America— The Perils of Ungoverned Territory and the Absence of the State

What should be conspicuously absent from the model of state failure is a measure for the *absence of the state.* Unfortunately, the Latinobarometer data does not include an appropriate measure for this concept; therefore, I was forced to omit it from my statistical analysis. Considering the importance this factor has on the relationship between state failure and political violence, I will be the first to admit that the model estimated suffers because of this omission. At the same time I did not want to move forward without delving deeper into the issue of ungoverned territory in the region, because this factor is critical to the existence of the drug trade and violent non-state actors in Latin America. Further, I am convinced addressing ungoverned territory in the region is the first step on a long road toward putting mechanisms in place to strengthen the state.

Case in point—creating an almost U-shape that begins with the border of Mexico and Guatemala, then runs through both Central and South America along the Pacific coast, and turning north at the border of Paraguay and Brazil to follow the north Atlantic coast line of South America before finally ending in Venezuela, there is a collective geographical space in Latin America that is littered with more patches of ungoverned territory than there is governed territory (See Figure 5.4).

Despite many futile and aborted attempts, stateless zones in Latin America are reflective of the inability of post-colonial governments to exercise sovereignty and authority over their territory all the way to their borders. This is why the most troubled regions of Latin America are typically situated along the borderlines[7] between two countries, both of which (countries) are generally suffering from endemic problems already. For example, the Tri-Border Area (TBA) between Brazil, Argentina, and Paraguay along with the border regions formed where Brazil meets Bolivia and Peru, Colombia meets Peru, Colombia meets Venezuela, and Venezuela meets Guyana all suffer from chronic ungovernability and an apparent lack of a state presence, given the disparities between the socio-economic and political indicators for the people living in these border regions when compared to the development indicators for the state as a whole. Given the host of challenges many Latin American states must confront, which range from corruption to economic development, among the hierarchy of importance, the border has become the least of the Latin American state's concern, and this is evident by the lack of governance in these regions.

7 Beyond border areas, there are a number of states where a great deal of its interior territory is ungoverned. For example, Guyana lacks both the financial resources and political capital to control over 80 percent of its territory. And the same can be said for neighboring Suriname as well as the majority of Haiti.

Figure 5.4 Ungoverned territory in Latin America

Recognized as one of the most visible ungoverned territories in Latin America, the towns and cities along the U.S.-Mexico border represent one of the most important gateways for the black market economy upon which Latin America thrives. Rival drug cartels have turned this border region into one of the most violent in Latin America in an effort to gain control over the extremely lucrative drug route into the United States.

Figure 5.5 Guatemala/Chipas–Mexico border
Note: Figure created using Smartdraw.

Although the border region between the U.S. and Mexico is one of the most visible and most discussed, the southern Pacific coastline of Mexico in the mountainous area between the states of Sinaloa and Durango along the Southern Sierra Madre mountain range is another pocket within Mexico suffering from drug cartel violence, and has long been considered a stateless zone.

Finally, the most salient region in Mexico where the state is all but absent is along the border of Chipas and Guatemala (See Figure 5.5). "The border separating Guatemala and Mexico is a more than six hundred mile long frontier that is plagued by poverty, violence, corruption, and an overall lack of a state presence" (Rabasa et al., 2007, p. 277). Both Guatemala and Mexico face significant security challenges in that region where organized criminal gangs outnumber the police personnel. The lack of a state presence is evident by the lack of governing institutions, physical infrastructure, and security. Poverty and illiteracy rates in Chipas are at its highest among Mexican states—less than 12 percent of the population are literate (Rabasa et al., 2007). While corruption remains an endemic problem in this state (Chiapas) and the provision of public goods, such as water, sewage, and a roadway system is among the worst in Mexico.

If Mexico appears to be in a precarious position, Guatemala fares no better. Actually, it is considered one of the worst in Latin America across almost every economic, political, and social indicator—and with regards to ungoverned territory it once again can be found at the bottom of the list. "A recent World Bank study notes that Guatemala performs at or near the bottom of several governance indicators, including political stability, government effectiveness, regulatory quality, rule of law, control of corruption, and accountability. Worse, government effectiveness and the rule of law have been on a steady decline since 2002" (Rabasa et al., 2007, p. 281). Guatemala has one of the highest poverty rates in Latin America with over half (56 percent) living in poverty. Further, only 18 percent of the population is literate, and it ranks 122nd out of 145 countries with regards to the prevalence of institutional corruption (World Bank, 2009; Global Corruption Perceptions Index, 2009). Almost every indicator of economic and political development echoes a trend with regards to Guatemala—the trend being that Guatemala is a failing state with pervasive lawlessness (Kahl, 2006). One of the greatest concerns for Guatemala is what scholars have referred to as the *Colombianization* of Guatemala, where this Central American nation could soon mirror the Colombia of a decade ago that was controlled not by the state authority but by criminals and narco-traffickers.

Within Central America, Guatemala is undoubtedly considered one of the worst-off states with regards to lack of governance within stateless regions, but Guatemala does not stand alone. Neighboring El Salvador, Honduras, and Nicaragua are also plagued by stretches of ungoverned territory, and with it, a host of subsequent problems. Nicaragua suffers from rampant trafficking operations, which in most areas of the state the leaders of the drug cartels function as de facto state authorities. The security of roads in Honduras is one of the worst, thus making road travel especially dangerous due to the lawless presence of organized criminals. As a result, state authorities often require a military escort in order to travel throughout their own country. In turn, El Salvador faces armed challenges along the border it shares with Honduras by two local trafficking groups—Los Perrones and the Cartel de Texis—which have corrupted the local government and police force, thus thwarting the national government's attempts to establish any measure of authority over this region.

Although I have examined these two regions at length throughout this chapter, unfortunately a discussion of ungoverned territory in Latin America would not be a thorough one without a discussion of Colombia and the Tri-Border Area (TBA) between Brazil, Argentina, and Paraguay. As I mentioned earlier in this chapter, a decade ago the Colombian government was forced to mount a strategic offensive against the FARC, which at that time represented the greatest security challenge to the state. Today, the dynamics of the violence in the country have seen only a marginal decrease; instead, the situation has deteriorated into one that involves not only the FARC, but also drug cartels and paramilitary operations, all of which struggle for control of the ungoverned territory along the Colombian–Venezuelan border that extends north into the Caribbean Sea and is largely used to traffic goods between Haiti and the Dominican Republic into Mexico and the United States (See Figure 5.6).

Another critical area that lacks the presence of the state is at the entry point into Central America through Panama known as Darien's Gap (See Figure 5.6). Darien's Gap is one of the oldest and most troubled ungoverned regions in

Latin America. Situated along the border between Panama and Colombia, it has long been a hub of criminal activity as it functions as a critical gateway between Central and South America and is used as a major trafficking portal for drugs, humans, and weapons between the two regions.

Second to the Colombian drug routes, the TBA of South America is one of the most active ungoverned regions in Latin America (See Figure 5.7). At risk of belaboring the point, the TBA is a hub of criminal activity, ranging from money laundering to all forms of trafficking. It has also come under scrutiny for harboring known terrorist organizations such as Hezbollah; however, the extent of Hezbollah's presence in the TBA has never been officially confirmed. Whether Hezbollah or any other terrorist organization is present in the region or not is less important than what the TBA represents and that is a stateless area where neither Brazil, Argentina, nor Paraguay have made any progress in removing the criminal organizations that utilize this space as a major port of criminal activity.

From the onset of this chapter, one would think that Latin America is simply a region of weak states, with few, if any on the brink of failure. Given the economic indicators for Latin America and the general stability of the region, when assessed collectively, one would not challenge such an assumption. However, a closer look at the internal dynamics of the region reveals some startling similarities with other regions, particularly sub-Saharan Africa, an undisputed region of failed states.

The majority of Latin American states must contend with ungoverned territory and the issues that arise because of its existence. The most notable concern is that the mere presence of a host of violent political groups, which exert authority within these spaces (of ungoverned territory), represents a direct challenge to the state's sovereignty. Collectively, the governments of Latin American states seem incapable of exerting even a minute measure of authority and security over not only vast stretches of rural territory, but also several densely populated urban areas that are considered ungoverned or under the control of violent political actors. As a consequence of this phenomenon, Latin American states are simply unable to provide the people of these regions (which represent a significant proportion of the Latin American population) with critical public goods and services.

The absence of the state, the lack of a state authority, deficiencies in the provision of public goods, and the absence of security—are all features of state failure, and all are present in Latin America, which is undoubtedly problematic for a region of fragile states that is continually contested by violent political actors. At first glance, while Latin America seems to be comprised of weak states, they are *resilient* weak states that have managed to avoid complete collapse. Yet, I argue, as I did with Haiti in *The Tragedy of Failure* (2010b) that fragile states, which lack a history of state "success" so to speak, require one major exogenous shock, and collapse is imminent. In the case of Haiti, that exogenous shock came in the form of the sadly tragic and devastating earthquake of 2010.

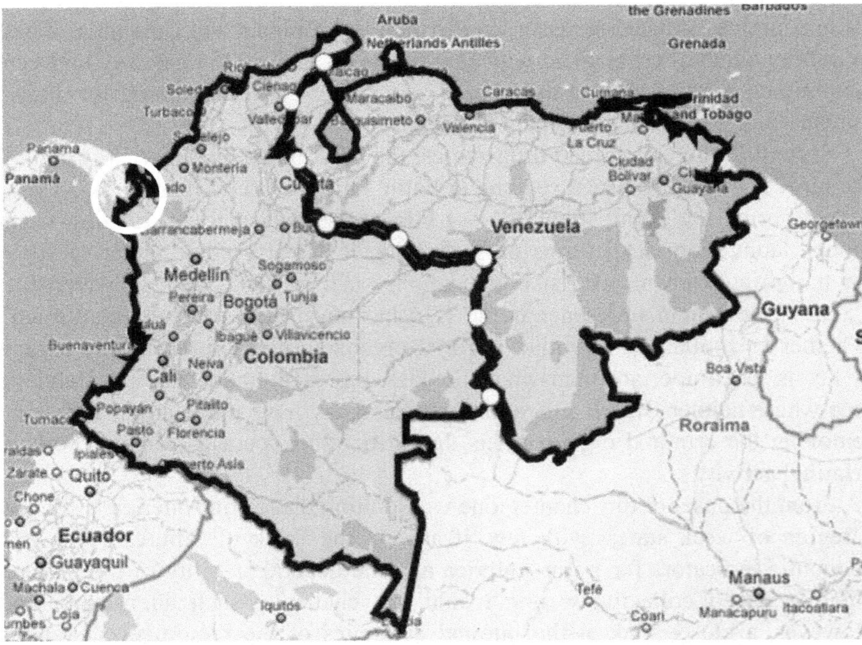

Figure 5.6 Darien's Gap and the Colombia–Venezuela border
Note: Figure created using Smartdraw.

The states of Latin America are not immune to such a fate, particularly the weakest of them (i.e. Guatemala, Colombia, Nicaragua, and Honduras), which is an obvious conclusion; yet what is less obvious is that states in crisis create a simultaneous vacuum/domino effect (Howard, 2008, 2010b). With the contagious nature of state failure, these border regions that have continually plagued Latin American governments could ultimately lead to the failure of the entire region, given the interconnectedness of these states along their borders.

Discussion

To open this discussion, I first would like to address the strengths of this chapter. The most important finding to emerge from this analysis is that the traditional model of state failure is supported by the data. Of the four features of state failure included in the model, all of them appear to have an impact on an individual's decision to support political violence. What that means for this collective work is that within Latin America, the climate of state failure has a contributing influence on the decision of an individual to support the use of political violence against the state. This finding is the core of this entire project, and thus it is encouraging that the statistical results appear to support this argument.

Figure 5.7 Tri-state border region of Paraguay, Brazil, and Argentina
Note: Figure created using Smartdraw.

Another noteworthy point is that the equation with the dependent variable, *Coup,* which would be considered the closest proxy of the concept of political violence, is the strongest equation of the two. I purposely estimated two equations, with two dependent variables (*Movement* and *Coup*) that move along a continuum from dissidence to an act of political violence. Undoubtedly, to support a coup would be considered an act of political violence, especially considering the democratic features of governance that are present in Latin America. Otherwise stated, the general assumption would be that Latin American states allow citizens to voice their dissatisfaction with the government through proper channels, given that they function as democracies. Thus, a coup, which is a radical, extreme action, should not be necessary in such a society, and yet the statistical results suggest that is not the case. It is important to note that military coups against democratic governments in Latin America are not unheard of. With the recent military coups in Honduras (2009) and Ecuador (2010, as well as 2000); and prior to that, Haiti (1991 and 2004), Guatemala (1993), Peru (1992), and Venezuela (1992 and 2002), all of these states witnessed coup d'états by either the military, popular uprising, or a combination of the two. Given the context of government transition from democracy to a military government and then back to some form of a democracy, it is quite possible the notion of a coup is not considered that extreme of a measure among Latin Americans when it comes to removing a democratically elected government. The findings certainly would suggest this.

Table 5.7 Hypotheses supported by the Logistical Regression analysis

Hypotheses Supported by Statistical Results	Variable and Concept Measured
Absence of the public good of security	Victim—Has been a victim of crime Csafe—Feels that their country is safe Concern—Concerned about becoming a victim of crime
State authority State legitimacy	Congress—Trust in Congress Govt—Trust in the govt in general Rigged—Elections are fraudulent Corrupt—The state ignores govt corruption
Provision of Public Goods	Hospitals—Dissatisfaction with medical services Schools—Dissatisfaction with public education Roads—Dissatisfaction with roadway system
Protection of private property	Property—Govt protects private property
Controls	Age—Respondent's age Education—Respondent's highest level of education Rural—Respondent lives in a rural area
Additional controls	Income—Inequities in income distribution Discrim—Presence of discrimination Trafficking—Drug trafficking is a major concern

Overall, the model estimated in this chapter illustrates that state failure is a powerful and important predictor of support for political violence and echoes the preceding chapters, which is the first step toward establishing that regardless of the region, there are general commonalities to be observed regarding the impact such extreme conditions have on an individual.

Therefore, to conclude this section, a general assessment of the state failure model is that it performs well considering the limitations of the data and the unique challenges that are inherent to analyzing a region that suffers from the presence of multiple state actors, which initially made establishing a linear relationship between state failure and political violence somewhat difficult.

Although it is certainly tempting to rush forward to the conclusion, there are intrinsic weaknesses to this analysis I wish to highlight that are essential to improving upon this work and research on this phenomenon as a whole. The first and probably the most obvious weakness is the use of social movements as a dependent variable. Many would argue that support for a social movement should not be considered an act of political violence. This is an argument I would not challenge, except I would beg those who make this argument to revisit the survey question presented in this text in the Methodology section. The question asks respondents the following: *Social movements are necessary mechanisms for the development of society?*

Again, my justification for including this variable as a proxy for political violence is largely based upon the research of Skocpol, Tilly, Huntington and Gurr, who identify social revolutions as transformative processes originating from state crisis

(Huntington, 1968; Gurr, 1970; Skocpol, 1979; Tilly, 1978, 2004). Non-violent protest and dissident behavior, I consider *necessary* for the development of society, yet social movements are generally precursors to violent social revolutions and in some cases civil war (i.e. Arab Spring). Further, Huntington notes these types of movements are considerably volatile and violence is easily triggered when tensions are high and there is a collective mass of frustrated individuals (1968).

Consequently, for a person to automatically consider social movements to be *necessary* to the development of society (given the alternatives i.e. non-violent protest, civil demonstrations, strikes, boycotts etc.), I would question the propensity of such individuals to be oriented toward action politics, and along that same reasoning, to be willing to take more radical actions to affect change.

Beyond my choice of dependent variables, I anticipate another criticism that will arise is the performance of certain measures of public goods, namely, why would dissatisfaction with the school system, the hospital system, and the roadway system compel a person to support political violence, but not access to water, electricity, or a sewage system? Of the public goods included in the model, one would think the latter three goods (water, electricity, and sewage) would be most important to individuals and that the lack of these goods would compel individuals to support acts of political violence.

A closer look at these variables reveals two issues, the first of which deals with measurement and the second involves access to goods. The measurement for the variables, *hospitals, schools, roads,* are all coded along the same scale that moves along a continuum from 1–4 where one represents being satisfied with the system and four indicates that a respondent is not satisfied with the system. The question is asked based upon the assumption that every respondent has access to these goods, which may not be the case, yet, with the exception of the variable *Roads,* there is no response category for access to this good. And even when I evaluate the variable that measures satisfaction with the roadway system, only 350 respondents, which is less than 2 percent of the sample, report not having access to this service, suggesting that if this is a consistent statistic across the remaining measures (for which this response category is not available, so the data are unavailable), only a marginal few do not have access to these goods.

The main reason why access is so important is because the three variables that measure public goods, that were not statistically significant, addressed this feature and were coded accordingly. Regarding water, sewage, and electricity, the respondent was asked if they themselves or a relative had access to these goods. Now I want to point out that even though the respondents were asked if they had access to these goods, it is important to note that the majority of them did. Ninety-seven percent of respondents reported having access to electricity, 86 percent reported having access to water, and 67 percent indicated they had access to a sewage system. Given these statistics, it is not surprising that the results were what they were. The data suggests that these individuals are not suffering from any lack of these basic public goods. I would argue regarding the variables, *hospitals, roads,* and *schools,* that because most of the respondents had either a favorable or unfavorable response regarding these services, that the majority of them would naturally have access to these goods and services. However, what we can see regarding the provision of public goods in Latin America is not if a person has access, because remember, Latin America generally performs well with regards to socio-economic and development indicators. What appears to be most important for the analysis of Latin America and this feature of state failure is *not* access, but *quality* of the goods and services provide. That diverges somewhat from our core hypothesis, but Latin America is a unique case that performs well on some indicators while failing at others, consequently, capturing these nuances in measurement should be taken into account. Otherwise stated, I believe the existing measurement of the variables *sewage*, *water*, and *electricity* are inappropriate for this particular analysis and lack critical information, which the findings suffer from. Had these variables been based upon a question which addressed satisfaction and not *simply* access, I believe the results would have been much different.

A final point to make regarding the findings is the lack of statistical support for all but one of the variables, which measures drugs, violence, and trafficking. I was certain these variables would be important to respondents, and thus would play an important role in the relationship between state failure and political violence. However, the statistical findings do not support this. And yet, there is no doubt in my mind that the drug cartels, the drug trade, and the violence of non-state actors have a significant impact on the people of Latin America and the relationship between state failure and support for political violence. Given my understanding of the political dynamics of Latin America, I refused to be deterred by the statistical findings, which led me to take a closer look at these variables. Not surprisingly, I found that the number of observations for these variables was simply too small to draw inferences from and the statistical results reflect this.

Of the approximately 19,000 individuals who responded to the question, 1.26 percent believes drug use in their country is a *major problem*; 1.04 percent believe the violence committed by non-state actors is a major problem; and 3.47 percent believe that the drug cartels are a major problem. This is compared to the only significant variable in the bunch, where 21 percent believe that the drug trade is a major problem.

A deeper look at each of these measures reveals why they did not perform in the model; however, I want to add that just because respondents did not state that these factors are *major* problems to them or even in their country does not in any way mean that is not the case; it only suggests that when forced to select a *single* answer, compared to other factors such as the economy or government corruption, the latter are more salient to them.

Finally, another point to consider is there may be an issue of endogeneity in the sense that as I suggested at the opening of this work if individuals do not distinguish between the motivations of violent groups (i.e. terrorist vs. guerilla fighter) then the lack of support for these variables in the model would actually lend support to that vein of thought. In other words, it was *I* who made the distinction here in this chapter that the narco-violence of gangs and cartels, which is purely economic driven and lacks a political motivation, is somehow different from the political violence of insurgents and guerilla fighters who direct their violence toward the state given their grievances which are rooted in political ideology. However, it is entirely possible that respondents see cartels and gangs as legitimate political groups that function as the opposition to the state. In many instances the gangs, cartels, and paramilitary organizations provide a source of employment and income to a segment of the population that are unskilled and undereducated (Shanty and Mishra, 2008). Further, it has been noted in this chapter that several cartels and gangs have displaced the central government in many regions as the local governing authority. Consequently, it is possible survey respondents do not consider the violence of these non-state actors to be a problem because of the important economic and political role they play in society, similar to that of Hamas in the West Bank and Gaza, and Hezbollah in Lebanon. If this dynamic is indeed present in Latin America then the broad definition I outlined at the opening of this work would hold, meaning that regardless of whether or not the actors are insurgents, rebels, guerillas, drug cartels, paramilitary organizations, revolutionaries, or terrorists, any strategic activity with the intent of inducing fear, based upon coercion, and for the purpose of threatening harm with the goal of forcing political or economic concessions, represents an act of terror and a form of political violence. Therefore, if the survey respondents support political violence against the state, as the statistical results suggest, then given the assumptions of the theoretical model, they also support the presence of the drug cartels, paramilitary groups, and gangs which have undermined and displaced the state authority in many regions. If that is the case, then what that means for this entire work is that, as I argued, the conflation of all forms of political violence is appropriate given that respondents do not make distinctions between the groups and their motivations. At the same time, what this means for this chapter is that the variables which identify gang violence and non-state actor violence as a major problem should have been omitted from the statistical analysis.

As I conclude this section, I acknowledge that there are strengths and weaknesses of this chapter, most of which I've worked to address. Beyond these strengths and weaknesses, I also encountered challenges in the analysis and writing of this chapter. The unavailability of an appropriate measure for the absence of the state being one of the biggest limitations I faced. At the same time, the region of Latin America in general represented a challenge since, unlike the preceding regions, the causal relationship between state failure and political violence became harder to establish in a theoretical sense, given the intervening factors of drug trafficking and the existence of violent non-state actors, which (at the time I believed) were exogenous to the specified relationship.

Yet, despite it all—the challenges, the weaknesses, even the limitations—I cannot understate the major finding of this text and that is failing and failed states are breeding grounds for political violence, in that respondents report support for the use of political violence against the state given the conditions of state fragility and failure. Even in Latin America, which "appears" to have resilient states—

despite that they are perpetually weak—the chronic features of state failure are present in the region and *have* given rise to political violence and domestic terrorist and security threats. The only question that remains is will this region eventually give rise to more deadly terrorist threats with trans-border targets in the West or beyond?

Conclusion

As discussed at the opening of this chapter, state failure in Latin America is not present within the region in its *classic* form. The absence of security, lack of state authority and legitimacy, ungoverned territory, and the inability to provide public goods have all been listed as features of state failure, and yet, if viewed as a whole, Latin America would not be considered a region with failed states—at least not initially. Many states within the region enjoy a measure of stability, economic viability and formal democratic institutions govern most.

Despite the successes of the region, its greatest challenge to stability is one that sparked the many communist movements and struggles for power in the sixties and seventies, and that is the disproportionate gap between the wealthy and the poor in Latin American society. Social inequality remains and has actually been aggravated by the displacement of authoritarian rule by democratic governments, as these new governments apply neoliberal ideals to the economy and society. The rise of capitalism and free market principles have only served to further alienate the poor. Poverty continues to rise in the region, along with the income disparities between the poor and the wealthy—a situation that has neither been addressed by structural reform or state action, nor will it as long as state weakness remains a pervasive reality for Latin America (Chesterman, Ignatieff, and Thakur, 2005).

To say that Latin America is a region of weak and failed states would imply that at one point they'd succeeded, but they never have. Since their infancy, Latin American states have *always* been weak, and the presence of contending non-state actors in the region give credence to the enduring frailty of Latin American states. Therefore, it is no surprise the region has given birth to such violent groups that include the FARC, the AUC, and the Sinaloa and Los Zetas drug cartels, to name a few. Unfortunately for Latin America, the region will only continue along this cyclical pattern of violence as long as institutional weakness is permissive.

The findings of this analysis echo the larger argument of this work, which is so clearly witnessed in the region of Latin America, where its states will forever be challenged for supremacy until they address the most critical features of state failure and that is a monopoly over security, violence, and territory.

Chapter 6
Beyond Failed States: Reflecting on State Failure and the Origins of Violence and the Future Threat of Transnational Terrorism

Conclusion

General Assessment

The process of understanding how fragile states in the developing world function as breeding grounds for terrorists, and actors that engage in political violence, is the central theme of this work. To apply the theoretical framework and develop the topics, *Failed States and the Origins of Violence* has focused solely on what I consider the regions of critical interest, given their propensity for state fragility and political violence—these regions are sub-Saharan Africa, the Middle East and North Africa, Southeast and South Asia, and Latin America. In each chapter, I conduct an analysis of the region of interest using statistical models of state failure and political violence developed specifically for this work to illustrate the salient nature of the relationship between these two phenomena.

In multiple statistical analyses, I find that citizens living within failing and failed states consider political violence to be a legitimate political tool. Thus, regardless of the region and ethno-religious differences between states, individuals' perspectives regarding the use of violence as an effective political instrument remain persistent among citizens of states that are on the brink of failure or that have failed.

In sub-Saharan Africa, where there is a prevalence of state failure, we observe the strongest support for this relationship between state failure and political violence. There is overwhelming popular support for political violence across the survey respondents. Regarding the Middle East and North Africa, the relationship between state fragility and political violence remains consistent, despite the use of proxy measures, which cannot completely capture the phenomenon of interest. Yet, despite the absence of a direct measure of support for political violence, similar to the one found in the Afrobarometer dataset, through the estimation of a series of statistical models, the findings largely remain consistent, which allows me to state with a measure of confidence that support for political violence in the Middle East and North Africa is driven by the conditions of state weakness and failure.

Even if the statistical model had not held up in the analysis, the political turmoil in this region of the world, as evidenced by the Arab Spring and Green Revolution, gives credence to this vein of thought. With the recent political uprisings in Iran, Egypt, Libya, and Syria, it has become apparent that every day average citizens are willing to support and engage in political violence given the conditions I have outlined in this work which represent the features of state weakness and failure.

Within Latin America we observe a complex relationship between the process of state fragility and the prevalence of political violence. Unlike sub-Saharan Africa, Latin America is not a region of failed states; and unlike the Middle East and North Africa, Latin America is not a region suffering from widespread outbreaks of political violence. Instead, the region of Latin America is plagued by a network of fragile states that suffer from pockets of violence and a pervasive culture of lawlessness, given the presence of a host of non-state actors who challenge the governments of Latin American states for sovereignty. Further, the violence that has broken out between these groups and the government has created a crisis of legitimacy for many Latin American states, particularly in rural areas where prominent drug cartels, such as the Zetas, operate as the state authority and *not* the government. As a result of this dynamic, Latin Americans living in these weak states indicate support for political violence against the embattled governments of their states, in response to the climate of instability and insecurity plaguing the region.

Southeast and South Asia are interesting cases because for the most part they are economically viable regions. Thus, one would assume that given continued economic growth and expansion, the political violence will eventually decline with the emergence of a strong middle class. While this is certainly the expected outcome, for now violence remains. The region still must contend with a number of destabilizing factors including: the conflict over Kashmir, the presence of al-Qaeda in the FATAS (Federally Administered Tribal Areas) of Pakistan, Jemaah Islamiyah in Indonesia, and the radicalization of the marginalized Muslim population who are discriminated against throughout the Southeast Asian region. Given these tenuous conditions, it is projected that the seeds of political violence in Southeast and South Asia could soon bear the fruit of transnational terrorist threats and internal conflict. Moreover, it has yet to be seen if the peace will hold in Sri Lanka, and what will eventually come of Afghanistan with the complete withdrawal of American troops in 2014. Therefore, despite the progress made in Southeast and South Asia, any hope for continued economic growth will be neutered, at least in the immediate future, if even one of these situations devolves into widespread violence, or internationally sponsored terrorist groups gain a stronghold in the region.

Limitations and Recommendations

The findings of this work provide evidence that individuals are willing to support or engage in political violence *against* the states in which they live that have failed or are failing. What this analysis falls short of doing is completely explaining how these same individuals go through the process of possibly having a legitimate cause for violence against the state to engaging in actual political violence and/or terrorism. That component of the decision-making process remains unexplored in this study and represents an avenue for future work.[1]

Finally, another limitation of this work is that it does not offer a comprehensive explanation as to why some failing and failed states breed political violence while others do not. In recent work, I have made an effort to address this, and find that as measured by this analysis, every failing and failed state must contend with some form of political violence (Howard and Morris, 2013). An examination of the 2012 Failed State Index (FSI) and the top 107 states that are ranked as very high alert, high alert, alert, and warning which this study classifies as a failed state and failing state, every single one of them report significant rankings (five or higher out of ten) for at least one (but in most cases both) of the following two indicators: 1) group grievances and 2) security apparatus which serve as indicators of political violence (See Appendices P and Q). What this finding suggests is that according to the 2012 FSI indicators and rankings, every failed and failing state on their list struggles with some form of political violence (See Appendices P and Q). What this work stops short of is distinguishing between the variant forms of political violence found within these failing and failed states, and the dynamics of state fragility that give rise to a narco-terrorist as opposed to an Islamic extremist, but I argue that is beyond the scope of this work as it examines the deeply rooted ideological or religious motivations of actors, which is a distinct vein of thought from the one that examines the socio-political origins of violence and its roots in state failure.

Another important point of note is the role that the protection of private property plays in the relationship between state failure and support for political violence. Although, due to the unavailability of data, this condition of state failure is only analyzed in Chapter 2 (sub-Saharan Africa) and Chapter 4 (Latin America), yet, in both chapters it is a strong predictor of support for political violence. As a feature of state failure, I argue that when the state fails to ensure private property guarantees that has far reaching socio-political implications, which is strongly supported by the statistical models. Thus, given the availability of data, I would like to further investigate the role of this variable in future models, because I believe it is one of the key indicators of the breakdown of the state.

---

1 Although, at the time of this writing, research has not examined the psychological impact living and existing in an environment of state weakness and failure has on the decision making process of an individual to engage in political violence and terrorism. However, work has been conducted on the decision making process of terrorists and terrorist organizations. See Brian Jenkins, 1979, 1981, 1982; Martha Crenshaw, 1986, 1988, 1990, 1994, 2000; Gordon McCormick, 2003; Ransom, Weaver, Barry G. Silverman, Hogeun Shin, and Richard Dubois, 2001; Ethan Bueno de Mesquita, 2011; Alexander Lee, 2011; Jacob Shapiro, 2012.

Finally, another limitation of this work is the weak findings to support the assertion that the absence of the state or ungoverned territory contributes to political violence. In Chapter 2, the case regarding sub-Saharan Africa, I fail to find support for this measure. The same is true for Chapter 4, the case regarding Southeast and South Asia. Chapter 5, the case of Latin America, no measure of the absence of the state/ungoverned territory is provided so I utilize case study investigation to build my argument, realizing that by having to do this there are certain limitations to the analysis. The only instance where the absence of the state/ungoverned territory is statistically significant is in Chapter 2, the case of the Middle East and North Africa; however, a number of proxy measures are utilized to capture the dependent condition of support for political violence, which raises measurement concerns. Therefore, taken as a whole, there is little evidence to support the assertion that the absence of the state/ungoverned territory contributes to support for political violence. I would further argue additional research is required to determine how this feature functions as a condition of state failure, because in complete opposition to existing studies, this work does not find empirical evidence to suggest that the absence of the state and ungoverned territory represent a sufficient indicator of state failure.

Nonetheless, logically it would make sense that non-state actors such as terrorists, rebel groups, and drug cartels benefit from the existence of ungoverned territory and the lack of a state presence. My belief is that this measure is indeed an indicator of state failure, and that as a feature of state failure, it has the potential to contribute to individual support for political violence. However, the measures used in this analysis, I argue, function as weak proxies for this condition. Thus, future research on this relationship will require more refined and precise measures of this concept to empirically reveal the importance of ungoverned territory/the absence of the state to the analytical model.

A Discussion of Larger Policy Implications and Future Research—Exploring State Failure As A Root Cause of Transnational and International Terrorist Threats

The core of this text is driven by the assertion that state weakness and failure have an impact on individual support for political violence and in certain cases terrorism. Throughout the process of this work I have illustrated that failing and failed states have given rise to political violence and domestic terrorist threats. In some cases, specifically that of the Middle East and North Africa, and South Asia, this work has provided evidence that some failing and failed states have also given rise to transnational terrorist threats. However, the main focus of this work has been the specific impact of state failure on individual support for political violence against the failing or failed state in which one lives. Nonetheless, at the opening of this work, I indicate that my intent was to also touch upon certain speculative suppositions regarding my predictions concerning the future breeding grounds for transnational terrorism. Within Chapter 2 (sub-Saharan Africa) and Chapter 4 (South East and South Asia), I discuss the potential for these regions to give rise to significant transnational threats given the current socio-political climate and economic conditions of those regions. At the same time; however, I acknowledge at no point do I empirically test the impact of state failure on support for political violence directed toward a state beyond that of the survey respondent's.

Nevertheless, as I look to continue this vein of research, future work will focus on broadening the argument made here to that of evaluating whether failing and failed states function as breeding grounds for all levels of political violence—domestic and transnational. The implication of such an empirical finding would further advance our understanding of the role failing and failed states play in fostering radical extremist thought and behavior. Given the foundation established by the research conducted in *Failed States and the Origins of Violence*, in the following section I discuss the context of such implications according to each region.

Latin America

Of all the regions where state weakness and political violence are a concern, this one is the least critical. Despite the prevalence of violence by the drug cartels and paramilitary groups, these organizations are focused solely on obtaining power within the state and financial control over the drug trade. Thus, there is no ideological or religious goal that drives groups such as the ELN and FARC in Colombia or the Sinaloa and Zetas in Mexico. Further, the existence of the West does not threaten them or their operations. Quite the opposite. The West has repeatedly sold arms and supported these cartels, rebel groups and paramilitaries, as evidenced by the Iran-Contra Affair, and the recently exposed Fast and Furious program. Many would even argue that because they lack a political motivator, these groups should not even be considered terrorist organizations.

My argument, one that I have firmly established throughout the course of this text, is that just because the U.S. State Department doesn't include a certain group on its list of terrorist organizations[2] or just because this group doesn't threaten Western interests doesn't mean they don't engage in political violence and terrorism. Furthermore, it has yet to be seen if the border violence will eventually spill over (more than it already has) into the United States from Mexico. And, while Latin America may not represent a critical threat to the West, because its organizations do not engage in transnational terrorism with targets against the West, the very proximity of Latin America to the United States should illustrate why the problem of porous borders and weak state authority should be of importance to the Western hemisphere, particularly the United States.

2 Although both the FARC and ELN are included on the U.S. State Department's list of foreign terrorist organizations.U.S. State Department (2011).http://www.state.gov/s/ct/rls/other/des/123085.htm. September 15.

Additionally, just as drugs and arms flow easily into the United States, so can terrorists, especially in the post 9/11 era, and despite the heightened scrutiny at seaports and airports and stricter visa entry guidelines. The U.S.-Mexico border remains one of the most accessible modes of entry into the United States, and with large stretches of ungoverned territory in Latin America now controlled by cartels, paramilitaries, and rebel groups—who is to say terrorists will not also take up residence in these ungoverned spaces from which they can plan and implement attacks, or worse yet, align themselves with one of the existing rebel organizations or drug cartels that have well established routes of entry into the United States. The political conditions within Latin America are ripe for any one of these scenarios; my only concern is that we have gone beyond the point of speculation and that terrorist groups have already begun to see the value of establishing a tangible presence in the ungoverned regions of Latin America where they can plan and implement strategic attacks.

Southeast and South Asia

Southeast and South Asia should be regions of concern for two reasons. First, in both Southeast and South Asia, states such as Afghanistan, Pakistan, Indonesia, and Sri Lanka have been the site of protracted violence and conflict, and at any point a crisis could reemerge once again from these contiguous regions. Second, both regions have and continue to be breeding grounds for terrorists and violent political dissent. South Asia has been the home to several terrorist factions that have found a safe haven in the lawless state of Afghanistan and the ungoverned tribal regions of Pakistan. The impunity Pakistan exhibited in its harboring of Osama bin Laden should serve as notice to the international community, especially considering the nuclear threat Pakistan represents. The instability of Pakistan has already been felt across its borders in India, and if the state should collapse completely, there is no doubt terrorist cells will become entrenched in Pakistan's lawless territory.

The precarious nature of Pakistan represents a critical threat to the stability of South Asia, which is why attention should remain focused on the region. At the same time, Southeast Asia should not escape notice either. With the exception of Singapore, speculation continues regarding the influx of terrorists into this region. Particularly, Indonesia and Cambodia are the two major states of interest.

Indonesia has been the site of notable terrorist attacks on Westerners, and for that reason alone, the state has come under close international scrutiny. There is no doubt that Indonesia sponsors and harbors international terrorists, with the political goal of attacking Western states and interests. Thus, the terrorist threat in Indonesia is a very real one.

However, the importance of Cambodia in the region has yet to be decided. I am convinced that the presence of JI in the region will only continue to grow, and with their numbers, so will their influence. Cambodia has largely escaped notice as a major state that harbors terrorists, even though it is well known that they do.

That could change if an international attack is found to have been planned in the state, or Western interests in Cambodia fall under attack, as was the case in Indonesia. At present, a radical transformation of the citizens of Cambodia has not taken place, so at this point Cambodia does not seem to be an *immediate* concern, but that could change given the growing strength of existing terrorist networks, and the continued weakness of the Cambodian state and its institutions of governance.

Sub-Saharan Africa

I opened this text with sub-Saharan for an important reason. Given that the incidence of state failure is so prevalent in this region I anticipated that for my argument to hold, sub-Saharan Africa's broken states would have to reveal strong evidential support for my hypothesis—that a climate of state failure fosters support for political violence. From Somalia to Sierra Leone, the tragic reality is that sub-Saharan's failed states have proven to be breeding grounds for terrorists and political violence. Thus far, the violent rebel groups that can be found across the region have waged a campaign of terror against its citizens, especially in the collapsed states of Sierra Leone, the DRC, and Somalia. The political violence of Joseph Kony and the LRA has been so severe across South Sudan, the DRC, but mainly Uganda that it has prompted the intervention of the African Union in order to bring an end to what has escalated into a tragic case of war crimes and human rights violations.

The situation in Somalia has been equally devastating to the nation and its people. Bitter struggles for power have led to the fragmentation of the entire state, which has created a climate of anarchy in all but a few pockets of the state. The rebel organizations, Rahanweyn Resistance Army (RRA) and Al-Shabaab have emerged as the most resilient groups and continue to engage in deadly attacks against the Somali government in a battle for further territorial autonomy. Essentially, the notion of state sovereignty no longer exists within Somalia, which is why of all the states in sub-Saharan Africa, it represents one of the greatest challenges and threats to the international community. For years Al-Shabaab has been connected to al-Qaeda, a relationship that continues today. Somalia is also a known sponsor of terrorists who have gone on to attack transnational targets. Somalia is essentially ungoverned, with large stretches of territory controlled by violent rebel organizations, and it is because of the absence of a state authority, with comprehensive legitimacy, that Somalia will remain a very real threat to the global community for many years to come.

Beyond Somalia and Uganda, the DRC is another state to watch closely. Despite a formal peace agreement, the Second Congo Civil War continues today as the violence between rebel groups and the Armed Forces of the Democratic Republic of Congo or FARDC remain at its highest. Little effort has been made to establish rule of law, as evidenced by the mass killings and heinous sexual violence perpetrated by all armed groups within the DRC. One of the greatest problems incurred as a result of the violence in the DRC—besides the obvious tragedy of the loss of human life—is that it has kept one of the poorest states in sub-Saharan Africa embroiled in conflict and subsequent poverty, which means the DRC is likely to remain a failed state for many years to come, with implications for not only the DRC, but also the region. Bordered by a number of failed states (Uganda, Angola, Rwanda), the violence in the DRC has already spilled over across its neighbors' borders into Zambia, Rwanda, and Uganda as well. Also, none would argue that it was the genocide in Rwanda that exacerbated the brewing conflict in the DRC when an already strained country was forced to absorb thousands of refugees in such a short period of time.

If ever Weiner's assessment of 'Bad Neighbors and Bad Neighborhoods' was true, the current situation in central Africa is a classic example (1996). Consequently, the failed states of sub-Saharan Africa are of tremendous importance to the context of this argument. Thus far, Africa's failed states have been the breeding grounds for political violence and groups that commit acts of terror against their own people, but not internationally sponsored terrorism.

I argue that could change, especially in light of the illegal economic connections that exist between these groups. As discussed in Chapter 2, it is no secret that those same 'blood diamonds' that fund internal conflicts in sub-Saharan Africa are also used to fund international terrorism. Just as it is no secret that al-Qaeda, Hamas, and Hezbollah have all done business with a number of rebel groups in Central and West Africa. What I pointed out in Chapter 2, I reemphasize here—Africa's broken states have yet to produce international terrorists, but I am convinced they soon will. The radicalization of Somalia provides one example of this, and Nigeria and Mali are both poised to follow a similar path. I expect, too, al-Qaeda will build upon the networks they have fostered in sub-Saharan Africa, as they come to realize the viability of a region that suffers from widespread state failure.

Sub-Saharan Africa's failed states are undoubtedly breeding grounds for deadly rebel groups, political violence, and domestic acts of terror; however, the region has the imminent potential of producing internationally sponsored terrorism, making Sub-Saharan Africa probably the most dangerous security threat to Western interests because the region has largely been ignored and that could prove to be the international community's gravest mistake.

Middle East and North Africa

The recent turmoil in the Middle East and North Africa should make this assessment relatively easy. Much like sub-Saharan Africa, the MENA region is plagued by both a collection of failed states and political violence. Also, the MENA region has the distinction of harboring terrorists, exporting radical violence and ideals, and producing some of the deadliest transnational terrorist organizations. Given the obvious convergence of both state fragility and political violence, my analysis of the MENA region *would* seem relatively straightforward—and it *is*—but how the Middle East and North Africa region ended up in its current predicament is what I explored in Chapter 3 and further elaborate upon here.

Autocratic regimes, ethno-religious conflict, and the radicalization of Islam have epitomized the region of the Middle East and North Africa for the past four decades. With the end of World War II, and the partitioning of this region by the Allied Powers, along with the subsequent creation of Israel, it was the confluence of these events that would usher in a new era within this region of the world. As a result of post World War II events; the Middle East and North Africa have come to be defined by their weak states, oppressive regimes, extremist religious ideology, and deadly acts of terrorism and political violence. And nowhere else in the world is the impact of state fragility on the psyche of those who inhabit these broken statesmore evident.

Frustrated by its military failure against Israel in the Six Day War, coupled with the perceived imperial power of the West through the process of globalization, noted scholar Bernard Lewis would point to these events as the trigger conditions that would lead to the emergence of some of the most notorious radical Islamic terrorist organizations such as the Muslim Brotherhood, Hamas, Hezbollah, al-Qaeda, the Palestinian Islamic Jihad, and Harakat al-Mujahidin.[3] These groups would usher in the fourth wave of terrorism, which according to Rapoport is the deadliest wave to date (2004).

The dynamic of state sponsors of terrorist groups in the Middle East is one of the endemic weaknesses that make strengthening the institutions of these states so difficult. When states such as Iran, Syria, and Yemen sponsor known terrorist organizations such as Hezbollah, Hamas, and al-Qaeda, it compromises the legitimacy of the state authority and in the case of Syria, further cripples a state laboring under the leadership of a weak, corrupt, illegitimate, and oppressive regime.

More specifically, the partnership between Hezbollah and the Lebanese government proved to be mutually beneficial, except when the interests of the two groups diverged. The Lebanese government's first preference was to secure the Israeli-Lebanese border and retain the Shibaa Farms territory seized by Israel during the 1967 war, [while] Hezbollah's first and ultimate preference was to destroy Israel, but also secure Lebanon's border with Israel (Dekmejian, 2007). Thus, between 1984 and 2006, when the Lebanese government was faced with mounting pressure from the United States and the global community to expel Hezbollah for its continuing terrorist agenda, the Lebanese government was both unable and unwilling to do so, given its lack of military power against Hezbollah and its reliance upon Hezbollah's strategic military might to secure Lebanon against Israel (Dekmejian, 2007). As a consequence, the Lebanese government was delivered a devastating blow—with the invasion of Israeli troops into Lebanon after Hezbollah kidnapped two Israeli soldiers and killed eight others—

3 Streeter, Sabin. (2005). *The Road to 9/11*. UK: Kundhardt Productions (film).

a blow that it had desperately sought to avoid, but just couldn't in the face of political constraints imposed by Hezbollah.

As was the case in Lebanon—a fate that Iran and Syria could soon suffer, given the continuing rise in power of Hezbollah—when a terrorist organization's interests are no longer aligned with that of the sponsoring state, it leaves that state open to retaliatory activities in response to the actions of the terrorist organization.

To preserve the concept of statehood and sovereignty in the region, efforts must first be made by regime leaders to withdraw support from terrorist organizations and expel them from their countries. Ideally, the next step would be to recognize the importance of political legitimacy by promoting democratic ideals, particularly in Saudi Arabia, Syria, Libya, and Iran. However, I realize such ideals are lofty ones. More importantly, I also recognize the more immediate economic concerns of the region must first be addressed before a comprehensive move toward democracy can be made. Yet even if democratic institutions could be established in the region, such a task would only be possible with the removal of radical Islamic terrorist groups who remain committed to creating a network of repressive and radical Islamic states across the region.

Moreover, I also acknowledge that many attempts at democracy, no matter how futile and half-hearted, have been attempted in the region with little or only marginal success. It has long been debated and widely accepted that the ideals of democracy are fundamentally incompatible with the cultural norms of the region. Further, as I discussed in Chapter 3, I remain convinced that democracy is not the answer. Pursuing comprehensive state building is the first and most important step. What do I mean by state building, if it is not the implementation of a system of democracy?

If state failure is defined by the absence of the state within large pockets of territorial boundaries, a weak state authority, the lack of security, the inability of the state to provide public goods and protect private property, and a lack of state legitimacy, then if these factors were addressed within the context of serious state building and not just as post-conflict afterthoughts to be pursued for awhile but then abandoned within months after a crisis, the region could possibly begin to move toward an open system of governance, which would address the dissent we have witnessed in the region in recent years. But more importantly, with comprehensive state building, the region would have the ability to develop its economic sector, which would begin to address the deeply rooted grievances over high rates of unemployment and high inflation.

I should point out that my recommendations for the MENA region are the same for all of the regions examined in this analysis. Granted, as I noted when discussing the Middle East and North Africa, that addressing economic concerns should come before addressing the political grievances, therefore, this recommendation should illustrate that each region has unique circumstances that require unique approaches.

In the case of sub-Saharan Africa, addressing the pervasive corruption and the culture of impunity that exists with regard to perpetrators of violence should be the first priority of that region. Not until these two factors are addressed can serious state building efforts be pursued in the region. As for Southeast and South Asia, where economic investment and development has the potential to bring about prosperity to these regions, it is important to fully address the grievances of existing factions that could derail this process. Establishing strong political institutions that constitutionally guarantee minority rights should be the first priority of these two regions that are on the path to economic growth. And finally, the absence of strong democratic institutions in Latin America has allowed for the black market economy to become a major economic force in the region, whereby many regimes rely upon the profits from drugs and human trafficking to fund their states. The region of Latin America must work to fully develop and strengthen their democratic institutions, while also making serious efforts to crack down on drug and human trafficking if there is to be any hope of developing a strong economic sector.

Final Thoughts

After World War II, and in light of the devastation of Germany and Japan, the international community understood the importance of rebuilding the state. Having ignored Germany after World War I, the global community recognized the consequences of turning a blind eye to the inherent crisis of state fragility. Consequently, efforts were made to develop states with strong economic and political institutions. This process of state building did not take place overnight. Instead, three decades would pass before Japan and Germany would be considered strong, stable nations.

Much has changed since World War II. The priorities of the international community have shifted. Providing immediate economic aid to states in crisis has become the primary strategy of the UN. Additional assistance in the form of military support has also been utilized as a strategy. However, long-term state building has largely been abandoned as we have witnessed in the Balkans, Afghanistan, and Iraq. Once a democratically elected government is in place and a critical mass of security forces are on the ground, the international community withdraws from the fledging state, regardless of how weak the government is and ill-equipped these newly trained security forces are to mediate contending factions, which still remain post-state failure.

The current strategy for dealing with states that have failed makes sense from a short-term fiscal standpoint. Relinquish and return authority to the state and the global community is thus absolved of any responsibility—that is, until the state fails again. Afghanistan, Somalia, the DRC are all failed states that at one point have been occupied by international forces only to be abandoned and re-occupied again when the situation within these states represents a global humanitarian threat in the form of trans-border conflict, forced migration, political violence and last but not least—terrorism.

I remain convinced that terrorism and political violence are just symptoms of a larger systemic problem: state failure. Regions that have been plagued by domestic terrorism and political violence will simply continue along this path as long as the states within these regions suffer from the crisis of state failure. The conditions within failing and failed states force citizens to turn to political violence as a legitimate alternative to achieve political concessions and obtain economic goods. As we look to the future of analyzing political violence and terrorism in the modern era, this is a troubling scenario, because as this work illustrates, no longer are those who support the use of political violence and terrorism *only* radicals and extremists existing on the fringes of society. There is the emergence of a new breed of terrorist—and that is the *seemingly* ordinary citizen.

Bibliography

Aarts, Paul. (1999). The Middle East: A Region without Regionalism or the End of Exceptionalism? *Third World Quarterly*, 20(5), pp. 911–25.

Abedin, Mahan. (2005). Al-Qaeda: In Decline or Preparing for the Next Attack: An Interview with Saad al-Faqih. *Spotlight on Terror*. The Jamestown Foundation, 3(5), June 15. http://jamestown.org/terrrorism.news/article.pjp?articleid=2369721. Accessed: December 8, 2008.

Abrahamsen, Rita and Williams, Michael (eds). (2007). The Privatisation and Globalisation of Security in Africa. *International Relations*, 21(2), June.

Abul Jobain, A. (1993). *Radical Islamic Terrorism or Political Islam?* Annandale, VA, USA: United Association for Studies and Research.

Abuza, Z. (2003a). *Militant Islam in Southeast Asia: Crucible of Terror*. Boulder: Lynne Rienner Publishers.

—— (2003b). Funding Terrorism in Southeast Asia: The Financial Network of Al Qaeda and Jemaah Islamiya. *Contemporary Southeast Asia: A Journal of International & Strategic Affairs*, 25(2), pp. 169–99.

Acharya, Amitav. (1993). A New Regional Order in Southeast Asia: ASEAN in the Post–Cold War Era. *International Institute for Strategic Studies*, Adelphi Paper No. 279, London.

Adamson, C. (1998). Tribute, Turf, Honor, and the American Street Gang: Patterns of Continuity and Change Since 1820. *Theoretical Criminology*, 2(1), pp. 57–84.

Addison, Michael. (2002). *Violent Politics: Strategies of Internal Conflict*. Basingstoke: Palgrave.

—— Afrobarometer. (2008). *Afrobarometer Dataset*. Lansing Michigan: Michigan State University. http://www.afrobarometer.org/data.html. Accessed: September 8, 2009.

Agier, Michel. (2004). Colombia. Violence versus Politics. In Fabrice Weissman (ed.), *In the Shadow of 'Just Wars.' Violence, Politics and Humanitarian Action*. Ithaca: Cornell University Press, pp. 228–46.

Ahmed, N. M. (2002). *The War on Freedom. How and Why America was Attacked, September 11th, 2001*. Joshua Tree, Calif.: Media Messenger Books.

Akers, R. L. (1998). *Social Learning and Social Structure: A General Theory of Crime and Deviance*. Boston, MA: Northwestern University Press.

Akers, R. L. and Gang, L. (1999). Age, Social Learning, and Social Bonding in Adolescent Substance Use. *Deviant Behavior*, 19, pp. 1–25.

Alagappa, M. (2003). *Asian Security Order: Instrumental and Normative Features*. Stanford, Calif.: Stanford University Press.

Alagappa, M. (2008). *The Long Shadow: Nuclear Weapons and Security in 21st Century Asia*. Stanford, Calif.: Stanford University Press.

Alao, Abiodun. (1999). Diamonds are Forever … but so also are Controversies: Diamonds and the Actors in Sierra Leone's Civil War. *Civil Wars*, 2(3), Autumn.

Alexander, Yonah and Allan S. Nanes. (eds). (1986). *Legislative Responses to Terrorism*. Dordrecht, Neth. and Boston, Mass.: MartinusNijhoff.

Alexander, Yonah and Swetnam, M. S. (1999). *Cyber Terrorism and Information Warfare*. Dobbs Ferry, N.Y.: Oceana Publications.

Allan, Richard. (1990). *Terrorism: Pragmatic International Deterrence and Cooperation*. New York: Institute for East-West Security Studies.

Allen, D. (1992). *Religion and Political Conflict in South Asia: India, Pakistan, and Sri Lanka*. Westport, Conn.: Greenwood Press.

Altheide, D. L. (2004). Consuming Terrorism. *Symbolic Interaction*, 27(3), pp. 289–308.

Amineh, M. P. and Houweling, H. (2005; 2004). *Central Eurasia in Global Politics* (2nd ed.). Leiden; Boston: Brill.

Amnesty International. (2004). *Malaysia–NasharuddinNasir: Detained without Trial in the "War on Terror."* London: Amnesty International, International Secretariat.

Anderson, Lisa. (1987). The State in the Middle East and North Africa. *Comparative Politics*, 20(1), October, pp. 1–18.

Ankersen, C. and O'Leary, M. (2007). *Understanding Global Terror*. Cambridge; Malden, MA: Polity Press.

Anzovin, S. (ed.). (1986). *Terrorism*. New York: H.W. Wilson.

—— Arabarometer. (2008). *Arabarometer Dataset*. http://www.arabbarometer.org/survey/survey.html. Accessed: November 24, 2009.

Ardila Galvis, Constanza. (2002). *The Heart of War in Colombia*. London: Kumarian Press.

Arena, M. P. and Arrigo, B. A. (2006). *The Terrorist Identity*. New York: New York University Press. Arias, Enrique Desmond. (2006). *Drugs and Democracy in Rio de Janeiro. Trafficking, Social Networks, and Public Security*. Chapel Hill: University of North Carolina Press.

Arias, Enrique Desmond. (2006). The Myth of Personal Security. Criminal Gangs, Dispute Resolution, and Identity in Rio de Janeiro's Favelas. *Latin American Politics and Society*, 48(4), pp. 53–81.

Art, R. J. and Richardson, L. (2007). *Democracy and Counterterrorism: Lessons from the Past*. Washington, D.C.: United States Institute of Peace Press.

—— Asymmetric Threats. (1998). In *Strategic Assessment*. Washington DC: Institute for National Security Studies.

Atran, S. (2003). Genesis of Suicide Terrorism. *Science*, 299(5612), pp. 1534–9.

Atzili, Boaz. (2006). When Good Fences Make Bad Neighbors: Fixed Borders, State Weakness, and International Conflict. *International Security*, 31(3), pp. 139–73.

Ayoob, Mohammed. (1996). State-Making, State-Breaking and State Failure: Explaining the Roots of 'Third World' Insecurity, in van de Goor, Luc et al. (eds),

Between Development and Destruction: An Enquiry into the Causes of Conflict in Post-Colonial States. New York: St. Martin's Press.

Azam, Jean-Paul. (2001). The Redistributive State and Conflicts in Africa. *The Journal of Peace Research*, 38(4), pp. 429–44.

Babbin, J. L. (2007). *In the Words of our Enemies*. Washington, DC: Regnery Pub.

Barak, Oren. (2003). Lebanon: Failure, Collapse, and Resuscitation, in Rotberg, Robert I. (ed.), *State Failure and State Weakness in a Time of Terror*. Cambridge, MA: World Peace Foundation.

Barnes, B. E. (2006). *Culture, Conflict, and Mediation in the Asian Pacific*. Lanham, Md.: University Press of America.

Bassiouni, M. Cherif. (2002). Legal Control of International Terrorism: A Policy-Oriented Assessment. *Harvard International Law Journal*, 43(1), pp. 83–103.

Bassiouni, M. Cherif. (2007). *International Extradition: United States Law and Practice*. 5th Edition. New York: Oxford University Press.

Bates, Robert. (1981). *Markets and States Tropical Africa: The Agricultural Basis of Agricultural Policies*. Berkeley and Los Angeles: University of California Press.

Bates, Robert. (2007). Political Conflict and State Failure, in Benno Ndulu, Stephen O'Connell, Robert Bates, Paul Collier and Charles Soludo (eds), *The Political Economy of Economic Growth in Africa, 1960–2000*. Cambridge: Cambridge University Press.

Bayart, Jean-François, Ellis, Stephen and Hibou, Béatrice. (1999). *Criminalisation of the State in Africa*. International African Institute: Oxford.

Beblawi, Hazem and Luiciani, Giacomo. (eds). (1987). *The Rentier State*. New York: Croom Helm.

Becker, Bronwyn E. and Luthar, Suniya S. (2002). Social-Emotional Factors Affecting Achievement Outcomes among Disadvantaged Students: Closing the Achievement Gap. *Educational Psychologist*, 37(4), pp. 197–214.

Benmelech, Efraim, Claude, Berrebi and Esteban F. Klor. (2010). Economic Costs of Harboring Terrorism. *Journal of Conflict Resolution,* 54(2), pp. 331–53.

Berdal, Mats and Keen, David. (1998). Violence and Economic Agendas in Civil Wars. *Millennium*, 26(3), pp. 795–818.

Berdal, Mats and Malone, David (eds). (2000). *Greed and Grievance: Economic Agendas in Civil Wars*. Boulder: Lynne Rienner.

Berliner, David C. (2005). Our Impoverished View of Educational Reform. *Teachers College Record.* August, 2. Available on-line: http://www.asu.edu/educ/epsl/EPRU/documents/EPSL-0508-116-EPRU.pdf.

Berman, Eric G. and Sams, Katie E. (2000). *Peacekeeping in Africa*. Geneva: United Nations Institute for Disarmament Research.

Beutel, Alejandro J. (2007). *Radicalization and Homegrown Terrorism in Western Muslim Communities: Lessons Learned for America* (Minaret of Freedom Institute: August). Available on-line: http://www.minaret.org/MPAC%20Back grounder.pdf.

Biersteker, T. J. and Eckert, S. E. (2007). *Countering the Financing of Terrorism*. London; New York: Routledge.

Bjelopera, Jerome P. and Randol, Mark A. (2010). *American Jihadist Terrorism: Combatting a Complex Threat* (Washington, DC: Congressional Research Service, December 7, 2010). Available on-line: http://www.fas.org/sgp/crs/terror/R41416.pdf.

Bjørgo, T. (2005). *Root Causes of Terrorism: Myths, Reality, and Ways Forward.* London; New York: Routledge.

Boas, Morten. (2001). Liberia and Sierra Leone—Dead Ringers? The Logic of Neopatrimonial Rule. *Third World Quarterly*, 22(5), pp. 697–723.

Boas, Morten and Dunn, Kevin C. (2007). *African Guerrillas: Raging Against the Machine*. Boulder: Lynne Rienner.

Bodansky, Yossef. (1999). *Bin Laden: The Man who Declared War on America.* Rocklin, Calif: Forum.

Boone, Catherine. (2007). Property and Constitutional Order: Land Tenure Reform and the Future of the African State. *African Affairs*, 106(425), pp. 557–86.

Borum, Randy. (2004). *Psychology of Terrorism*. Tampa: University of South Florida.

Brady, David. (2003). Rethinking the Sociological Measurement of Poverty. *Social Forces*, 81(3), pp. 715–51.

Braun, Herbert. (1994). *Our Guerrillas, Our Sidewalks. A Journey into the Violence of Colombia*. Boulder: University Press of Colorado.

Brisard, Jean-Charles. (2002). *Terrorism Financing: Roots and Trends of Saudi Terrorism Financing*. New York: JCB Consulting.

Broch-Due, Vigdis. (2005). *Violence and Belonging: The Quest for Identity in Post-colonial Africa*. New York: Routledge.

Brosio, Giorgio and Zanola, Roberto. (2007). Violence and its Impact on Democracy in Colombia, in Alain Marciano and Jean Michel Josselin (eds), *Democracy, Freedom and Coercion: A Law and Economics Approach*. London: MPG Books, pp. 130–52.

Brown, Daniel W. (1996). *Rethinking Traditions in Modern Islamic Thought*. Cambridge UK: Cambridge University Press.

Brown, J. K. (2003). *Warfare in the 21st Century*. New York: H.W. Wilson.

Brown, Michael (ed.). (1993). *Ethnic Conflict and International Security*. Princeton: Princeton University Press.

Brunnée, Jutta and Toope, Stephen J. (2004). Slouching Towards New 'Just' Wars: The Hegemon after September 11th. *International Relations*, 18, pp. 405–23.

Burghart, D. L., Sabonis-Helf, T. and National Defense University. (2004). *In the Tracks of Tamerlane: Central Asia's Path to the 21st Century*. Washington, D.C.: Center for Technology and National Security Policy, National Defense University.

Byman, Daniel and Kenneth, Pollack. (2008). Iraq's Long-Term Impact on Jihadist Terrorism. *The ANNALS of the American Academy of Political and Social Science*, 618(1), pp. 55–68.

Callaghy, Thomas M. (2001). From Reshaping to Resizing a Failing State: The Case of the Congo/Zaïre, in Brendan O'Leary, et al. (eds), *Right-Sizing the State: The Politics of Moving Borders*. Oxford: Oxford University Press.

Callaghy, Thomas, Kassimir, Ronald and Latham, Robert (eds). (2001). *Intervention and Transnationalism in Africa*. Cambridge: Cambridge University Press.

Campbell, K. M. and Flournoy, M. A. (2001). *To Prevail: An American Strategy for the Campaign Against Terrorism*. Washington, D.C.: CSIS Press.

Chadwick, Elizabeth. (1996). *Self-determination, Terrorism, and the International Humanitarian Law of Armed Conflict*. The Hague, Boston Mass.: MartinusNijhoff.

Chakrabarti, R. (2009). *The Other India: Realities of an Emerging Power*. Los Angeles: Sage.

Chaliand, G. and Blin, A. (2007). *The History of Terrorism: From Antiquity to al Qaeda*. Berkeley: University of California Press.

Chalk, Peter, Rabasa, Angel, Rosenau, William and Piggott, Leanne. (2009). *The Evolving Terrorist Threat to Southeast Asia: A Net Assessment*. Santa Monica, CA: RAND Corporation, http://www.rand.org/pubs/monographs/MG846.

Chandler, David. (2006). *Empire in Denial: The Politics of State Building*. London: Pluto Press.

Charters, David A. (1994). Conclusions: Security and Liberty in Balance—Countering Terrorism in the Democratic Context, in D. A. Charters (ed.), *The Deadly Sin of Terrorism: Its Effect on Democracy and Civil Liberties in Six Countries*. Westport, CT: Greenwood Press.

Chasdi, Richard. (1999). *Serenade of Suffering: A Portrait of Middle Eastern Terrorism 1968–1993*. Lanham, MD: Lexington Books.

Chasdi, Richard. (2002). *Tapestry of Terror: A Portrait of Middle Eastern Terrorism 1994–1999*. Lanham, MD: Lexington Books.

Chesterman, Simon. (2003). *Just War or Just Peace: Humanitarian Intervention and International Law*. New York: Oxford University Press.

Chesterman, Simon, Ignatieff, Michael and Thakur, Ramesh (eds). (2005). *Making States Work: State Failure and the Crisis of Governance*. Tokyo: United Nations University Press.

Chomsky, Noam. (1988). *The Culture of Terrorism*. Boston: South End Press.

Chrétien, Jean-Pierre. (2003). *The Great Lakes of Africa: Two Thousand Years of History*. New York: Zone Books.

Christie, Clive J. (1996). *A Modern History of Southeast Asia: Decolonization, Nationalism and Separatism*. London: I. B. Tauris.

Chua, A. (2003). *World on Fire: How Exporting Free Market Democracy Breeds Ethnic Hatred and Global Instability* (1st ed.). New York: Doubleday.

CIA – The World Factbook. (2009). https://www.cia.gov/library/publications/the-world-factbook/rankorder/2001rank.html. Accessed: March 21, 2010.

Cilluffo, Frank (ed.). (2001). *Combating Chemical, Biological, Radiological, and Nuclear Terrorism: A Comprehensive Strategy: A Report of the CSIS Homeland Defense Project*. Washington DC: Center for Strategic and International Studies.

Clapham, Christopher. (2002). Problems of Peace Enforcement: Lessons to be Drawn from Multinational Peacekeeping Operations in Ongoing Conflicts in Africa, in Tunde Zack-Williams, Diane Frost and Alex Thomson (eds), *Africa in Crisis: New Challenges and Possibilities*. Sterling, VA: Pluto Press, pp. 196–215.

Clarance, W. (2007). *Ethnic Warfare in Sri Lanka and the UN Crisis*. London; Ann Arbor, MI: Pluto Press.

Cliffe, Lionel and Luckham, Robin. (1999). Complex Political Emergencies and the Failure of the State: Failure and the Fate of the State. *Third World Quarterly*, 20(1), pp. 27–50.

Clutterbuck, R. L. and Clutterbuck, R. L. (1994). *Terrorism in an Unstable World*. London; New York: Routledge.

Collier, Paul. (1999). Doing Well out of War. Paper presented at the Conference on Economic Agendas in Civil Wars, April 26–27, London. Available on-line: http://econ.worldbank.org/files/13200_CollierDoingWell.pdf/.

Collier, Paul, Elliot, Lani, Hegre, Havard, Hoeffler, Anke, Reynal-Querol, Martha and Sambanis, Nicholas. (2003). *Breaking the Conflict Trap: Civil War and Development Policy*. Washington DC: World Bank.

Collier, Paul and Hoeffler, Anke. (1998). On Economic Causes of Civil War. *Oxford Economic Papers*, 50(4), pp. 563–73.

—— (1999). Justice-seeking and Loot-seeking in Civil War. Washington, DC: World Bank. Available on-line: http://econ.worldbank.org/files/13203_CH JusticeSeeking.pdf/.

—— (2002). On the Incidence of Civil War in Africa. *Journal of Conflict Resolution*, 46(1), pp. 13–28.

—— (2004). Greed and Grievance in Civil War. *Oxford Economic Papers*, 56(4), pp. 563–95.

Collins, A. (2003). *Security and Southeast Asia: Domestic, Regional, and Global Issues*. Boulder, Colo.: Lynne Rienner Publishers.

Combs, Cindy C. (1997). *Terrorism in the Twenty-first Century*. Upper Saddle River, N.J.: Prentice Hall.

Cooley, John K. (1999). *Unholy Wars: Afghanistan, America, and International Terrorism*. London; Sterling, Va.: Pluto Press.

Cox, M. (2009). *Social Capital and Peace-building: Creating and Resolving Conflict with Trust and Social Networks*. London; New York: Routledge.

Cragin, Kim, Chalk, Peter, Daly, Sara A. and Jackson, Brian A. (2007). *Sharing the Dragon's Teeth: Terrorist Groups and the Exchange of New Technologies*. RAND Corporation: Santa Monica, CA.

Craig, Captain D. W. (1988). *Asymmetrical Warfare and the Transnational Threat: Relearning the Lessons from Vietnam*. Ontario: Canadian Forces College.

Crelinsten, Ronald D. (1978). *Terrorism and Criminal Justice: An International Perspective*. Lexington, Mass.: Lexington Books.

Crenshaw, Martha (ed.). (1983). *Terrorism, Legitimacy, and Power: The Consequences of Political Violence*. Middletown, Conn.: Wesleyan University Press.

Crenshaw, Martha. (1981). The Causes of Terrorism. *Comparative Politics*, 13, pp. 379–99.

Crenshaw, Martha. (1995). *Terrorism in Context*. University Park, Pa.: Pennsylvania State University Press.

Crenshaw, Martha. (2001). Why America? The Globalization of Civil War. *Current History*, 100, pp. 425–32.

Crenshaw, Martha. (2007). The Logic of Terrorism, in Mahan, Susan and Griset, Pamela L (eds), *Terrorism in Perspective*. Thousand Oaks, CA: Sage Publications, pp. 24–46.

Crenshaw, Martha. (2011). *Explaining Terrorism: Causes, Processes, and Consequences*. New York: Routledge.

Crosston, M. I. (2006). *Fostering Fundamentalism*. Aldershot, England; Burlington, VT: Ashgate.

Crotty, W. J. (2005). *Democratic Development & Political Terrorism: The Global Perspective*. Boston: Northeastern University Press.

Daniels, Ronald J., Patrick, Macklem and Kent, Roach (eds). (2001). *The Security of Freedom: Essays on Canada's Anti-Terrorism Bill*. Toronto: University of Toronto Press.

Danziger, Sheldon H. and Weinberg, Daniel H. (1994). The Historical Record: Trends in Family Income, Inequality, and Poverty, in Danziger, Sheldon H., Sandefur, Gary D. and Weinberg, Daniel. H. (eds), *Confronting Poverty: Prescriptions for Change*. New York: Russell Sage Foundation, pp. 18–50.

Darwish, Nonie. (2008). *Cruel and Usual Punishment: The Terrifying Global Implications of Islamic Law*. Nashville: Thomas Nelson Publishers.

Davies, T. R. (1973). Aggression, Violence, Revolution and War, in Jeanne N. Knutson (ed.), *Handbook of Political Psychology*. San Francisco: Jossey-Bass, pp. 234–60.

Davis, J. (2004). *The Global War on Terrorism: Assessing the American Response*. Hauppauge, N.Y.: Nova Science.

Dawisha, K. and Parrott, B. (1997). *Conflict, Cleavage, and Change in Central Asia and the Caucasus*. Cambridge, U.K.; New York, NY, USA: Cambridge University Press.

DeVault, Ryan Christopher. (2009). Mexico Political Collapse Could be on Horizon, According to U.S. Joint Forces Report. *Associated Content*, January 14. http://www.associatedcontent.com/article/1388155/mexico_political_collapse_could_be.html?cat=9.

Debiel, Tobias and Axel, Klein. (2002). *Fragile Peace: State Failure, Violence and Development in Crisis Regions*. London: Zed Books Ltd.

Dekmejian R. Hrair. (2007). *Spectrum of Terror*. Washington DC: CQ Press.

Deng, Francis M. and Zartman, William I. (2002). *A Strategic Vision for Africa: The Kampala Movement*. Brookings Institution Press, Washington.

De Waal, Alex. (1997). *Famine Crimes: Politics and the Disaster Relief Industry in Africa*. London: The International African Institute.

De Waal, Alex (ed.). (2002). *Demilitarizing the Mind: African Agendas for Peace and Security*. Trenton: Africa World Press.

Diaz, Elizabeth. (2008). Analysis: Mexico's Tijuana Cartel Weaker as Ex-Boss Comes Home. *Reuters*. March 14.

Dien, Mawillzzi. (2004). *Islamic Law: From Historical Foundations to Contemporary Practice*. Notre Dame: University of Notre Dame Press.

Dishman, Chris. (2001). Terrorism, Crime, and Transformation. *Studies in Conflict and Terrorism*, 24(1), pp. 43–58.

Docking, Tim. (2001). *Peacekeeping in Africa*. Special Report No. 66. Washington: United States Institute of Peace, 13 February.

Donno, Daniela and Russett, Bruce. (2004). Islam, Authoritarianism, and Female Empowerment: What are the Linkages? Typescript. Department of Political Science, Yale University.

Dosch, J. (2007). *The Changing Dynamics of Southeast Asian Politics*. Boulder, Colo.: Lynne Rienner Publishers.

Doyle, Michael and Sambanis, Nicholas. (2006). *Making War and Building Peace*. Princeton: Princeton University Press.

Duffield, Mark. (2001). *Global Governance and the New Wars: The Merging of Development and Security*. London: Zed Books.

Duffy, Helen. (2001). National Constitutional Compatibility and the International Criminal Court. *Duke Journal of Comparative and International Law*, 11(5), pp. 5–38.

Duffy, Helen. (2005). *The 'War on Terror' and the Framework of International Law*. Cambridge, UK: Cambridge University Press.

Durch, William J. (ed.). (1993). Part Four: Peacekeeping in Africa. In *The Evolution of UN Peacekeeping: Case Studies and Comparative Analysis*. New York: St. Martin's Press, pp. 315–434.

Easterly, William. (2000). *Can Institutions Resolve Conflict?* Washington, DC: The World Bank.

Ehrenfeld, Rachel. (2002). Funding Terrorism. *Confronting Terrorism*. Available on-line: http://library.lanl.gov/cgi-bin/getdoc?event=CT2002&document=30.

Elliot, D. D. and Menard, S. (1996). Delinquent Friends and Delinquent Behavior: Temporal and Developmental Patterns, in D. Hawkins (ed.), *Delinquency and Crime: Current Theories*. Cambridge: Cambridge University Press, pp. 28–67.

Enders, W. and Sandler, T. (2000). Is Transnational Terrorism becoming more Threatening? *Journal of Conflict Resolution*, 44, pp. 307–32.

Enders, W. and Sandler, T. (2002). Patterns of Transnational Terrorism, 1970–1999: Alternative Time-Series Estimates. *International Studies Quarterly*, 46(2), pp. 145–65.

Esty, Daniel C., Goldstone, Jack A., Gurr, Ted Robert, Harff, Barbara, Levy, Marc, Dabelko, Geoffrey D., Surko, Pamela T. and Unger, Alan N. (1998). *State Failure Task Force Report: Phase II Findings*. McLean, VA: Science Applications International Corporation. 31 July.

Eubank, William Lee and Weinberg, Leonard. (1994). Does Democracy Encourage Terrorism? *Terrorism and Political Violence*, 6(4), pp. 417–43.

Eubank, William Lee and Weinberg, Leonard. (1998). Terrorism and Democracy: What Recent Events Disclose. *Terrorism and Political Violence*, 10(1), pp. 108–18.

Eubank, William Lee and Weinberg, Leonard. (2001). Terrorism and Democracy: Perpetrators and Victims. *Terrorism and Political Violence*, 13(1), pp. 155–64.

Eyerman, Joe. (1998). Terrorism and Democratic States: Soft Targets or Accessible Systems. *International Interactions*, 24(2), pp. 151–70.

Fair, Christine and Shepherd, Bryan. (2006). Who Supports Terrorism? Evidence from Fourteen Muslim Countries. *Studies in Conflict and Terrorism*, 29, pp. 51–74.

Farah, Douglas. (2004). *Blood from Stones: The Secret Financial Network of Terror*. Broadway Books: New York, NY.

Fearon, James D. and David Laitin. (2004). Neotrusteeship and the Problem of Weak States. *International Security*, 28(4), pp. 5–43.

Fields, R., Elbedour, S. and Hein, F. A. (2003). The Palestinian Suicide Bomber, in C. E. Stout and K. Schwab (eds), *The Psychology of Terrorism*, 2. Westport, CT: Praeger, pp. 193–223.

Findlay, Trevor. (1996). Turning the Corner in Southeast Asia, in Michael E. Brown (ed.), *The International Dimensions of Internal Conflict*. Cambridge, Mass.: MIT Press, pp. 173–204.

Fitzgerald, E. V. K., Stewart, F. and Venugopal, R. (2006). *Globalization, Violent Conflict and Self-determination*. New York: Palgrave Macmillan.

Flannery, Daniel J. and Huff, Ronald C. (eds). (1999). *Youth Violence: Prevention, Intervention, and Social Policy*. Washington, D.C.: American Psychiatric Press.

Foot, R. (2004). *Human Rights and Counter-terrorism in America's Asia Policy*. Oxford; New York: Oxford University Press for the International Institute for Strategic Studies.

Foreign Policy and the Fund for Peace. (2011). *The Failed State Index*. New York, NY: Foreign Policy.

Francis, David J. (ed.). (2008). *Peace and Conflict in Africa*. London: Zed Books.

Francis, David J. (2006). *Uniting Africa: Building Regional Peace and Security Systems*. Aldershot: Ashgate.

Francis, David J. (ed.). (2005). *Civil Militia: Africa's Intractable Security Menace*. Aldershot: Ashgate, pp. 1–12.

Franke, Benedict. (2007). Enabling a Continent to Help Itself: U.S. Military Capacity Building and Africa's Emerging Security Structure. *Strategic Insights*, VI(1).

Franks, Jason. (2006). *Rethinking the Roots of Terrorism*. Palgrave Macmillian: New York: NY.

Freedman, Lawrence (ed.). (2002). *Superterrorism: Policy Responses*. Blackwell Publishing: Oxford, UK.

Galtung, Johan. (2005). *Pax Pacifica: Terrorism, the Pacific Hemisphere, Globalisation and Peace Studies*. London: Pluto Press.
Gambetta, D. (2005). *Making Sense of Suicide Missions*. Oxford; New York: Oxford University Press.
Ghosh, P. S. (1997). *Rivalry and Revolution in South and East Asia*. Aldershot, Hants, England; Brookfield, Vt., USA: Ashgate.
Giraldo, J. K. and Trinkunas, H. A. (2007). *Terrorism Financing and State Responses*. Stanford, Calif.: Stanford University Press.
—— (2009). Global Barometer Round One Official Data File. *Global Barometer*. http://www.jdsurvey.net/gbs/GBSData.jsp.
—— (2010). Global Corruption Perceptions Index. http://www.transparency.org/policy_research/surveys_indices/cpi/2010. Accessed August 2, 2011.
Goldstone, Jack A., Gurr, Ted Robert, Harff, Barbara, Levy, Marc A., Marshall, Monty G., Bates, Robert H., Epstein, David L., Kahl, Colin H., Surko, Pamela T., Ulfelder, John C. and Alan N. Unger. In consultation with Matthew Christenson, Geoffrey D. Dabelko, Daniel C. Esty and Parris, Thomas M. (2000). *State Failure Task Force Report: Phase III Findings*. McLean, VA: Science Applications International Corporation. 30 September.
Go, J. and Foster, A. L. (2003). *The American Colonial State in the Philippines: Global Perspectives*. Durham: Duke University Press.
Goldstone, Jack A. (2008). Pathways to State Failure. *Conflict Management and Peace Science*, 25, pp. 285–96.
Gompert, David C., Richardson, Courtney, Kugler, Richard L. and Bernard, Clifford H. (2005). Learning From Darfur. Building a Net-capable African Force to Stop Mass Killings. National Defense University Center for Technology and National Security Policy, July.
Goodhand, Jonathon. (2003). Enduring Disorder and Persistent Poverty: A Review of the Linkages Between War and Chronic Poverty. *World Development*, 31(3).
Goodson, Larry P. (2001). *Afghanistan's Endless War: State Failure, Regional Politics, and the Rise of the Taliban*. Seattle: University of Washington Press.
Gordon, B. K. (1966). *The Dimensions of Conflict in Southeast Asia*. Englewood Cliffs, N.J.: Prentice-Hall.
Greaves, Rose L. (1993). Themes in British Policy towards Afghanistan in its Relation to Indian Frontier Defense, 1798–1947. *Asian Affairs*, 24(1), pp. 30–46.
Gregg, Mills and Herbst, Jeffrey. (2007). Africa, Terrorism and AFRICOM, Royal United Services Institute for Defence and Security Studies Research (RUSI), 152(2), pp. 40–44.
Grzymala-Busse, Anna and Jones Luong, Pauline. (2002). Reconceptualizing the State: Lessons from Post-Communism. *Politics and Society*, 30(4), pp. 592–54.
Gurr, Ted Robert. (1970). *Why Men Rebel*. Princeton: Princeton University Press.
—— (1993). *Minorities at Risk: A Global View of Ethno-political Conflict*. Washington, DC: U.S. Institute of Peace Press.
Halliday, F. (2002). *Two Hours that Shook the World: September 11, 2001: Causes and Consequences*. London: Saqi Books.

Hamilton, Daniel (ed.). (2006). *Terrorism and International Relations*. Johns Hopkins University Press: Baltimore, MD.

Hegre, Havard, Ellingsen, Tanja, Gates, Scott and Gleditsch, Nils Petter. (2001). Toward a Democratic Civil Peace? Democracy, Political Change, and Civil War, 1816–1992. *American Political Science Review*, 95(1), pp. 33–48.

Hegre, Havard (ed.). (2004). Duration and Termination of Civil War [special issue]. *Journal of Peace Research*, 41(5).

Heiberg, M., O'Leary, B. and Tirman, J. (2007). *Terror, Insurgency, and the State: Ending Protracted Conflicts*. Philadelphia: University of Pennsylvania Press.

Herbst, Jeffrey. (1996). Responding to State Failure in Africa. *International Security*, 21(3), pp. 120–44.

Hippel, Karin von (ed.). (2002). The Roots of Terrorism: Probing the Myths in Lawrence Freedman. *Superterrorism: Policy Responses*, Special Issue of *Political Quarterly*, Blackwell Publishing, pp. 25–39.

Hironaka, Ann. (2005). *Neverending Wars: The International Community, Weak States, and the Perpetuation of Civil War*. Cambridge, MA: Harvard University Press.

Hirsch, John L. (2001). *Sierra Leone: Diamonds and the Struggle for Democracy* Boulder: Lynne Rienner.

Hirsch, John L. (2001). War in Sierra Leone. *Survival*, 43(3).

Hoffman, Bruce. (2006). *Inside Terrorism*. Columbia University Press: New York: NY.

Hoge, J. F. and Rose, G. (2001). *How did this Happen?: Terrorism and the New War* (1st ed.). New York: Public Affairs.

Holmes, Stephen. (1997). What Russia Teaches Us Now: How Weak States Threaten Freedom. *The American Prospect*, 8(33), pp. 30–39.

Homer-Dixon, Thomas F. (1999). *Environment, Scarcity and Violence*. Princeton, NJ: Princeton University Press.

Hopkins, E. (2008). Inequality, Happiness and Relative Concerns: What Actually is their Relationship? *Journal of Economic Inequality*, 6(4), pp. 351–72.

Horgan, John. (2003). The Search for a Terrorist Personality, in A. Silke (ed.), *Terrorists, Victims and Society: Psychological Perspectives on Terrorism and its Consequences*. New York: Wiley, pp. 3–27.

Horgan, John and Kurt, Braddock. (2012). *Terrorism Studies: A Reader*. New York: Routledge.

Hor, M. Y. M., Ramraj, V. V. and Roach, K. (2005). *Global Anti-terrorism Law and Policy*. Cambridge; New York: Cambridge University Press.

Horowitz, S. A. and Heo, U. (2003). *Conflict in Asia: Korea, China-Taiwan, and India- Pakistan*. Westport, Conn.: Praeger.

Howard, Tiffiany. (2008). Revisiting State Failure: Developing a Causal Model of State Failure Based Upon Theoretical Insight. *Civil Wars*, 10(2), pp. 125–46.

Howard, Tiffiany. (2010a). Failed States and the Spread of Terrorism in sub-Saharan Africa. *Studies in Conflict and Terrorism*, 33(11), pp. 960–88.

Howard, Tiffiany. (2010b). *The Tragedy of Failure: Evaluating State Failure and its Impact on the Spread of Refugees, Terrorism, and War*. Santa Barbara, CA: Praeger Security International-ABC/CLIO.

Howard, Tiffiany and Morris, Brendan. (2013). Pathways to State Failure: Greed or Grievance? Presented at the Western Political Science Association Annual Conference, March 25–April 2, 2013, Hollywood CA.

Howe, H. (2001). *Ambiguous Order: Military Forces in African States*. Boulder: Lynne Rienner.

Hubbard, David G. (1983). The Psychodynamics of Terrorism, in Yonah Alexander, T. Adeniran and R. A. Kilmarx (eds), *International Violence*. New York: Praeger, pp. 45–53.

Hübschle, A. (2007). Terrorist Financing in Southern Africa: Are We Making a Mountain Out of a Molehill? Institute for Security Studies, ISS Paper 132, January. http://www.iss.co.za/dynamic/administration/file_manager/file_links/PAPER132.PDF?link_id=14&slink_id=4094&link_type=12&slink_type=23&tmpl_id=3.

Hudson, Rex A. (1999). *The Sociology and Psychology of Terrorism: Who Becomes a Terrorist and Why?* Washington, DC: Library of Congress, Federal Research Division.

Human Development Reports-HDI Rankings. (2009). http://www. hdr.undp.org/en/statistics/. Accessed: March 23, 2010.

Huntington, Samuel. (1968). *Political Order in Changing Societies*. Yale University Press: Ithaca, NY.

—— (1991). *The Third Wave: Democratization in the Late Twentieth Century*. London: Oklahoma University Press.

—— (1996). *The Clash of Civilizations and the Remaking of World Order*. New York: Simon & Schuster.

Inglehart, Ronald. (1997). *Modernization and Postmodernization: Cultural, Economic, and Political Change in 43 Societies*. Princeton, NJ: Princeton University Press.

International Monetary Fund-Principal Global Indicators. (2009). http://www.principalglobalindicators.org/. Accessed: March 23, 2010.

Iqbal, Zaryab and Zorn, Christopher. (2003). The Political Economy of Assassination, 1946–2000. Paper prepared for presentation at the Annual Meeting of the Midwest Political Science Association, 3–6 April, Chicago.

Jackson, Robert H. and Rosberg, C. G. (1982). *Personal Rule in Black Africa*. Berkeley, CA: University of Berkeley Press.

Jackson, Robert H. (1993). *States in a Changing World*. Oxford: Carendon Press.

Jain, P., O'Leary, G. and Patrikeeff, F. (2002). *Crisis and Conflict in Asia: Local, Regional and International Responses*. Huntington, N.Y.: Nova Science Publishers.

Jalal, A. (2008). *Partisans of Allah: Jihad in south Asia*. Cambridge.: Harvard University Press.

Janke, P. (1994). *Ethnic and Religious Conflicts: Europe and Asia*. Aldershot, Hants, England; Brookfield, Vt., USA: Dartmouth.

Jenkins, Brian M. (1979). Terrorists at the Threshold, in E. Nobles Lowe and Harry D. Shargel (eds), *Legal and Other Aspects of Terrorism*. New York: Practicing Law Institute.

Johnson, Chalmers. (1978). Perspectives on Terrorism, reprinted in Walter Laqueur (ed.), *The Terrorism Reader*. New York: New American Library.

Johnson, R. (2005). *A Region in Turmoil: South Asian Conflicts since 1947*. London: Reaktion Books.

Johnson, Toni. (2010). Threat of Homegrown Islamist Terrorism. Council on Foreign Relations, December 10. Available on-line: http://www.cfr.org/terrorism/threat-homegrown-islamist-terrorism/p11509#p4.

Jones, Sidney. (2004). Indonesia Backgrounder: Jihad in Central Sulawesi. *International Crisis Group Report*, 74, February 3.

Kahl, Colin. (2006). *States, Scarcity, and Civil Strife in the Developing World*. Princeton: Princeton University Press.

Kahler, Miles. (2002). Networks and Failed States: September 11 and the Long Twentieth Century. Paper presented at the annual meeting of the American Political Science Association, 5–7 September, Boston.

Kaplan, David E. (2003). The Saudi Connection: How Billions in Oil Money Spawned a Global Terror Network. *US News and World Report*, December 15.

Kedourie, Elie. (1994). *Democracy and Arab Political Culture*. London: Frank Cass.

Keen, David. (2000). War and Peace: What's the Difference. *International Peacekeeping*, 7(4), pp. 1–22.

Keen, David. (2003). *The Economic Functions of Violence in Civil Wars*, Adelphi Paper 320, Oxford: OUP.

Kendall, Diana. (2005). *Sociology in Our Times*. New York: Thomson Wadsworth.

Khalilzad, Z., Lesser, I. O., United States, Project Air Force and Rand Corporation. (1998). *Sources of Conflict in the 21st Century: Regional Futures and U.S. Strategy*. Santa Monica, CA: Rand. Retrieved from http://www.rand.org/pubs/monographreports/MR897/.

Khashan, Hilal. (1997). The New World Order and the Tempo of Militant Islam. *British Journal of Middle East Studies*, 24(1), pp. 5–24.

King, Gary and Zheng, Langche. (2001). Improving Forecasts of State Failure. *World Politics*, 53(4), pp. 623–58.

King, P., King, S. and Antinolfi, G. (2005). *International Economics and International Economic Policy: A reader* (4th ed.). Boston: McGraw-Hill/Irwin.

Kingman, Kees. (2002). Demobilization, Reintegration and Peace-building in Africa. *International Peacekeeping*, 9, pp. 181–201.

Klare, Michael. (2002). *Resource Wars: The New Landscape of Global Conflict*. New York: Owl Books.

Klein, Malcom and Maxson, Cheryl. (2006). *Street Gang Patterns and Policies*. Oxford: Oxford University Press.

Koonings, Kees and Kruijt, Dirk. (2004). *Armed Actors: Organized Violence and State Failure in Latin America*. London: Zed Books.

Kramer, Martin. (1996). Islam and Democracy, in Martin Kramer (ed.), *Arab Awakening & Islamic Revival: The Politics of Ideas in the Middle East*. New Brunswick, N J: Transaction Publishers, pp. 265–78.

Krasner, Stephen D. (2004). Sharing Sovereignty: New Institutions for Collapsed and Failing States. *International Security*, 29(4), pp. 85–120.

Kreijen, Gerard. (2004). *State Failure, Sovereignty and Effectiveness*. Leiden, The Netherlands: Martinus Nijhoff Publishers.

Krueger, Alan B. (2003 May 29). Cash Rewards and Poverty alone do not Explain Terrorism. *New York Times*, p. C2.

Krueger, Alan B. and Maleckova, Jitka. (2002). Education, Poverty, Political Violence, and Terrorism: Is There a Causal Connection? NBER Working Paper 9074.

Krueger, Alan B. and Maleckova, Jitka. (2003). Education, Poverty, Political Violence and Terrorism: Is there a Causal Connection? *Journal of Economic Perspectives*, 112(4), pp. 725–53.

Kuegler, A. (2009). A Curse of Comparison? Evidence on Reference Groups for Relative Income Concerns. Policy Research Working Paper 4820, Development Economics Vice-Presidency The World Bank. Washington DC.

Laitin, David D. and Shapiro, Jacob N. (2007). The Sources of Terrorism: An Ecological and Organizational Perspective, in Philip Keefer and Norman Loayza (eds), *Terrorism and Economic Development*. Cambridge: Cambridge University Press.

Laqueur, W. (2003). *No End to War: Terrorism in the Twenty-first Century*. New York: Continuum.

—— (2008). Latinobarometer Dataset. http://www.latinobarometro.org/latino/latinobarometro.jsp.

Leatherwood, David G. (2001). Peacekeeping in West Africa. *Joint Force Quarterly*, 29 (Autumn–Winter 2001–2002), pp. 76–81.

LeBillon, Philippe. (2001). The Political Ecology of War: Natural Resources and Armed Conflicts. *Political Geography*, 20(5), pp. 561–84.

Lee, Alexander. (2011). Who Becomes a Terrorist? *World Politics*, 63(2), pp. 203–45.

Lennon, A. T. (2003). *The Battle for Hearts and Minds: Using Soft Power to Undermine Terrorist Networks*. Cambridge, Mass.: MIT Press.

Leung, K. and Tjosvold, D. (1998). *Conflict Management in the Asia Pacific: Assumptions and Approaches in Diverse Cultures*. Singapore; New York: J. Wiley & Sons, Asia.

Lewis, Bernard. (1987). The Shi'a in Islamic History, in M. Kramer (ed.), *Resistance and revolution*. Boulder, CO: Westview Press.

Li, Quan. (2005). Does Democracy Produce or Reduce Transnational Terrorist Incidents? *Journal of Conflict Resolution*, 49(2), pp. 278–97.

Li, Quan, and Schaub, Drew. (2004). Economic Globalization and Transnational Terrorism: A Pooled Time-series Analysis. *Journal of Conflict Resolution*, 48(2), pp. 230–58.

Lichbach, Mark. (1990). Will Rational People Rebel Against Inequality? Samson's Choice. *American Journal of Political Science*, 34 (November), pp. 1049–75.

Lim, T. G., Valencia, M. J. and United Nations University. (1990). *Conflict over Natural Resources in Southeast Asia and the Pacific*. Singapore; New York: Oxford University Press.

Linden, Edward. (2002). *World Terrorism*. Nova Science: New York, NY.

Long, David. (1990). *The Anatomy of Terrorism*. New York: Free Press.

—— (2006). *Measuring State Fragility*. U.S. Agency for International Development. Washington DC.

Lustick, Ian S. (2001). Thresholds of Opportunity and Barriers to Change in the Right-Sizing of States, in O'Leary, Brendan; Ian S. Lustick; and Thomas Callaghy (eds), *Right-Sizing the State: The Politics of Moving Borders*. Oxford: Oxford University Press.

MacQueen, Norrie. (2002). *United Nations Peacekeeping in Africa Since 1960*. New York: Longman.

Mahajan, R. (2002). *The New Crusade: America's War on Terrorism*. New York: Monthly Review Press.

Makinda, Samuel. (2006). African Thinkers and the Global Security Agenda, in Makumi Mwagiru and Okello Oculli (eds), *Rethinking Global Security: An African Perspective?* Nairobi: Heinrich Böll Foundation, pp. 21–37.

Malaquias, Assis. (2002). Peace Operations in Africa: Preserving the Brittle State? *Journal of International Affairs*, 55, pp. 415–40.

Margolin, Joseph. (1977). Psychological Perspectives in Terrorism, in Yonah Alexander and Seymour Maxwell Finger (eds), *Terrorism: Interdisciplinary Perspectives*. New York: John Jay, pp. 273–74.

Marten, Kimberly. (2006). Warlordism in Comparative Perspective. *International Security*, 31(3) Winter 2006/07, pp. 41–73.

Martin, R. C. (1987). Religious Violence in Islam: Towards an Understanding of the Discourse on Jihad in Modern Egypt, in P. Wilkinson and A. Stewarts (eds), *Contemporary Research on Terrorism*. U.K.: Aberdeen University Press.

Martin, J. R. (2002). *Defeating Terrorism*. Carlisle, PA: Strategic Studies Institute, U.S. Army War College.

Mazrui, Ali. (1977). *Africa's International Relations: The Diplomacy of Dependency and Change*. London: Heinemann.

Mbadinga, Moussounga I. (2001). The Inter-African Mission to Monitor the Implementation of the Bangui Agreements (MISAB). *International Peacekeeping*, 8, pp. 21–37.

McGarry, J. and O'Leary, B. (1993). *The Politics of Ethnic Conflict Regulation: Case Studies of Protracted Ethnic Conflicts*. London; New York: Routledge.

McGilvray, D. B. (2008). *Crucible of Conflict: Tamil and Muslim Society on the East Coast of Sri Lanka*. Durham: Duke University Press.
Menkhaus, Ken. (2002). Somalia: Next Up in the War on Terrorism, *CSIS Africa Notes*, 6, January. www.csis.org/component/option,com_csis_pubs/task,view/id,2139/type,3/. Accessed: February 12, 2009.
Millard, M. (2004). *Jihad in Paradise*. Armonk, N.Y.: M.E. Sharpe.
Miliken, Jennifer and Krause, Keith. (2002). State Failure, State Collapse, and State Reconstruction: Concepts, Lessons and Strategies. *Development and Change*, 33, pp. 753–74.
Miliken, Jennifer. (2003). *State Failure, Collapse and Reconstruction*. New York: Blackwell Publishing.
MIPT Terrorism Knowledge Database. Global Incidences of Terrorism by Country and Region, 2000–2006. (2006). http://www.terrorisminfo.mipt.org/incidentcalendar.asp. Accessed: April 23, 2010.
Moghadam, A. (2003). Palestinian Suicide Terrorism in the Second Intifada: Motivations and Organizational Aspects. *Studies in Conflict and Terrorism*, 26, pp. 65–92.
Moran, D. (2006; 2001). *Wars of National Liberation*. Washington, D.C.: Smithsonian Books.
Morgan, Robin. (2001). *The Demon Lover: The Roots of Terrorism*. New York: Washington Square Press.
Mudimbe, V. Y. (1988). *The Invention of Africa: Gnosis, Philosophy, and the Order of Knowledge*. London: James Curry.
Mudimbe, V. Y. (1994). *The Idea of Africa*. London: James Curry.
Mulikita, Njunga-Michael. (2000). Enhancing Human Security in Africa: What Role for the International Community? *Peacekeeping & International Relations*, 29, pp. 12–13, 16–18.
Murithi, Timothy. (2008). The African Union's Evolving Role in Peace Operations. *African Security Review*, 17(1), pp. 70–82.
Murithi, Tim. (2005). *The African Union: Pan-Africanism, Peacebuilding and Development*. Ashgate Publishing Ltd: Aldershot.
Muravchik, Joshua. (2001). Freedom and the Arab world. *The Weekly Standard* (31 December).
Murray, W. (2006). *Strategic Challenges for Counterinsurgency and the Global War on Terrorism*. Carlisle, PA: Strategic Studies Institute, U.S. Army War College.
Narine, S. (2002). *Explaining ASEAN: Regionalism in Southeast Asia*. Boulder, Colo.: Lynne Rienner Publishers.
Nathan, Ambassador S. R. (1997). Terrorism in the Asia-Pacific Region: Nature, Manifestation, Counter-Measures. Paper presented at the 11th Asia-Pacific Roundtable, Kuala Lumpur, June 5–8.
Nelles, W. C. (2003). *Comparative Education, Terrorism, and Human Security: From Critical Pedagogy to Peace-building?* (1st ed.). New York: Palgrave Macmillan.

Newman, Edward. (2007). Weak States, State Failure and Terrroism. *Terrorism and Political Violence*, 19(4), pp. 463–88.
Nhema, A. and Zeleza, P. T. (2008a). *The Resolution of African Conflicts: The Management of Conflict Resolution & Post-Conflict Reconstruction.* James Currey: London.
Nhema, A. and Zeleza, P. T. (2008b). *The Roots of African Conflicts: The Causes and Costs.* Oxford.
Nir, Ori. (2005). Saudi Jihadists Play a growing Part in Iraq Insurgency, U.S. Generals Say, *Jewish Daily Forward*, June 17. http://www.forward.com/articles/saudi-jihadists-play-a-growing-part-in-iraq-insurg/. Accessed: December 7, 2008.
O'Hanlon, Michael E. (2002). Saving Lives with Force: An Agenda for Expanding the ACRI. *Journal of International Affairs*, 55, pp. 289–300.
Okumu, Wafula. (2003). Humanitarian International NGOs and African Conflicts. *International Peacekeeping*, 10, pp. 120–37.
Oliker, O., Szayna, T. S., Arroyo Center, Rand Corporation and United States. (2003). *Faultlines of Conflict in Central Asia and the South Caucasus: Implications for the U.S. Army.* Santa Monica, CA: RAND Arroyo Center. Retrieved from http://www.rand.org/pubs/monograph_reports/MR1598/.
Ollapally, D. M. (2008). *The Politics of Extremism in South Asia.* Cambridge, UK; New York: Cambridge University Press.
Olonisakin, Funmi. (2000). *Reinventing Peacekeeping in Africa.* Boston: Kluwer Law International.
Olson, Mancur. (1965). *The Logic of Collective Action.* Cambridge, MA: Harvard University Press.
—— (1982). *The Rise and Decline of Nations: Economic Growth, Stagflation, and Social Rigidities.* New Haven, CT: Yale University Press.
—— (1993). Dictatorship, Democracy, and Development. *American Political Science Review*, 87, pp. 567–76.
—— (2000). The Criminal Metaphor. *Power and Prosperity.* New Haven, CT: Yale University Press.
Oots, Kent Layne and Wiegele, Thomas C. (1985). Terrorist and Victim: Psychiatric and Physiological Approaches from a Social Science Perspective. *Terrorism: An International Journal*, 8(1), pp. 1–32.
Orfield, G. and Lee, C. (2005). *Why Segregation Matters: Poverty and Educational Inequality.* Cambridge, MA: Harvard University. The Civil Rights Project.
Ortiz, Roman. (2002). Insurgent Strategies in the Post-Cold War: The Case of the Revolutionary Armed Forces of Colombia. *Studies in Conflict and Terrorism*, 25, pp. 127–43.
—— (2003). Diaspora. *Semana*, November 30, Bogota, Colombia.
Ottaway, Marina. (2002). Rebuilding Institutions in Collapsed States. *Development and Change*, 33(5), pp. 1001–1023.
Pakenham, Thomas. (1991). *The Scramble for Africa: 1876–1912.* London: Abacus.

Palmer, M. and Palmer, P. (2004). *At the Heart of Terror: Islam, Jihadists, and America's War on Terrorism*. Lanham, MD: Rowman & Littlefield Publishers.

Passas, N. (2006). Commodities and Terrorist Financing: Focus on Diamonds. *European Journal on Criminal Policy and Research*, 12(1), pp. 1–33.

—— (2002). Illicit Diamonds, Conflict and Terrorism: The Role of U.S. Agencies in Fighting the Conflict Diamond Trade. 13 February, http://hsgac.senate.gov/021302witness.htm.

Patrick, S. (2006). Weak States and Global Threats: Fact or Fiction? *Washington Quarterly*, 29(2), pp. 27–53.

Peebles, P. (2006). *The History of Sri Lanka*. Westport, Conn.: Greenwood Press.

Peimani, H. (2003). *Falling Terrorism and Rising Conflicts: The Afghan "Contribution" to Polarization and Confrontation in West and South Asia*. Westport, Conn.: Praeger.

—— (2009). *Conflict and Security in Central Asia and the Caucasus*. Santa Barbara, Calif.: Abc-Clio.

Peters, J. E., United States, Project Air Force and Rand Corporation. (2006). *War and Escalation in South Asia*. Santa Monica, CA: Rand.

Pettigrew, J. (1995). *The Sikhs of the Punjab: Unheard Voices of State and Guerilla Violence*. London; Atlantic Highlands, N.J.: Zed Books.

Piazza, James A. (2006). Rooted in Poverty?: Terrorism, Poor Economic Development and Social Cleavages. *Terrorism and Political Violence*, 18, pp. 159–77.

—— (2007). Draining the Swamp: Democracy Promotion, State Failure and Terrorism in 19 Middle Eastern States. *Studies in Conflict and Terrorism*, 30, pp. 521–39.

Political Instability Task Force. *Episodes of Political Instability/State Failure, 1995–2009*. http://globalpolicy.gmu.edu/pitf/. Accessed: April 21, 2010.

Pratap, A. (2003). *Island of Blood: Frontline Reports from Sri Lanka, Afghanistan and Other South Asian Flashpoints*. New York: Penguin Books.

Prober, Joshua. (2005). Accounting for Terror: Debunking the Paradigm of Inexpensive Terrorism. Washington Institute for Near East Policy. PolicyWatch #1041.

Putnam, Robert. (1993). *Making Democracy Work: Civic Traditions in Modern Italy*. Princeton, NJ: Princeton University Press.

Rabasa, Angel, Boraz, Steven, Chalk, Peter, Cragin, Kim, Karasik, Theofore W., Moroney, Jennifer D. P., O'Brien, Kevin A. and Peters, John E. (2007). *Ungoverned Territories: Understanding and Reducing Terrorism Risks*. RAND Corporation: Santa Monica, CA.

Rapoport, David. (1999). Terrorism. In *Encyclopedia of Violence, Peace, and Conflict*, Volume 3. San Diego: Academic Publishers, pp. 497–510.

Rapoport, David C. (2001). The Fourth Wave: September 11 in the History of Terrorism. *Current History*, pp. 419–24.

Rapoport, David C. (2004). The Four Waves of Terrorism, in Cronin, Audrey and Ludes, James (eds), *Attacking Terrorism*. Georgetown University. Center for Peace and Security Studies.

Reno, William. (1995). *Corruption and State Politics in Sierra Leone*. New York NY: Cambridge University Press.

Reno, William. (1999). *Warlord Politics in African States*. Boulder CO: Lynne Rienner.

Reveron, D. S. and Murer, J. S. (2006). *Flashpoints in the War on Terrorism*. New York: Routledge.

Rice, Susan E. and Patrick, Stewart. (2008). *Index of State Weakness in the Developing World*. Foreign Policy; Washington, DC.: Brookings.

Roberts, J. J. (2003). *The Origins of Conflict in Afghanistan*. Westport, Conn.: Praeger.

Rotberg, Robert. (1999). *Creating Peace in Sri Lanka: Civil War and Reconciliation*. Washington DC: Brookings Institution Press.

Rotberg, Robert. (2002). The New Nature of Nation-state Failure. *The Washington Quarterly*, 25(3), pp. 85–96.

Rotberg, Robert (ed.). (2003). *State Failure and State Weakness in a Time of Terror*. Cambridge, Mass.: World Peace Foundation; Washington, D.C.: Brookings Institution Press.

Rotberg, Robert (ed.). (2004). *When States Fail: Causes and Consequences*. Cambridge, Mass.: World Peace Foundation; Washington, D.C.: Brookings Institution Press.

Roth, M. P. and Sever, M. (2007). The Kurdish Workers Party (PKK) as Criminal Syndicate: Funding Terrorism through Organized Crime, a Case Study. *Studies in Conflict & Terrorism*, 30(10), pp. 901–20.

Rubin, Barry M. (2002). *The Tragedy of the Middle East*. Cambridge, UK: Cambridge University Press.

Rubin, Barry M. and Rubin, Judith C. (2008). *Chronologies of Modern Terrorism*. Armonk, N.Y.: M.E. Sharpe.

Rubin, Barnett R. (2002). *The Fragmentation of Afghanistan: State formation and Collapse in the International System*. 2nd edition. New Haven: Yale University Press.

Rumer, B. Z. (2002). *Central Asia: A Gathering Storm?* Armonk, N.Y.: M.E. Sharpe.

Sachs, Jeffrey D. and Warner, Andrew M. (1995). Natural Resource Abundance and Economic Growth. NBER Working Paper 5318, National Bureau of Economic Research, Cambridge, MA.

Schmid, Alex. (1992). Terrorism and Democracy. *Terrorism and Political Violence*, 4(4), pp. 14–25.

Seifer, Kathryn. (2006). *How Children Become Violent: Keeping Your Kids out of Gangs, Terrorist Organizations, and Cults*. Boston, MA: Acanthus Publishing.

Sen, Amartya. (1999). *Development as Freedom*. Oxford: Oxford University Press.

Shanty, Frank and Mishra, Patit Paban. (2007). *Organized Crime: From Trafficking to Terrorism*. Vol. 1. Santa Barbara, CA: ABC-CLIO.

Sidel, J. T. (2006). *Riots, Pogroms, Jihad: Religious Violence in Indonesia*. Ithaca: Cornell University Press.

Sievers, A. M. (1974). *The Mystical World of Indonesia: Culture & Economic Development in Conflict*. Baltimore: Johns Hopkins University Press.

Silber, Jacques and Verme, Paolo. (2010). Distributional Change, Reference Groups and the Measurement of Relative Deprivation, Chapter 9, in *Research on Economic Inequality*, Volume 18, *Studies in Applied Welfare Analysis*, J. Bishop (ed.), pp. 197–217.

Silber, Jacques and Verme, Paolo. (2012). Relative Deprivation, Reference Groups and the Assessment of Standard of Living. *World Bank Working Papers*. Available: http://elibrary.worldbank.org/content/workingpaper/10.1596/1813–9450–5930. Silke, Andrew. (2003). Becoming a Terrorist, in A. Silke (ed.), *Terrorists, Victims and Society: Psychological Perspectives on Terrorism and its Consequences*. New York: Wiley, pp. 29–53.

—— (2003). The Psychology of Suicidal Terrorism, in A. Silke (ed.), *Terrorists, Victims and Society: Psychological Perspectives on Terrorism and its Consequences*. New York: Wiley, pp. 93–108.

Sinclair, A. (2003). *An Anatomy of Terror: A History of Terrorism*. London: Macmillan.

Singh, G. (2000). *Ethnic Conflict in India: A Case-study of Punjab*. New York: St. Martin's Press.

Sirrs, J. R., Abedin, M., Heffelfinger, C. and Jamestown Foundation. (2004). *Unmasking Terror: A Global Review of Terrorist Activities*. Washington, D.C.: Jamestown Foundation.

Skocpol, Theda. (1979). *States and Social Revolutions: A Comparative Analysis of France, Russia, and China*. New York and Cambridge: Cambridge University Press.

Smith, Stephen C. (2005). *Ending Global Poverty: A Guide to What Works*. New York: Palgrave Macmillan.

Solimano, Andres. (2004). Political Violence and Economic Development in Latin America: Issues and Evidence. *Serie Macroeconomíadel Desarrollo/ Macroeconomics of Development*, No. 30, Economic Development Division, United Nations, Cepal-Eclac, August.

Sorli, Miriam, Gleditsch, Nils Peter and Strand, Havard. (2005). Why is there so much Conflict in the Middle East. *Journal of Conflict Resolution*, 49(1), pp. 141–65.

Spencer, Jonathan (ed.). (1990). *Sri Lanka: History and the Roots of Conflict*. New York: Routledge.

Sperling, J., Malik, Y. K. and Louscher, D. J. (1998). *Zones of Amity, Zones of Enmity: The Prospects for Economic and Military Security in Asia*. Leiden; Boston, Mass: Brill.

Sri Raman, J. (2004). *Flashpoint how the U.S., India and Pakistan brought us to the Brink of Nuclear War*. Monroe, Me.: Common Courage Press.

State Failure Task Force. (2003). *Consolidated State Failure Events*, http://cidcm.umd.edu/stfail.Number of international terrorist incidents. Accessed: April 23, 2010.

Takeyh, Ray and Nikolas Gvosdev. (2002). Do Terrorist Networks Need a Home? *The Washington Quarterly*, 25(3), pp. 97–108.

Taylor, Ian and Williams, Paul (eds). (2004). *Africa in International Politics: External Involvement on the Continent*. New York Routledge.

Taylor M. and Horgan J. (eds). (2000). *The Future of Terrorism*. London: Frank Cass.

Thee, M. and California State University, Los Angeles. (1982). *Towards a New Conceptualization of Neutrality: A Strategy for Conflict Resolution in Asia*. Los Angeles, Calif.: Center for the Study of Armament and Disarmament, California State University.

Thomas, R. G. C. (1992). *Perspectives on Kashmir: The Roots of Conflict in South Asia*. Boulder, Colo.: Westview Press.

Thrupkaew, Noy. (2004). Follow the (Saudi) Money. *American Prospect*, 15(8).

Tikusis, P. (2009). On the Relationship between Weak States and Terrorism. *Behavioral Sciences of Terrorism and Political Aggression*, 1(1), pp. 66–79.

Tilak, Jandhyala B. G. (2002). Education and Poverty. *Journal of Human Development*, 3(2), pp. 191–207.

Tilly, Charles. (1978). *From Mobilization to Revolution*. Reading, Massachusetts: Addison-Wesley.

Tilly, Charles. (1992). *Coercion, Capital, and European States*. Cambridge, MA: Blackwell Press.

Tilly, Charles. (2004). Social Movements and Democratisation, in Anna-Maija Castrén, Markku Lonkila and Matti Peltonen (eds), *Between Sociology and History. Essays on Microhistory, Collective Action, and Nation-Building*. Helsinki: SKS/Finnish Literature Society.

Tirman, J. (2004). *The Maze of Fear: Security and Migration after 911*. New York: New Press.

Tunde, Zack-Williams; Diane Frost; and Alex Thomson (eds). (2002). *Africa in Crisis: New Challenges and Possibilities*. London, Pluto Press.

Urdal, Henrik. (2006). A Clash of Generations? Youth Bulges and Political Violence. *International Studies Quarterly*, 50(3), pp. 607–30.

—— (2008). Population, Resources and Violent Conflict: A Sub-national Study of India 1956 2002. *Journal of Conflict Resolution*, 52(4), pp. 590–617.

UNHCR Global Report. (2010). United Nations Publications. http://www.unhcr.org/gr10/index.html#/home. Accessed: August 12, 2011.

United States Congress House Committee on Foreign Affairs Subcommittee on the Middle East and South Asia. (2008). Counternarcotics strategy and police training in Afghanistan: Hearing before the subcommittee on the Middle East and South Asia of the committee on foreign affairs, house of representatives, one hundred tenth congress, first session, October 4, 2007. Washington: U.S. G.P.O. Retrieved from http://purl.access.gpo.gov/GPO/LPS90865.

United States Congress House Committee on Foreign Affairs Subcommittee on the Middle East and South Asia. (2008). Political crises in South Asia: Pakistan, Bangladesh, Sri Lanka and Nepal: Hearing before the subcommittee on the Middle East and South Asia of the committee on foreign affairs, house of representatives, one hundred tenth congress, first session, August 1, 2007. Washington: U.S. G.P.O. Retrieved from http://purl.access.gpo.gov/GPO/LPS90864.

United States Congress House Committee on International Relations—Subcommittee on Asia and the Pacific. (2004). The challenge of terrorism in Asia and the Pacific: Joint hearing before the subcommittee on Asia and the Pacific and the subcommittee on international terrorism, nonproliferation and human rights of the committee on international relations, house of representatives, one hundred eighth congress, first session, October 29, 2003. Washington: U.S. G.P.O. Retrieved from http://purl.access.gpo.gov/GPO/LPS44653.

United States Congress House Committee on International Relations—Subcommittee on Asia and the Pacific. (2004). Developments in Burma: Joint hearing before the subcommittee on Asia and the Pacific and the subcommittee on international terrorism, nonproliferation, and human rights of the committee on international relations, house of representatives, one hundred eighth congress, second session, March 25, 2004. Washington: U.S. G.P.O. Retrieved from http://purl.access.gpo.gov/GPO/LPS54354.

United States Congress House Committee on International Relations—Subcommittee on International Terrorism, Nonproliferation, and Human Rights. (2004). Human rights in Burma: Fifteen years post military coup: Joint hearings before the subcommittee on international terrorism, nonproliferation and human rights and the subcommittee on Asia and the Pacific of the committee on international relations, house of representatives, one hundred eighth congress, first session, October 1 and 2, 2003. Washington: U.S. G.P.O. Retrieved from http://purl.access.gpo.gov/GPO/LPS44397.

United States Department of State—Office of the Coordinator for Counterterrorism Country Reports on Terrorism—Chapter 8—Foreign Terrorist Organizations April 2009. http://www.state.gov/s/ct/rls/crt/2009/65275.htm. Accessed: May 23, 2010.

United States Department of State. (2003). Patterns of Global Terrorism. http://www.state.gov/s/ct/rls/pgtrpt/2003/33777.htm. Accessed: April 23, 2010.

United States Department of State. (2003). Patterns of Global Terrorism. http://www.state.gov/s/ct/rls/pgtrpt/2003/33777.htm. Accessed: April 23, 2010.

Urdal, Henrik and Bo, Malmberg. (2008). *Demography and the Changing Global Geography of Internal Armed Conflict*. Mimeo: PRIO, Oslo.

Urdal, Henrik and Hoelscher, Kristian. (2009). Urban Youth Bulges and Social Disorder: An Empirical Study of Asian and Sub-Saharan African Cities. World Bank Policy Research Working Paper 5110. Washington, D.C.: World Bank.

Van Creveld, Martin. (1999). *The Rise and Decline of the State*. Cambridge: Cambridge University Press.

Varshney, A. (2002). *Ethnic Conflict and Civic Life: Hindus and Muslims in India*. New Haven, Conn.: Yale University Press.

Vaughn, Bruce, Chanlett-Avery, Emma, Cronin, Richard, Manyin, Mark and Niksch, Larry. (2005). *Terrorism in Southeast Asia*. Washington DC: The Library of Congress-Congressional Research Service: Foreign Affairs, Defense and Trade Division. (February 7). http://www.fas.org/sgp/crs/terror/RL31672.pdf/. Accessed: May 23, 2010.

Verma, V. (2002). *Malaysia, State and Civil Society in Transition*. Boulder, Colo.: Lynne Rienner.

Walker, Clive. (1992). *The Prevention of Terrorism in British Law*. Second edition. Manchester, G.B. and New York: Manchester University Press and St. Martin's Press.

Walker, Iain and Smith, Heather J. (2001). *Relative Deprivation: Specification, Development, and Integration*. Cambridge: Cambridge University Press.

Weiner, Myron. (1996). Bad Neighbors, Bad Neighborhoods, an Inquiry into the Causes of Refugee Flows. *International Security*, 21(l), pp. 5–42.

Wickramasinghe, Nira. (2006). *Sri Lanka in the Modern Age – A History of Contested Identities*. Honolulu: University of Hawai'i Press.

Widner, Jennifer A. (1995). States and Statelessness in Late Twentieth-century Africa. *Daedalus*, 124(3), pp. 129–53.

Wilkinson, Paul. (2000). The Strategic Implications of Terrorism, in M. L. Sondhi (ed.), *Terrorism and Political Violence: A Sourcebook*. India: Har-anand Publications, pp. 19–49.

Wilson, A. J. (1988). *The Break-up of Sri Lanka: The Sinhalese-tamil Conflict*. Honolulu: University of Hawaii Press.

Windsor, Jennifer L. (2003). Promoting Democratization can Combat Terrorism. *Washington Quarterly*, 26, pp. 43–58.

Winslow, Deborah and Woost, Michael D. (eds). (2004). *Economy, Culture and Civil War in Sri Lanka*. Bloomington: Indiana University Press.

Wishnick, E. (2002). *Growing U.S. Security Interests in Central Asia*. Carlisle, PA: Strategic Studies Institute, U.S. Army War College.

Wishnick, E. (2004). *Strategic Consequences of the Iraq War*. Carlisle Barracks, PA: Strategic Studies Institute, U.S. Army War College.

WOLA/Center of Inter-American Studies and Programs of the Instituto Tecnológico Autónomo de México (ITAM). (2007). Transnational Youth Gangs in Central America, Mexico, and the United States, Executive Summary, February.

Wolseth, Jon and Babb, Florence. (2008). Youth and Cultural Politics in Latin America, in *Latin American Perspectives*, 35(4), pp. 3–14.

Woltering, Robert A. F. L. (2002). The Roots of lslamist Popularity. *Third World Quarterly*, 23(6), pp. 1133–43.

World Bank. (2009). *World Development Report 2009*. Oxford: Oxford University Press.

World Bank—World Development Indicators. (2009). http://www.data.worldbank.org/indicator. Accessed: March 24, 2010.

World Health Organization. (2002). *World Report on Violence and Health*. Geneva: World Health Organization.

Young, Crawford. (2002). Deciphering Disorder in Africa: Is Identity the Key? *World Politics*, (54) July, pp. 532–57.

Zacher, M. W. and Milne, R. S. (1974). *Conflict and Stability in Southeast Asia* (1st ed.). Garden City, N.Y.: Anchor Press.

Zack-Williams, Tunde, Frost, Diane and Thompson, Alex (eds). (2002). *Africa in Crisis*. Pluto Press: London.

Zanini, Michele. (1999). Middle Eastern Terrorism and Netwar. *Studies in Conflict and Terrorism*, 22 (3), pp. 247–56.

Zartman, I. William. (1995). *Collapsed States: The Disintegration and Restoration of Legitimate Authority*. Boulder, CO: Lynne Rienner.

Zartman, I. William. (2004). Posing the Problem of State Collapse, in Zartman, I. William (ed.), *Collapsed States: The Disintegration and Restoration of Legitimate Authority*. Boulder CO: Lynne Rienner.

Appendices

Appendix A Chapter 2, Descriptive statistics

Variable	Observations	Mean	Std. Dev.	Min	Max
Violence	23993	.1896803	.3920563	0	1
Security1	24290	.7142445	1.154027	0	4
Security2	24310	.2035788	.6049248	0	4
Presence1	24207	.4823398	.907163	0	3
Presence2	24206	.1816905	.5812226	0	3
Presence3	20736	1.041667	1.104477	0	4
Corrupt1	19685	1.173787	.9253391	0	3
Corrupt2	19960	1.248697	.8737496	0	3
Corrupt3	20562	1.278134	.9010785	0	3
Corrupt4	20271	1.352721	.8658986	0	3
Corrupt5	20280	1.349162	.8793982	0	3
Legitimate1	22219	1.530492	.9100338	0	3
Legitimate2	22187	1.541308	.9762087	0	3
Goods1	25347	1.134296	1.381171	0	4
Goods2	24568	2.563538	1.256931	0	4
Goods3	25048	2.45297	1.045318	0	4
Property	23654	2.040374	.6894866	0	5
Gender	25397	.4998622	.5000098	0	1
Persecon	25308	2.606211	1.189938	1	5
Education	25305	3.117803	1.995429	0	9
Ethnic	22000	3.161864	.9888373	1	5
Urban	25397	.618262	.4858224	0	1

Appendix B Chapter 2, Marginal change in variables of significance—support for political violence

Variable	Marginal Change	Percentage Change	Support for Hypotheses
Security2	.028	2.8	Yes
Presence3	.015	1.5	No
Corrupt1	.029	2.9	Yes
Legitimate2	-.010	-1	Yes
Goods2	-.008	-0.8	Yes
Goods3	-.009	-0.9	Yes
Property	.021	2.1	Yes
PersEcon	.009	0.9	No
Education	.008	0.8	Yes*
Ethnic	-.012	-1.2	No

Note: The marginal effect indicates an increase in the predicted probability of the dependent variable according to one standard deviation change in the independent variable, holding all other variables constant.

* In the case of this analysis, education can be interpreted in either direction as a variable concept that supports the hypothesis.

Appendix C Chapter 2, Control variables

1. Education
Question: What is the highest level of education you have completed?
Variable Label: Education of respondent
Values: 0-9, 98-99, -1
Value Labels: 0=No formal schooling, 1=Informal schooling (including Koranic schooling), 2=Some primary schooling, 3=Primary school completed, 4=Some secondary school/ High school, 5=Secondary school completed/High school, 6=Post-secondary qualifications, other than university e.g. a diploma or degree from a technical/polytechnic/college, 7=Some university, 8=University completed, 9=Post-graduate, 98=Refused to Answer, 99=Don't Know, -1=Missing Data
* *In order to estimate the model, I code the values of "98" and "99" as Missing Data*
2. Personal Economic/Living Conditions
Question: In general, how would you describe: your own present living conditions?
Variable Label: Your present living conditions
Values: 1-5, 9, 998, -1
Value Labels: 1=Very bad, 2=Fairly bad, 3=Neither good nor bad, 4=Fairly good, 5=Very good, 9=Don't Know, 998=Refused to Answer, -1=Missing Data
* *In order to estimate the model, I code the values of "9" and "98" as Missing Data*

Appendix C *Concluded*

3. Gender
Question Number: Q101
Question: Respondent's gender
Variable Label: Gender of respondent
Values: 1, 2
Value Labels: 1=Male, 2=Female
Note: Answered by interviewer.
* *In order to estimate the model, I label the values so that "0" equals male and "1" equals female*
4. Ethnic Group's Economic Status
Question: Think about the condition of ___________ [respondent's identity group] Are their economic conditions worse, the same as, or better than other groups in this country?
Variable Label: Ethnic group's economic conditions
Values: 1–5, 7, 9, 98, -1
Value Labels: 1=Much Better, 2=Better, 3=Same, 4=Worse, 5=Much Worse, 7=Not Applicable, 9=Don't Know, 98=Refused to Answer, -1=Missing Data
Note: Interviewer probed for strength of opinion. If respondent had not identified a group on question 79, this question was marked as "Not Applicable."
* *In order to estimate the model, I code the values of "7," "9," and "98" as Missing Data*
5. Respondent is From an Urban or Rural Area
Question: Do you come from a rural or urban area?
Variable Label: Interviewer urban or rural
Values: 1, 2
Value Labels: 1=Rural, 2=Urban
Note: Answered by interviewer.
* *In order to estimate the model, I label the values so that "0" equals rural and "1" equals urban*

Appendix D Chapter 3, Descriptive statistics

Variable	Observations	Mean	Std. Dev.	Min	Max
Violence1a	5901	.114	.317	0	1
Violence1b	5791	.138	.345	0	1
Violence1c	5452	.238	.426	0	1
Violence1d	5267	.235	.424	0	1
Violence1e	5027	.152	.359	0	1
Violence2	5013	.577	.494	0	1
Violence3	6373	.143	.350	0	1
Security1	7979	1.99	.721	1	4
Presence1	7974	2.72	1.11	0	4
Presence2	7800	2.51	1.43	0	4
Presence3	7984	2.25	1.14	0	4
Presence4	7847	1.81	1.40	0	4
Presence 5	7700	1.43	1.16	0	4
Trustt1	7616	2.59	1.12	1	4
Trustt2	7603	2.58	1.09	1	4
Trustt3	7582	2.78	1.09	1	4
Trustt4	7737	2.42	1.10	1	4
Trustt5	7239	3.13	1.01	1	4
Legitimate1	6439	2.32	1.17	1	4
Corrupt1	7547	2.64	.830	1	4
Goods1	5342	2.54	1.04	1	4
Autocracy1	6451	.057	.233	0	1
Autocracy2	6258	.1011	.302	0	1
EconDev1	6451	.574	.494	0	1
EconDev2	7877	2.86	.894	1	4
Religion1	7616	2.05	.995	1	4
Religion2	6820	2.37	1.13	1	4
Education	8098	3.75	1.73	1	7
Gender	8119	.492	.499	0	1
Employment	8054	.479	.499	0	1
Age	6799	35.9	13.1	18	90

Appendix E Chapter 3, Control variables

1. Education
Question Number: Q703
Variable Label: Education of respondent
Value Labels: 1=Illiterate, 2=Elementary, 3=Primary, 4=Secondary, 5=College Diploma (Two Years), 6=Bachelors, 7=Masters or higher, 97=Not Clear
* *In order to estimate the model, I code the value of "97" as Missing Data*
2. Employment Status
Question Number: Q704
Variable Label: Employment Status of Respondent
Value Labels: 1=Employed, 2=Not Employed, 97=Not Clear
* *In order to estimate the model, I label the values so that "0" equals not employed and "1" equals employed. I then code the value of "97" as Missing Data*
3. Gender
Question Number: Q702
Question: Respondent's gender
Variable Label: Gender of respondent
Values: 1, 2
Value Labels: 1=Male, 2=Female
* *In order to estimate the model, I label the values so that "0" equals male and "1" equals female*
4. Age
Question Number: Q701
Question: Respondent's age
Variable Label: Age of respondent
Values: 18-90
Value Labels: N/A

Appendix F Chapter 4, Descriptive statistics

Variable	Observations	Mean	Std. Dev.	Min	Max
Violence	7717	.0218	.1125	0	1
Trust1	7456	2.976	.8429	1	4
Trust2	7404	2.889	.8275	1	4
Trust3	7350	2.832	.8229	1	4
Trust4	7521	2.936	.7540	1	4
Security1	7719	2.126	.6129	0	3
Security2	6702	.0503	.2185	0	1
Legitimate1	7090	2.169	.8827	0	3
Corrupt1	5930	2.242	.8875	1	4
Corrupt2	6765	2.332	.8593	1	4
Goods1	7552	2.610	1.119	0	4
Goods2	7674	2.823	.8609	0	4
Goods3	7614	2.234	1.313	0	4
Presence1	7712	1.646	.8811	1	3
Presence2	7688	1.395	.7499	1	3
Age	7774	.4969	.5000	0	1
Gender	7768	41.72	14.97	17	95
PersEcon	7769	4.992	2.315	1	10
Education	7596	2.737	.8714	1	4
Urban	5164	3.580	1.539	1	6

Appendix G Chapter 4, Control variables

1. Education
Question Number: se005
Variable Label: Education
Value Labels: 1=No formal education, 2=Incomplete primary/elementary, 3=Complete primary/elementary, 4=Incomplete secondary/high school: technical/vocational type, 5=Complete secondary/high school: technical/vocational type, 6=Incomplete secondary/high school, 7=Complete secondary/high school, 8=Some University Education, 9=University Education Completed, 10=Post-graduate Degree, 99=Decline to answer
* *In order to estimate the model, I code the value of "99" as Missing Data*

Appendix G *Concluded*

2. Economic Status
Question Number: seii9a
Variable Label: Does the total income of your home allow you to satisfactorily cover your needs
Value Labels: 0=Not Applicable, 1=Covers the needs well, we can save, 2=Covers the needs alright, without much difficulty, 3=Does not cover the needs, there are difficulties, 4=Does not cover the needs, there are great difficulties, 7=Do not understand the question, 8=Can't Choose, 9=Decline to Answer
* *In order to estimate the model, I code the values "0," "7," "8," and "9" as Missing Data*
3. Gender
Question Number: se002
Question: Respondent's gender
Variable Label: Gender of respondent
Values: 1, 2
Value Labels: 1=Male, 2=Female
* *In order to estimate the model, I label the values so that "0" equals male and "1" equals female.*
4. Age
Question Number: se003a
Question: Respondent's age
Variable Label: Age of respondent
Values: 17-95, 99=Refused to Answer
Value Labels: N/A
* *In order to estimate the model, I code the value of "99" as Missing Data*
5. Respondent is From an Urban or Rural Area
Question Number: irii4
Variable Label/Question: Interviewer: Which of the following levels within the country does the respondent live?
Value Labels: 1=Capital of megacity, 2=Regional center or other major city, 3=Small city or town, 4=Village or countryside, 5=Suburb, 6=Remote Area
Note: Answered by interviewer.
* *In order to estimate the model, I recode the variable so that 1=Capital or megacity, 2=Regional center or other major city, 3=Small city or town, 4=Suburb, 5=Village or countryside, 6=Remote Area.*
* *I made the decision to switch the values for Suburb and Village or countryside due to the belief that that was a coding area. The prevalent assumption is that a suburb is just beyond a large city, and is thus closer to the urban center than a village or the countryside.*

Appendix H Chapter 4, Marginal change in variables of statistical and substantive significance for support for political violence

Variable	Marginal Change	Support For Hypotheses
Trust in Local Government	-.004	Yes
Corruption at Local Level	.004	Yes
Public Good of Medical Treatment	-.004	Yes
Gender	.006	Yes

Note: The marginal effect indicates an increase in the predicted probability of the dependent variable according to one standard deviation change in the independent variable, holding all other variables constant.

Appendix I Episodes of political instability/state failure, 1995–2009

Ethnic War		Revolutionary War		Adverse Regime Change	
Afghanistan	**1992–X***	**Afghanistan**	**1992–X***	Afghanistan	2001–02
India	**1990–X**	**India**	**2001–X**	Bangladesh	2007–07
Indonesia	1997–99	Indonesia	1998–99	Nepal	2002–02
Indonesia	1998–05				
Myanmar	**1961–X**				
Pakistan	**2004–X**				
Philippines	**1972–X**				
Sri Lanka	**1983–X**				
Thailand	**2004–X**				

Source: Political Instability Task Force, http://globalpolicy.gmu.edu/pitf/. Accessed April 21, 2010.
Note: An "X" indicates that the episode was ongoing as of early 2009; an asterisk (*) denotes cases that are listed as both Ethnic and Revolutionary Wars.

Appendix J Number of known terrorist organizations within each country, 2006

Rank	State	Number	Region
# 1	**Afghanistan**	**13**	**South Asia**
# 2	**Pakistan**	**12**	**South Asia**
# 3	Lebanon	10	Middle East
# 4	**India**	**9**	**South Asia**
# 5	Ireland	8	W. Europe
# 6	United Kingdom	7	W. Europe
# 7	Israel	6	Middle East
# 7	Iraq	6	Middle East
# 9	**Philippines**	**5**	**SE Asia**
# 9	Turkey	5	Eurasia
# 11	Russia	4	E. Europe
# 11	Syria	4	Middle East
# 13	Colombia	3	Latin America
# 13	Yemen	3	Middle East
# 13	Peru	3	Latin America
# 13	Italy	3	W. Europe
# 17	Kyrgyzstan	2	Eurasia
# 17	Spain	2	W. Europe
# 17	Canada	2	N. America
# 27	Mauritania	2	North Africa

Source: US Department of State—Office of the Coordinator for Counterterrorism Country Reports on Terrorism—Chapter 8—Foreign Terrorist Organizations April 2006. http://www.state.gov/s/ct/rls/crt/2005/65275.htm. Accessed, May 23, 2010, compiled by author.

Note: The Middle East has five states, while W. Europe and Southeast Asia/South Asia have the second highest number of terrorist organizations with four states from their respective region.

Appendix K Chapter 5, Control variables

1. Education
Question: What level of education do you have?
Variable Name: Education
Value Labels: 0=No formal schooling, 1/12=Number of years of schooling, 13=Incomplete Technical Degree, 14=Completed Technical Degree, 15=Incomplete University, 16=Completed University
2. Economic Situation
Question 1: In general, how would you describe your present economic situation and that of your family?
Variable Name: Econ
Value Labels: 1=Very good, 2=Good, 3=About Average, 4=Bad, 5=Very bad, 0=Did Not Answer, 8=Don't Know
* *In order to estimate the model, I code the values of "0" and "8" as Missing Data*
Question 2: Does the salary you receive and your total family income allow you to cover your needs in a satisfactory manner?
Variable Name: Salary
Value Labels: 1=It is sufficient and we can save, 2=It is just sufficient, without major problems, 3=It is not sufficient and we have problems, 4=It is not sufficient and we have big problems, 0=Did Not Answer, 8=Don't Know
* *In order to estimate the model, I code the values of "0" and "8" as Missing Data*
3. Gender
Question: Respondent's gender
Variable Name: Gender
Values: 1, 2
Value Labels: 1=Male, 2=Female
Note: Answered by interviewer.
* *In order to estimate the model, I label the values so that "0" equals male and "1" equals female*
4. Ethnicity
Question: What ethnicity or race do you best identify with?
Variable Name: Ethnic
Value Labels: 1=Asian 2=Black, 3=Indigenous, 4=Mestizo, 5=Mulatto, 6=White, 0=Did Not Answer, 8=Don't Know
Note: Answered by interviewer.
* *In order to estimate the model, I code the values of "0" and "8" as Missing Data*
5. Respondent is From an Urban or Rural Area
Variable Label: Size of Town
Variable Name: Town

Appendix K *Continued*

Value Labels: 1=Up to 5,000 inhabitants, 2=5,001-10,000 inhabitants, 3=10,001-20,000 inhabitants, 4=20,001-40,000 inhabitants, 5=40,001-50,000 inhabitants, 6=50,001-100,000 inhabitants, 7=100,001or more inhabitants, 8=the capital
6. Age
Variable Label: Age of Respondent
Variable Name: Age
Values: 16-98
Value Labels: N/A
7. Employment Status
Variable Label: Employment Status of Respondent
Variable Name: Job
Value Labels: 1=Independent/Self-Employed, 2=Salaried Employee in a Public Company, 3=Salaried Employee in a Private Company, 4=Temporarily Out of Work, 5=Retired, 6=Don't Work/Home Caretaker, 7=Student
* *In order to estimate the model, I set the values 4=Temporarily Out of Work, and 6=Don't Work/Home Caretaker to "0" which equals unemployed because these respondents are not actively in the work force, nor have they retired from active work. All other values I code as "1" which equals employed.*
8. Income Distribution
Question: How fair would you say income distribution is in your country?
Variable Name: Income
Value Labels: 1=Very fair, 2=Fair, 3=Unfair, 4=Very Unfair, 0=Did Not Answer, 8=Don't Know
* *In order to estimate the model, I code the values of "0" and "8" as Missing Data*
9. Discrimination
Question: Would you describe yourself as part of a group that is discriminated against in (country)?
Variable Name:Discrim
Value Labels: 1=Yes, 2=No, 0=Did Not Answer or Don't Know
* *In order to estimate the model, I code the value "0" as Missing Data, and set value "2" to "0"*
10. Drugs and Drug Trafficking
Question 1: In your opinion drug trafficking is the most important concern in the country?
Variable Name: Trafficking
Value Labels: 0=Did Not Answer, 1=Yes, 2=List of Problems,* 96=Others, 97=No Problem, 98=Don't Know
* *In order to estimate the model, I code the values "0" and "98" as Missing Data, and set values "2," "96," and "97" to "0"*

Appendix K ***Concluded***

Question 2: In your opinion drug use is the most important concern in the country?
Variable Name: Druguse1
Value Labels: 0=Did Not Answer, 1=Yes, 2=List of Problems,** 96=Others, 97=No Problem, 98=Don't Know
* *In order to estimate the model, I code the values "0" and "98" as Missing Data, and set values "2," "96," and "97" to "0"*
11. Gangs and Violence
Question 1: In your opinion gang violence is the most important concern in the country?
Variable Name: Gangs
Value Labels: 0=Did Not Answer, 1=Yes, 2=List of Problems,*** 96=Others, 97=No Problem, 98=Don't Know
* *In order to estimate the model, I code the values "0" and "98" as Missing Data, and set values "2," "96," and "97" to "0"*
Question 2: In your opinion violence (terrorism, political violence, guerilla groups) is the most important concern in the country?
Variable Name: Viol
Value Labels: 0=Did Not Answer, 1=Yes, 2=List of Problems,**** 96=Others, 97=No Problem, 98=Don't Know
* *In order to estimate the model, I code the values "0" and "98" as Missing Data, and set values "2," "96," and "97" to "0"*

Notes: * This variable is derived from the open survey question Q2st, where respondents provide their own answer, which varies by respondent and includes a list of twenty-eight responses. I recode the variable as a dummy measure where this variable becomes an indicator of drug trafficking concerns.

** This variable is derived from the open survey question Q2st, where respondents provide their own answer, which varies by respondent and includes a list of twenty-eight responses. I recode the variable as a dummy measure where this variable becomes an indicator of drug use concerns.

*** This variable is derived from the open survey question Q2st, where respondents provide their own answer, which varies by respondent and includes a list of twenty-eight responses. I recode the variable as a dummy measure where this variable becomes an indicator of concerns regarding gang violence.

**** This variable is derived from the open survey question Q2st, where respondents provide their own answer, which varies by respondent and includes a list of twenty-eight responses. I recode the variable as a dummy measure where this variable becomes an indicator of concerns regarding violence.

Appendix L Chapter 5, Descriptive statistics

Variable	Observations	Mean	Std. Dev.	Min	Max
Protest	18871	.159	.367	0	1
Movement	18240	.655	.475	0	1
Coup	18082	.463	.499	0	1
Crime	20204	3.04	1.05	0	4
Victim	19916	.391	.488	0	1
CSafe	19857	2.48	.677	1	3
NSafe	19721	2.27	.741	1	3
Concern	19998	1.93	.929	0	3
Govt	19993	1.39	.992	0	3
Congress	19414	1.17	.915	0	3
Courts	19370	1.12	.891	0	3
Army	17611	1.39	.945	0	3
Admin	19319	1.17	.849	0	3
Local	19633	1.26	.883	0	3
Rigged	18216	.505	.499	0	1
Corrupt	19247	2.75	.930	1	4
Water	19930	.857	.350	0	1
Sewage	19882	.670	.470	0	1
Electric	20058	.972	.166	0	1
Hospital	19904	2.55	.897	1	4
Schools	19925	2.43	.880	1	4
Roads	19984	2.57	.976	0	4
Property	19412	2.56	.984	1	4
Education	20204	8.14	4.71	0	16
Econ	20127	2.98	.818	1	5
Salary	19828	2.63	.828	1	4
Town	20204	5.56	2.08	1	8
Gender	20204	.522	.499	0	1
Age	20204	40.3	16.6	16	98
Job	20204	.687	.464	0	1
Income	19194	3.00	.736	1	4
Discrim	19399	.177	.381	0	1
Trafficking	19012	.206	.404	0	1
Viol	19012	.010	.102	0	1
Gangs	19012	.035	.183	0	1
Druguse1	19012	.013	.112	0	1

Appendix M Chapter 5, Marginal change in variables of statistical and substantive significance for support for political violence (coup)

Variable	Marginal Change	Support For Hypotheses
Trust in local government	-.004	Yes
Corruption at local level	.004	Yes
Public good of medical treatment	-.004	Yes
Gender	.006	Yes

Note: The marginal effect indicates an increase in the predicted probability of the dependent variable according to one standard deviation change in the independent variable, holding all other variables constant.

Appendix N Binary logit estimates of support for political violence—merged Global Barometer data (2009)

Variable	Polviol2—Military Should Displace Government
Security1	-.115***(.039)
Security2	-.023(.036)
Presence1	-.142(.093)
Presence2	.036(.107)
Presence3	-.142***(.039)
Presence4	.120(.114)
Presence5	-.022(.120)
Presence6	.100(.109)
Trust1	.058**(.026)
Trust2	-.009(.022)
Trust3	-.065**(.027)
Trust4	.031(.024)
Trust5	.107***(.025)
Trust6	-.059**(.028)
Trust7	.095***(.031)
Trust8	.021(.027)
Trust9	-.009(.021)
Gender	.181***(.056)
Age	-.105***(.019)
Education	-.289***(.020)
Income	.004(.024)
Constant	-.094(.263)
Observations	8736
Pseudo R2	.0517
LR	436.94
Prob>	.000

Note: *** p < .01 for two-tailed test; ** p < .05 for two-tailed test; * p <0.1 for two-tailed test; standard errors in parentheses.

Appendix O Hypotheses supported by the Logistical Regression analysis—merged Global Barometer dataset

Hypotheses
Security
State Authority
State Presence
Control Measures: • Gender • Age • Education • Socioeconomic Status

Note: Appropriate measures for public goods and private property were not available in the merged data file so those variables were omitted from the model.

Appendix P The Failed State Index top failing and failed states with political violence concerns (as measured by group grievance and security apparatus scores)

Rank	Country	Group Grievance	Security Apparatus
1	Somalia	9.6	10.0
2	Congo (D. R.)	9.3	9.7
3	Sudan	10.0	9.7
3n/r	South Sudan*	10.0	9.7
4	Chad	9.1	8.9
5	Zimbabwe	8.7	8.7
6	Afghanistan	9.4	9.7
7	Haiti	7.0	8.2
8	Yemen	9.0	9.7
9	Iraq	9.7	9.9
10	Central African Republic	8.5	9.6
11	Cote d'Ivoire	9.0	8.9
12	Guinea	7.9	9.4
13	Pakistan	9.6	9.3
14	Nigeria	9.7	9.2
15	Guinea Bissau	5.7	9.4
16	Kenya	8.9	7.6
17	Ethiopia	8.1	8.1
18	Burundi	8.0	7.4
18	Niger	7.7	8.2
20	Uganda	7.7	8.3
21	Myanmar	8.7	7.5

Appendix P ***Continued***

Rank	Country	Group Grievance	Security Apparatus
22	North Korea	6.6	8.1
23	Eritrea	6.4	7.8
23	Syria	9.2	8.5
25	Liberia	6.5	7.0
26	Cameroon	7.5	7.9
27	Nepal	9.0	7.5
28	Timor-Leste	6.8	8.3
29	Bangladesh	8.9	7.6
29	Sri Lanka	9.1	8.2
31	Sierra Leone	6.2	5.7
31	Egypt	8.8	7.0
33	Congo (Republic)	6.3	7.0
34	Iran	8.6	8.3
35	Rwanda	8.5	5.5
36	Malawi	5.7	5.1
37	Cambodia	7.3	6.5
38	Mauritania	7.5	7.7
39	Togo	5.1	7.3
39	Uzbekistan	7.7	8.2
41	Burkina Faso	5.2	7.1
41	Kyrgyzstan	8.4	7.4
43	Equatorial Guinea	6.6	7.8
44	Zambia	6.3	5.3
45	Lebanon	8.4	8.4
46	Tajikistan	6.9	7.1
47	Solomon Islands	6.8	6.7
48	Laos	6.3	6.9
48	Angola	6.5	5.9
50	Libya	7.0	9.0
51	Georgia	8.3	7.6
52	Colombia	7.2	7.0
53	Dijbouti	6.5	6.5
54	Papua New Guinea	6.9	6.3
55	Swaziland	3.6	6.3
56	Philippines	7.6	8.4
57	Comoros	5.3	7.5
58	Madagascar	5.2	6.9
59	Mozambique	4.9	6.8
59	Bhutan	7.6	5.9
61	Israel/West Bank	9.5	6.8
62	Bolivia	7.4	6.5

Appendix P ***Continued***

Rank	Country	Group Grievance	Security Apparatus
63	Indonesia	7.1	7.1
63	Gambia	3.7	5.8
65	Fiji	7.6	7.0
66	Tanzania	5.8	5.8
67	Ecuador	6.9	6.5
68	Azerbaijan	7.2	6.7
69	Nicaragua	6.2	5.9
70	Guatemala	7.1	7.3
71	Senegal	6.0	6.3
72	Lesotho	4.7	5.5
73	Moldova	6.3	7.5
74	Benin	3.6	6.0
75	Honduras	5.6	7.0
76	China	7.9	6.0
77	Algeria	8.1	7.1
78	India	7.9	7.5
79	Mali	6.0	7.1
79	Bosnia and Herzegovina	8.0	6.7
81	Turkmenistan	6.4	7.2
82	Venezuela	6.7	6.7
83	Russia	7.9	8.2
84	Thailand	7.8	7.3
85	Turkey	8.6	7.7
85	Belarus	6.5	6.0
87	Morocco	6.8	6.6
88	Maldives	4.9	5.7
89	Serbia	7.9	6.4
90	Jordan	7.0	5.7
91	Cape Verde	4.2	5.7
92	Gabon	3.3	5.7
93	El Salvador	6.0	6.7
94	Tunisia	5.6	7.5
95	Dominican Republic	5.8	5.5
96	Vietnam	6.0	5.7
97	Sao Tome	4.8	5.8
98	Mexico	5.8	7.7
99	Peru	7.1	6.9
100	Saudi Arabia	7.7	7.2
101	Cuba	4.8	6.6
102	Armenia	5.7	5.2
103	Micronesia	4.2	5.4

Appendix P ***Concluded***

Rank	Country	Group Grievance	Security Apparatus
104	Guyana	6.2	6.1
105	Suriname	6.1	5.8
106	Namibia	5.6	5.2
107	Paraguay	6.2	6.1
107	Kazakhstan	6.5	6.3

Note: The scores are measured from 1-10, therefore, a six or higher represents a high score across the variables: 1) Group Grievance, 2) Uneven Economic Development and 3) Poverty and Economic Decline.

Appendix Q FSI social indicators: group grievance and security apparatus (measures of political violence)

Group Grievance	Security Apparatus
FSI Definition: When tension and violence exists between groups, the state's ability to provide security is undermined and fear and further violence may ensue.	*FSI Definition*: The security apparatus should have a monopoly on the use of legitimate force. The social contract is weakened where this is affected by competing groups.
Includes pressures and measures related to: • Discrimination • Powerlessness • Ethnic Violence • Communal Violence • Sectarian Violence • Religious Violence	*Includes pressures and measures related to*: • Internal Conflict • Small Arms Proliferation • Riots and Protests • Fatalities from Conflict • Military Coups • Rebel Activity • Militancy • Bombings • Political Prisoners

Source: 2012 Failed State Index. http://www.foreignpolicy.com/failed_states_index_2012_interactive.